STUDIES IN COMMONWEALTH POLITICS AND HISTORY
No. 1

Lion Rampant

Lion Rampant

Essays in the Study of British Imperialism

D. A. Low

*Director of the Research School of Pacific Studies,
The Australian National University*

Cass paperbacks

Paperback edition 1974

First published in 1973 by
FRANK CASS & COMPANY LIMITED
67 Great Russell Street, London WC1B 3BT

And in the United States of America by
Frank Cass and Co. Ltd.
c/o International Scholarly Book Services, Inc.
P.O. Box 4347, Portland, Oregon 97208

ISBN 0 7146 2986 3 (hardback)
ISBN 0 7146 4010 7 (paperback)

Printed in Great Britain

Contents

For

ANGELA

Foreword

Legatee of a vast empire, the Commonwealth still carries the imprint of its past. And in doing so it may be said to have a collective identity which, in a very varying degree, each of its members exhibits. This, we believe, can sustain a collective inquiry into the political history and institutions of countries which were once governed within the British Empire and we note signs of a revival of interest in this field. In recent years 'area studies' have been encouraged, but there is also a sense in which the Commonwealth is itself a region, bounded not by geography but history, and imperial history in particular. Seen thus the region cannot exclude areas into which empire overspilled as in the Sudan, or areas now outside the Commonwealth such as South Africa and Burma, or the unique case of Ireland. No account of the dilemmas which face the government of Canada or Nigeria or India—or indeed of the United Kingdom—which examines the present in relation to the past can be complete which omits some consideration of this 'imperial dimension'. Without in any sense trying to claim that there is a 'political culture' common to all Commonwealth countries it is certainly the case that some of the institutions, some part of the political life, and a certain element in the political beliefs of many Commonwealth leaders, can be said to derive from the import of institutions, practices and beliefs from Britain into its former colonies.

Nor is the Commonwealth merely a useful category of study. It is also a community of scholars, many of them teaching and writing within the growing number of universities throughout the member countries who share an interest in the consequences of imperial experience and have common traditions of study.

The present series of books is intended to express that interest and those traditions. They are presented not as a guide to the Commonwealth as a corporate entity, but as studies either in the politics and recent history of its member states or of themes which are of common interest to several of the countries concerned. Within the Commonwealth there is great variety—of geographical setting, of cultural context, of economic development and social life; they provide the challenge to comparative study, while the elements of common experience make the task manageable. A cross-nation study of administrative reforms or of legislative behaviour is both facilitated and given added meaning; so also is an examination of the external relations of one or more member states; even a single country study, say on Guyana, is bound to throw light on problems which are echoed in Malaya and Sri Lanka. The series will bring together—and, we hope, stimulate—studies of these kinds carried out by both established and younger scholars. In doing so, it can make its distinctive contribution to an understanding of the changing contemporary world.

It would have been difficult to find a more appropriate volume with which to begin the series than this collection of thought-provoking essays by a scholar who has the rare distinction of having done substantial work in both African and Asian settings.

DENNIS AUSTIN
W. H. MORRIS-JONES

January 1973

Preface

In the making of this book I have incurred many debts. Chapter 1 is based on the article called 'Lion Rampant', which Professor Kenneth Robinson published in the *Journal of Commonwealth Studies*, Vol. II, No. 3, November 1964, pp. 235–52. I am grateful to the present editors for permission to include an amended version of it here. Chapter 2 was once read to a seminar at the Institute of Development Studies at the University of Sussex, and I am grateful to the Institute for permission to republish something very close to the version which appeared in its *Communication Series,* No. 51. Chapter 4 owes more than may at first be apparent to the unusual opportunity I had in April 1969 to take part in a small seminar called by the secretariat of the World Council of Churches at the Selly Oak Colleges, Birmingham, to discuss its remarkable series of *World Studies of Churches in Mission.* For the rest, several of my colleagues at Sussex have been good enough to provide me with comments on one or more of my chapters in draft, and I would like to thank in particular Duncan Forrester, Donald Winch, Helmut Pappé, John Burrow, Richard Brown and Bruce Graham. I am similarly indebted to Sir Keith Hancock, Ravinder Kumar, Tony Kirk-Greene, John Ballard, Geoff Oddie, Tom Metcalf, Colin Leys, and Dick Cashmore.

I very much doubt, however, if these essays would ever have been produced but for the invitation I had to spend the Fall of 1967 at the University of Chicago. To Edward Shils, Barney Cohn, Tom and Margaret Fallers, Ari Zolberg, Lloyd and Suzanne Rudolph, Clifford Geertz, John Hope Franklin, Ralph Austen, and other members of its Department of History, and of its Committees for the Comparative Study of New Nations, for African Studies and for South Asian Studies, I am greatly indebted for a memorable three months. However, these essays would never have been finished but for the kindness of Trevor Reese and, in particular, W. H. Morris-Jones in arranging four special seminars for me at the Institute of Commonwealth Studies in London in the summer term of 1970. At many points throughout Chapters 2 to 5 I am much indebted to the comments which were made by those who were good enough to attend, even if I have occasionally stuck to my guns.

My greatest debts—bar those to my nomadic family—are, however, to Makerere College, Uganda, which gave me the opportunity to develop an interest in Africa; to the Australian National University which enabled me to take an interest in India, and to the University of Sussex which allowed me to attempt to combine the two. Once again Yvonne Wood has made it possible (with help this time from Margaret Beard and Nancy Davies) for others to read what I have written.

D. A. Low

Clare Hall, Cambridge
January 1972

Introduction

This book is a *ballon d'essai*. 'Imperialism,' Sir Keith Hancock wrote back in 1940, 'is no word for scholars. The emotional echoes which it arouses are too violent and contradictory. It does not convey a precise meaning.' In the intervening decades his injunction has been little heeded. In the aftermath of Gallagher and Robinson's stimulating, if somewhat idiosyncratic, *Africa and the Victorians*, it was tempting to believe that David Fieldhouse had come close to summing up a by now rather protracted debate. But No. It persists as lively as ever. Fieldhouse indeed has been subjected to a blistering onslaught which takes the discussion right back to its twentieth-century origins in J. A. Hobson.[1]

Apart, however, from the issues to which Hancock referred, there are a number of problems connected with this debate. In particular, the vehemence with which it has been conducted has led to the quite unwarranted presumption, amongst polemicists and many historians alike, that when considering the phenomenon of Imperialism the only issues to be discussed concern the impetus of the West towards it. We are still therefore regaled with books and articles which go over the well-trodden ground once again, often apparently oblivious to the many other issues which their compendious titles suggest. This certainly constitutes one of the problems to be discussed. But it really is astonishing that it should have been allowed to engross the whole discussion to quite the degree that it has. There are surely other matters to be considered as well. At all events this book is a modest attempt to insist that there are; and in a genuinely exploratory, introductory and tentative way, to make some suggestions as to what some of them might be.

It should, of course, be said straightaway that several of the major issues concerning the phenomenon of Imperialism have long since been systematically discussed by specialists. We have had for a start the massive *Survey of British Commonwealth*

Affairs[2] by Hancock and Mansergh, and then such magisterial books as Richard Koebner's on the concept of *Empire,*[3] and Philip Curtin's on the (British) *Image of Africa.*[4] In more recent years the whole subject has been greatly enlivened as well by a steady stream of informative monographs. The intellectual sophistication of some of these has been very high. Without them no further systemisation of the kind attempted here would be feasible. The whole discussion, moreover, of what previously passed for imperial history has in recent decades been greatly improved by the insistence that the history of areas subjected to imperial rule should first be looked at in their own right before there is any suggestion that imperial rule may have been a critical variable.[5] A subtlety has entered into the discussion here which was not to be found even a few years back.[6] Not that there is not still disagreement as to whether the imperial impact is or is not to be considered important,[7] or at all events is to be seen more as a response than an initiative[8] (and it is not by any means those of imperialist stock alone who express caution here).[9] Beyond this there have been some useful general accounts of the conflict between nationalism and imperial rule;[10] and of other matters besides.[11] Despite all the temptations I have not sought to go over any of this ground here.

Nor have I attempted to deal with a number of other issues which spring very readily to mind in considering the study of Imperialism—concerning, for example, the revolts against imperial rule,[12] or the development of colonial economies.[13] Upon this latter point the work of A. G. Frank on Latin America brings forward once again the argument about the actual *under*-development of colonial economies,[14] which to someone interested in India raises in a new and sharper form a famous nineteenth-century debate there.[15]

Two further issues cry out for attention as well, if only one were daring enough to square up to them. In the first place there is the vast subject of societal change in colonial territories under western imperial rule. (What was it, that is, that happened to society in Burma or Uganda, as compared with what happened in Afghanistan or Ethiopia?).[16] And in the second place there is the arresting question of what it was actually like to be subject to imperial rule.[17] What did it *feel* like?

In the interim before these larger issues find their expositors, this book attempts to open up what seem at present to be some of the more tractable matters. In half a dozen essays it takes half a dozen topics and by varying the approach on each occasion suggests the kind of intellectual enquiry into them which it begins to seem possible to undertake. Each of course deserves a whole book to itself. The purpose of the present volume is at once more modest and more ambitious: to suggest by taking a number of examples in quick succession the very variety of the topics which require further elucidation. Should it succeed in injecting some greater variety into the more general debates about Imperialism, its primary purpose will have been very well served.

The discussion is almost entirely confined to the British Empire. Indeed, even within this there is little or no mention of the white colonies, the Caribbean, Ceylon, South-east Asia or the Pacific. Throughout I have drawn in the main from my own more specialist reading on East Africa and South Asia. To judge from Eric Stokes's 'Traditional resistance movements and Afro-Asian nationalism: the context of the 1857 Mutiny Rebellion in India',[18] this can be a fruitful proceeding. Comparative history has of course its limitations; but its heuristic value is hard to gainsay. Sometimes the contrasts are as illuminating as the likenesses, and in the present case the importance of events in one region for those in another frequently turns out to have been very much greater than those who confine their attention to one of them tend to appreciate. The arguments about administrative 'single-seatedness' in India, not to mention the triumph of the Indian nationalist movement, were quite vital in Africa later on; and my own view would be that a recent anthropological paper on 'African Conversion', admirable as it was so far as it went, would have been greatly improved if, in considering why converts to Christianity were secured in Africa, it had referred to something more than that obfuscating cliché about 'the mystical religions of the East' when considering the paucity of such converts in India.[19]

It is upon these and certain other topics that the chapters which follow are focused. The first is concerned to suggest that attention needs to be given to the issue of why imperial rule came to be accepted as a fact of life in the countries which became subject to empire. A 'typology of initial imperial situations' is offered, and suggestions are made both about the different elements which buttressed the authority of the imperial power, and about the measuring of the precise incidence of imperial authority in its different stages. The second chapter traces the thinking of British imperialists over the best part of two centuries on the question of whether or not they should make any moves to change the condition of the societies under their rule, and if so how, and in what direction; and it is suggested that not only can three eras of thinking be discerned here, but that British thinking about Africa was much more closely related to British thinking about India than is generally realised. The third chapter develops one of the issues discussed in the first chapter, and by means of three instances in succession takes up the question of what happened to the traditional rulerships that became subject to British imperial dominion. It suggests that they passed through two crises, the first at the advent of empire, the second at its conclusion, and it asks why some traditional rulerships fared better in these crises than others, and suggests some possible answers.

In the fourth chapter the focus is shifted considerably. Attention is directed to the fact that Christian missions came to have a specially advantageous period for their proselytisation during the period when the British Empire was in control of India and large parts of Tropical Africa, and the question is raised (and some answers are suggested) about why so few converts were secured for Christianity in India in these favourable circumstances as compared with the great many secured in Africa.

The fifth chapter takes a much more strictly chronological theme than any of the others. It seeks to delineate the interactions in the great confrontation between the British Raj and the Indian national movement in the first half of this century. It attempts to point to what were and what were not its critical aspects, and it then traces the implications of, and the developments from, this story for Africa. In particular it is suggested that the two stories have to be seen in sequence if one is to have a proper understanding of at least the second. In the final chapter, various ways of visualising the condition and the inheritance of the post-imperial regimes are outlined, and in the end it is suggested that the post-independence concerns of the successor regimes should now raise new questions about their previous imperial periods for historians to consider.

As it has turned out, British imperial officials never seem to have been very far from the reckoning. Clearly their position was always a delicate one. Perhaps, therefore, this is the place to proffer a clear-eyed commentary upon men in such situations. It comes from Tolstoy's *War and Peace*, Book XI, Chapter XV, and runs as follows:[20]

> 'In quiet and untroubled times it seems to every administrator that it is only by his efforts that the whole population under his rule is kept going, and in this consciousness of being indispensable every administrator finds the chief reward of his labour and efforts. While the sea of history remains calm the ruler-administrator in his frail bark, holding on with a boat-hook to the ship of the people, and himself moving, naturally imagines that his efforts move the ship he is holding on to. But as soon as a storm arises and the sea begins to heave and the ship to move, such a delusion is no longer possible. The ship moves independently with its own enormous motion, the boat-hook no longer reaches the moving vessel, and suddenly the administrator, instead of appearing a ruler and a source of power, becomes an insignificant, useless, feeble man.'

NOTES

1. W. K. Hancock, *Survey of British Commonwealth Affairs,* London, 1940, Vol. II, Part 1, p. 1; J. A. Gallagher and R. E. Robinson with Alice Denny, *Africa and the Victorians*, London, 1961; D. K. Fieldhouse, '"Imperialism": an historiographical revision', *Economic History Review*, XIV, 1961, pp. 187–209; D. K. Fieldhouse, *The Theory of Capitalist Imperialism*, London, 1967; A. P. Thornton, *Doctrines of Imperialism*, London, 1967; Keith Sinclair 'Hobson and Lenin in Jahore: Colonial Office policy towards British concessionaires and investors, 1878–1907', *Modern Asian Studies*, I, 1967, pp. 335–53; D. C. M. Platt, 'Economic Factors in British Policy during the New Imperialism', *Past and Present*, No. 39, 1968, pp. 120–38; A. G. Hopkins, 'Economic Imperialism in West Africa: Lagos 1880–92', *Economic History Review*, XXI, 1968, pp. 508–606; Eric Stokes, 'Late Nineteenth-Century Colonial Expansion and the Attack on Economic Imperialism: a case of mistaken identity?', *Historical Journal*, XII, 1969, pp. 285–301; Hans-Ulrich Wehler, 'Bismarck's Imperialism 1862–1890', *Past and*

Present, No. 48, pp. 119–55; George Lichtheim, *Imperialism*, London, 1971; Hugh Stretton, *The Political Sciences*, London, 1969, Ch. 4; J. A. Hobson, *Imperialism: a Study*, London, 1902. The other classics are V. I. Lenin, *Imperialism, the Highest Stage of Capitalism*, 1917, and Joseph Schumpeter, *Imperialism and Social Classes.*

2. Loc. cit., et seq.
3. R. Koebner, *Empire*, Cambridge, 1961; R. Koebner and Schmidt, *Imperialism: the Story and Significance of a Political Word 1840–1960*, Cambridge, 1964.
4. P. D. Curtin, *The Image of Africa*, London, 1965.
5. The classical statement is in J. C. van Leur, *Indonesian Trade and Society: Essays in Asian Social and Economic History*, translated by J. S. Holmes and A. van Marle, The Hague/Bandung, 1955.
6. There was an unedifying dispute over South-east Asian history. A more satisfactory statement was by John R. W. Smail, 'On the possibility of an autonomous history of modern South-east Asia'. *Journal of South East Asian History*, II, 2, 1961, pp. 72 ff.
7. See, for example, P. H. M. Van den Dungen's chapter on the Punjab in D. A. Low (ed.), *Soundings in Modern South Asian History*, London, 1968, and cf. A. G. Frank, footnote 14 below.
8. See, for example, John Iliffe, *Tanganyika under German Rule 1905–1912*, Cambridge, 1969.
9. I have in mind both Ravinder Kumar in Low, *Soundings*, and Jacob Ajayi in L. H. Gann and Peter Duignan, *Colonialism in Africa*, Vol. I, Cambridge, 1969, the last chapter.
10. Rupert Emerson, *From Empire to Nation*, Harvard, 1960; Fatma Mansur, *Process of Independence*, London, 1962.
11. E.g. Martin Wight, *The Development of the Legislative Council, 1606–1945*, London, 1946; A. P. Thornton, *The Imperial Idea and its Enemies*, London, 1959; and Max Beloff, *Imperial Sunset*, Vol. I, London, 1969.
12. See Mazrui's 'Postlude: Towards a Theory of Protest' in R. I. Rotberg and A. A. Mazrui, *Protest and Power in Black Power*, New York, 1970, p. 1185 ff.
13. My colleagues C. C. Wrigley and E. A. Brett are completing studies in the history of the East African colonial economies.
14. A. G. Frank, *Capitalism and Underdevelopment in Latin America* and *Latin America: Underdevelopment or Revolution*, New York, 1969. See also Robert I. Rhodes, *Imperialism and Underdevelopment: a Reader*, London, 1970.
15. The classic statement was in Dadabhai Naoroji, *Poverty and Un-British Rule in India*, London, 1901.
16. The 'reader' compiled by Immanuel Wallerstein, *Social Change: The Colonial Situation*, New York, 1966, illustrates the difficulties.
17. Does one start with Jawaharlal Nehru's *Autobiography*, or with the dedication to Nirad Chaudhuri's *Autobiography of an Unknown Indian*, London, 1951?

• •

18. *Past and Present*, 48, August 1970, pp. 100–18.
19. Robin Horton, 'African Conversion', *Africa*, XLI, 2, April 1971, pp. 85–108.
20. Mr. (now Dr.) Richard Cashmore first gave me this to read in 1956 in his District Officer's bungalow at Chuka in Kenya while he discussed a projected patrol against some Mau Mau fighters in the forests of Mount Kenya with two armed police officers.

1

Empire and Authority

When they discuss questions of political power and political authority, most political scientists are able to refer to a substantial corpus of literature. There is no such corpus of literature about imperial authority.[1] There is plenty of writing about the doctrine of indirect rule. Most of this skirts, however, the central issues of imperial authority. Among historians there is now a growing literature about 'resistance' and 'revolt'.[2] But what of the long intervals when there was next to none such? One vital problem concerning imperial authority has of course received attention (a tremendous amount of attention indeed) from both political scientists and historians alike, namely the question why and how it has now been so largely overthrown. By and large we think we know the answer to this. We explain it by the rise of nationalism. But the truth probably is that we have not really gone nearly as far as we think we have in fathoming it adequately. For we have still to learn a great deal more about that other question, namely, not why imperial rule has been overthrown, but why it was in the first place (and let us for the moment beg the question here) accepted.

The essential issue in all this can be very simply illustrated with just one question. How was it possible that 760 British members of the ruling Indian Civil Service could as late as 1939, in the face of the massive force of the Indian national movement led by Gandhi 'hold down' 378 million Indians?[3] For all the work done on British administration in India, and upon Indian nationalism, we cannot yet—and by 'we' I mean chiefly 'we historians'—answer that question. We can note that the Indian army, the Indian police and the Indian provincial services remained remarkably 'loyal' to the British through each of the Indian National Congress's successive Civil Disobedience movements against the Raj,[4] and with Percival Spear[5] we may recall that 'the uncommitted majority of the [Indian] articulate class . . . still stopped short of violence and revolution' as late as 1942 when Gandhi launched his explosive 'Quit India' movement. But we still remain abysmally ignorant about how the Raj's political domination was articulated beneath the British district officer through various networks of locally prominent families, subordinate Indian bureaucracies, and rural dominant castes, and until we know a great deal more about this, any account of Indian politics in the British period will be open to substantial amendment.[6] It is not the purpose of this present chapter to try to close the gap. But this is very much the kind of issue which will eventually require elucidation, even when, as at present, it only seems possible to reconnoitre some of the issues to which it relates.

This chapter accordingly seeks to do no more than three things. To offer in the first place a typology—if the term may be allowed—of initial imperial situations: secondly, to discuss some of the factors which, in the British Empire at least, went to the establishment of its authority over Asian and African peoples: and then thirdly to consider, on the basis of some historical studies of Uganda, the significance for an imperial historian of the points which look as if they need to be made about the 'intensity' of imperial power.

Initial Imperial Situations

From a consideration of a substantial number of instances it would seem that one can differentiate between three different kinds of initial imperial situation:

1. Where an imperial power superseded a pre-existing political authority
2. Where an imperial power established its dominance over a pre-existing political authority which continued to exist, but under its dominance; and
3. Where there were no distinctly political authorities to be either superseded or subordinated, only stateless societies, so that the imperial power was engaged in the extremely difficult task of creating a distinctly political authority for the first time.

A few words about each will be in order.

The situation where an imperial power superseded a pre-existing political authority did not necessarily involve the supersession by the imperial power of a political authority which was previously paramount. The East India Company, for instance, for half a century and more after the Battle of Plassey (1757) continued to acknowledge the paramountcy of the successors of the Mughal Emperors. They superseded, however, those who were the Emperors' subordinates. In Bengal, for instance, they superseded the Nawab as the Mughal Emperor's Dewan there. In general, however, this first type of imperial situation came into existence where the imperial power did supersede a pre-existing paramount authority. The remnant of the authority of the Mughal Emperors in India was in fact eventually done away with, and in due course British Emperors of India succeeded Mughal Emperors as the paramount power there. In India this was a protracted proceeding. It began with Warren Hastings's efforts to secure the safety of the British East India Company during the wars of the 1770s and 1780s, which had the effect of making the Company the pre-eminent 'country power' in India. Only with Wellesley and Marquess Hastings in the first twenty years of the nineteenth century, however, did the Company, by superseding several of the other 'country powers', establish itself as paramount in most parts of India east of the Indus valley; and even then it continued until 1857 to grant a certain (albeit drastically reduced) status to the Kings of Delhi (as the lineal successors to the Mughals were called):[7] while it was not until the 1840s that it finally superseded the rulers of Sind and the Punjab to the westward.[8]

Nevertheless India, or to be precise British India—as distinct from the Indian Princely States—probably provides the classic example of this type of initial imperial situation in the British Empire. In India the British succeeded to the paramount traditional authority of the Indian State. One can see the point here very clearly in the operation of the Indian land revenue system. In India there was an intimate relation between land and taxation (there was no such relation in Africa, where the basic taxation was not land revenue, but first the hut tax and then the poll tax), and what happened was that the British simply took over the traditional role of the Indian State in regard to land, and claimed—and received—the share (or at least something which approximated to the share) of the produce of the soil which had traditionally been the State's perquisite.[9]

But this same imperial situation was to be found occasionally in Africa as well. In Southern Rhodesia, for instance, Rhodes and the British South Africa Company in the 1890s succeeded Lobengula, the paramount chief of the major tribe, the Ndebele, as the paramount authority between the Limpopo and the Zambezi. In two wars—the Ndebele War of 1893 and the Ndebele Rebellion of 1896—the Ndebele were severely defeated, and their traditional political authorities destroyed. The royal salute of the Ndebele was the cry 'Bayete'. When in 1902 Rhodes was buried in the Matopo Hills in Southern Rhodesia, his body was carried to its hill-top tomb by Ndebele warriors crying 'Bayete, Bayete'; Rhodes was given, that is, the Ndebele royal salute.[10] The last paramount chief of the Ndebele was thus, in a very real sense, not Lobengula, but Rhodes; and the thinking of the Ndebele seems to have been that this white man, despite all that he had done to them, had succeeded by right of conquest (a right the Ndebele themselves fully recognised, for they had often profited from it themselves) to political authority over them. In Southern Rhodesia, as in British India, imperial power thus rested, in the first instance, upon the supersession by the imperial power of a pre-existing political authority. And this seems very often to have been the basis of French imperial power, since the French do not appear to have been as ready as the British to work the second kind of imperial situation.

This was the situation in which an imperial power did not supersede a pre-existing political authority, but established its dominance over a pre-existing political authority which continued to exist under its dominance. The classic form here was represented by those situations in which a 'native state' continued to exist under the aegis of the imperial power (though there were other variants as well). The point to be stressed is that, in terms of the autonomy which the native state enjoyed, there were many variations to be found in this second type of imperial situation. If some of these—for the British Empire at least—were placed upon a scale, it might run something like this. At one end there were the Persian Gulf Sheikhdoms. Here British control was limited to control over their foreign relations: there was no interference with their internal administration.[11] Next there came the Princely States of the British Empire in India. Here again, British authorities controlled their external relations, but not their internal affairs. The British did, however, claim to exercise 'paramountcy' over the Princely States, and this amounted to an assertion of the right to interfere in internal affairs if they were convinced that maladministration and/or injustice were rampant.[12]

In Africa, British dominance generally amounted to more than this. Here we can pick out four more situations all further up the scale. First Egypt, where, in the days of Cromer and his successors, a clear separation was supposed to exist between the British diplomatic representatives on the one hand and the Egyptian Government on the other. Cromer, after all, was officially never anything more than British Consul-General in Cairo, and Egypt continued throughout his period to be part of the Ottoman Empire. *De facto*, of course, Cromer was 'Viceroy' of Egypt. What was more, the Egyptian Government had British officials attached to its ministries whose advice had to be accepted, so that in practice there was substantially more direct British control over the internal affairs of Egypt than in normal circumstances there ever was over the Indian States.[13]

The kingdoms of Uganda presented a somewhat parallel, though clearly distinct, situation. Here, by contrast with Egypt in Cromer's day, a British Protectorate existed: and by a treaty signed in 1900 (an extraordinarily ambiguous treaty as it happened) the authorities of the foremost native state, Buganda, were required 'to cooperate loyally with Her Majesty's Government in the organisation and administration of the kingdom'. For the most part, however, no British officials worked, as they did in Egypt, within the native state government, and to an even greater extent than in Egypt there were two parallel structures of government operating side by side.[14] It is a little difficult to decide whether Buganda should be placed above or below Egypt, but at all events it stood somewhere near the middle of the scale.

Next would be placed Northern Nigeria, the nursery (in the horticultural sense) of Lord Lugard's theories of Indirect Rule. Here his purpose was to establish *one* structure of government:[15] a contrast with both Egypt and Buganda. Certainly relations between the British and the Northern Nigerian Emirates were not—as with the Uganda kingdoms—governed by Treaty and so to some degree limited. The governments of the Northern Nigerian emirates were directly subject to British authority. Addressing the conquered of Sokoto in Northern Nigeria on 21 March 1903, Lugard declared:

> 'Now these are the words which I, the High Commissioner, have to say for the future. The Fulani in old times under Dan Fodio conquered this country. They took the right to rule over it, to levy taxes, to depose kings and to create kings. They in turn have by defeat lost their rule which has come into the hands of the British. All these things which I have said the Fulani by conquest took the right to do now pass to the British. Every Sultan and Emir and the principal officers of State will be appointed by the High Commissioner throughout all this country. The High Commissioner will be guided by the usual laws of succession and the wishes of the people and chiefs, but will set them aside if he desires for good cause to do so. The Emirs and Chiefs who are appointed will rule over the people as of old time and take such taxes as are approved by the High Commissioner, but they will obey the laws of the Governor and will act in accordance with the advice of the Resident.'[16]

At the same time—and this will have been noted in the extract—the Government of the Emirs was to be preserved under the authority of the British.

In Zanzibar the position was different again; and its place would be right towards the other end of the scale. During the British period, the government of the island was conducted in the name of His Highness the Sultan. In fact (unlike Buganda, unlike Egypt, unlike Northern Nigeria), the Sultan's Government was composed entirely of British officials. Thus the British Resident was at once British Representative to, and First Minister of, the Government of His Highness the Sultan.[17] Malaya had its own variations, but by and large the Resident system there was more akin to that in Zanzibar than to that in India or upon the African mainland. The formal position of the Resident varied in each state. In theory he was only there to 'advise'. But, as one British official put it, this was 'one of those fictions in which we seem to delight';

and the Pangkor Engagement of January 1874, by which the Sultan and chiefs of the state of Perak, for example, bound themselves to the British, openly stated in Article VI that the Resident's 'advice must be asked and acted upon on all questions other than those touching Malay religion and custom'. And the truth was (as the late Dr. Emma Sadka, the prime authority upon all of this, put it) that the 'administration of the native states were organised and directed by the Residents, under the control of the Governor, and subject to the general authority of the Secretary of State; the Resident and his staff collected and administered the revenue, organised the police, administered justice, and framed and carried out policy in all its aspects'.[18]

Two things were, of course, at work here. The British employed the native state as an instrument of their authority. But at the same time they tended to leave to the local indigenous authority control over matters which were of little importance to them.

At one end of the scale—the Persian Gulf/Indian States end—the relationship may be described as 'quasi-diplomatic': at the other end, the Zanzibar/Malaya end, it was a more directly 'administrative' relationship. For those regimes somewhere near the centre of the scale it was never quite certain whether it was more of the one or more of the other, and an analysis of the political relationships in these situations revolves around a precise identification of the extent of the quasi-diplomatic and more directly administrative elements in them. The situation could be exceedingly confusing. One British officer in Buganda once said of one of his conversations with its Native Ministers: 'When this advice was given to them with an order to get to work at once, agreement was instant.'[19]

Another British officer in Uganda set out in general terms the principles underlying the native state system:

> 'It has always been the practice of England to govern her distant dominions, as apart from her colonies, wherever feasible by the system of Protectorates; by which system their administrators are placed under the native Prince who governs by the advice of a native Protector. The advantages are obvious; for the people through force of habit, love for the person, or the prestige of his

office, naturally submit to the orders of their Prince. The Prince himself through the instinct of self-preservation if through nothing else, usually willingly obeys the orders of his protector, and those orders are further disguised under the name of advice, and are conveyed in such manner as to as little as possible destroy his prestige or wound his susceptibilities. By this means pressure when it is necessary, is brought to bear on one person only, the Prince, and not on the whole population. Even when the Prince withholds his ready cooperation from his protector, the cases of Egypt, of Zanzibar and of Uganda tend to prove that the system can still be employed with a full measure of success.'[20]

A cruder statement of the position was set out in 1892 in a letter from Sir John Kirk, formerly British Consul-General in Zanzibar, in reply to an enquiry from the British Foreign Office about the succession to the Zanzibar sultanate.

> 'The question is' Kirk declared, 'do we wish a strong man on the throne? Will an ambitious, but soured, man fall into our ways after he is in power? Or will he then do like Seyyid Barghash [a former Sultan of Zanzibar], and say that promises given by a private person can have no binding force when that individual is placed by God to rule in trust the faithful? It needs no casuistry for a Mohammedan to absolve himself from the binding nature of any such bond, so that we must place no reliance on the effect promises made beforehand will have, but trust to the means we hold to keeping the new Ruler under our hand. If we set aside Barghash's son I think we cannot do better than go back to the son of the Ruler of Muscat, the parent State. But history shows that we are free to choose from any branch of the family the man who suits us best, for we are the "longest sword", and we have become the electors and patrons to the throne.'[21]

It should be added that situations one and two could co-exist. That became apparent in the quotation on page 13 from Lugard. The British had superseded the Fulani in Northern Nigeria as the paramount power, but they would retain each individual Fulani Emirate as a subordinate polity. In Uganda there was a similar case. East of the Kingdom of Buganda there were a number of smaller kingdoms which now make up Busoga. Here, before the British advent, Buganda had enjoyed a position of paramount authority. In the 1890s the British superseded the Baganda as the paramount authority in

Busoga,[22] but retained, for a time, the Busoga kingdoms as subordinate polities. Similarly in India: the British superseded the Mughals as paramount power; but they retained a large number of Princely States as subordinate polities.

Sometimes there could be movements from situation two to situation one. This was the essence of the Lawrences' proceedings in the Punjab in the aftermath of the two Sikh Wars in the 1840s, as it was of British relations with the remnant of the Nawabi of Oudh. During the first half of the nineteenth century, Oudh continued to exist as a 'native state' with a British Resident. But annexation occurred in 1856, and the former Nawabi was then finally done away with.[23] For reasons to which we must return (see Chapter 3 below), there do not seem to have been similar movements in the relationship between the British and African 'native states'. But there was one very clear example of this switch in the changing relationship between the French and the Hova kingdom of Madagascar in the 1880s and 1890s.[24]

We may now turn to the third initial imperial situation. This, it will be remembered, was the one in which there were no pre-existing political authorities either to supersede or to subordinate. To give just one example of this, Dr. Paula Brown may be quoted on the Chimbu of New Guinea. Here, there were 'no traditional fixed office-holders responsible for specified tasks. . . . There was no real specialisation in leadership functions. . . . No leader can be sure that his opinion will be respected, that his orders will be obeyed, that he will be helped in avenging his wrongs, that his suggestion to hold a ceremony will be taken up, or that the points he makes in a bragging speech to another tribe will be supported by his fellow-tribesmen.'[25] This is the situation that the social anthropologists have called the stateless society.[26] It presented as many variations as the native states—from migrant food gatherers such as the Australian aborigines,[27] to various peoples in northern Ghana, northern Rhodesia, eastern Nigeria, the southern Sudan, and Kenya.[28]

It should be emphasised here that imperial authority in such situations was exceedingly difficult to establish, partly because the social units were often very small indeed, but largely because the notion of a distinctly political authority, as Dr.

Brown has made clear (and many others of us could confirm), did not exist, and had to be created for the first time. The problem, as one British officer in Kenya put it in 1905, was 'to get the natives, as a whole, to recognise any one individual member of their tribe as a person of authority over them.'[29] Accounts of such imperial situations are replete with the attempts of the imperial authority to pick out someone who had some kind of traditional authority—ritual, oracular, military, or gerontocratic—and make him a chief. In New Guinea such chiefs were called *tultuls* and *luluais*; in Kenya they were sometimes given the grandiloquent title of 'paramount chief', though they were nothing of the kind. It is interesting to note, too, how frequently imperial authorities in such situations were forced to fall back upon an ex-policeman, an ex-interpreter, or a caravan headman for their subordinate agents; and how frequently such men, who were solely dependent upon their native wit and the backing of the imperial authority for their position, became excessively masterful. One can glimpse some of the other issues which such a situation presented by asking whether the establishment of Australian authority in New Guinea would not have proceeded very much faster (it took well over half a century to bring the whole of Papua and eastern New Guinea under Australian control) had New Guinea been ruled by a Sultan or an Emir or a Kabaka who could have been conquered.

In offering this typology two points should perhaps be added. First, it should be made clear that nothing has been said so far about military conquest. In saying, for example, that in initial imperial situation type three, imperial authority was exceedingly difficult to establish, the discussion has been confined to the position after the initial 'conquest' had taken place. Conquest in such situations was generally very easily effected. It was usually very much more difficult in those areas where there had been a pre-existing political authority. But all this is another issue. Secondly, all modern imperial powers from the West were quick to advance a legal and rational basis for their authority. Thus in Southern Rhodesia it was not the behaviour of the Ndebele at Rhodes's funeral that counted for its European rulers, but the Matabeleland Order in Council of 1894 and the British legal enactments which succeeded it. In British India the Government of India was the supreme political authority in British eyes not because it was the heir to the Mughals, but because it was—in the famous phrase—'the Government established by law in British India'. Where, moreover, there were Native States much reliance was placed upon treaties, agreements, sanads, and so forth.[30] But where these did not exist the legal luminaries were not put out. The preamble to the British Foreign Jurisdiction Act of 1890 (the basic law for British Protectorates) stated that 'by treaty, grant, *usage, sufferance and other lawful means*, Her Majesty has power and jurisdiction within the said Territories' (emphasis added). All this, of course, was of great consequence during the heyday of imperial rule; imperial rulers always emphasised the legal basis of their authority at the expense of its political basis. It was also of consequence in the transition to independence. Where the legal basis of supreme authority was not complicated by special legal enactments with Native States the process was technically—and often politically—much less complicated.[31] In other words, it looks as if it was less difficult to move into national independence from initial situations one and three than from situation two. But again all this constitutes a whole subject in iself.[32]

The Establishment of Authority

We now turn to the second main topic and consider some of the factors which went to the establishment of imperial authority in its British variant in Africa and in India. And we may begin with the conclusion to which the discussion of the first topic would seem to point. For it looks as if in very many areas one of the main reasons for the successful establishment of imperial authority in the early stages was that it gathered to itself a legitimacy which was traditional. Certainly the task for imperial empire-builders was very much more difficult where there was no traditional authority to lay their hands upon. Certainly, too, imperial authorities never for very long tolerated the existence of traditionally legitimate political authorities which were not under their wing.[33] What is more, they—especially British imperial authorities—were exceedingly careful to build into the structure of their imperial authority institutions which had a traditional legitimacy wherever these existed. In India they frequently worked through *rajas, zamindars*, and village headmen of one sort or another. In Africa they were constantly on the look out for Chiefs. Such political constructs became particularly effective wherever the notions of subordination and superordination (the 'premise of inequality' as Jacques Maquet has called it)[34] existed. People (in the phrase of the Uganda official quoted above) 'through force of habit, love for the person, or the prestige of his office, naturally submit to the orders of their Prince'; crucial elements of the traditional order remained and the people continued to obey them. In such situations, another Uganda official wrote, the right way to proceed, was 'by the Administration strengthening the authority of the king with his people whilst at the same time acquiring by political conduct on the part of its representative, a controlling influence over the King'.

The question then is why did the Prince submit? Why did the Emir, the Nawab, the Sultan, the Kabaka—and their chiefs—submit?

In a great many cases historians have still to explain why. I can only report on my own researches on southern Uganda. There, by the nineteenth century, there were over twenty African kingdoms of some substance. Most of them became subject to British imperial authority between 1890 and 1900. But there was no case in which a previously dominant authority made a successful rapprochement with the British invaders; in general, settlements were made by the British with rulers and chiefs who were not dominant prior to the British arrival, but became secured by means of an alliance with the British. Since these people succeeded to traditional offices in ways which were by no means untraditional—it was quite normal to procure help from abroad—their position was fully legitimate in the eyes of their own people. These rulers and chiefs, moreover, were ready to acknowledge the imperial authority of the British, because this was the best guarantee of their own hold on the traditionally legitimate offices which they now held within their own kingdoms. As a result, British imperial authority in the Uganda kingdoms came to depend upon an alliance with rulers and with chiefs who, with British support, occupied traditionally legitimate offices of state. It is in this se that one may affirm that imperial authority very often depended for its success upon taking unto itself local authorities who were traditionally legitimate. The men actually concerned were very often newcomers, but there was nothing illegitimate in that.[35]

Indeed, to continue the Uganda story for a moment, and in passing hint at another point; what happened in Buganda in the 1890s was that the British made a highly fruitful alliance with a new generation of young chiefs who were in opposition to a generation of old chiefs. The imperial situation, however—and this issue must be left to one side here—was itself always changing, and imperial authority, if it was to be preserved, had to react to these changes. By the 1920s the young Baganda chiefs of the 1890s had grown old, and there was a new generation of young chiefs. There were also by that time various strains in the alliance between the British and the Baganda, which was the key to the British position there. In the 1920s, however, the British re-established their previous alliance, by making a new alliance with the young chiefs against the old—and the young men of the 1890s who were now ageing were one by one removed from office. There was also by this time a new generation of British administrators; and for twenty years from the mid-1920s to the mid-1940s the British position in Buganda clearly depended upon the new alliance between new administrator and new chief. When in the 1940s and 1950s there was a crisis in the relationship between Britain and Buganda— and it had many aspects—one of the reasons was that this time, when it came to the pinch, the British instead of backing the young men against the old, as they had done on the two previous occasions, started by backing the old men against the young. There was then a very significant corollary: beginning in the middle 1940s and extending through the 1950s, the British, for the first time, had to build rural police stations throughout Buganda for their Protectorate Government Police; these had never before been necessary for the maintenance of British authority.[36]

The important point is that imperial authority was most successfully established wherever it was able to work with the grain of the colonial peoples' own notions of legitimacy: and for various reasons it was able to do this on a substantial number of occasions. But the establishment of a nexus between imperial authorities and traditionally legitimate indigenous authorities was only one of the foundations of imperial authority. We must now consider some of the others.

First, force. Apologists of empire have tended to underestimate the use of force. It is perfectly true that many imperial administrators were very cautious about resorting to it. 'It is our most positive injunction,' the Directors of the East India Company wrote to the Governor of Madras in 1805, 'that force be never resorted to against any of the poligars . . . until every lenient and conciliatory measure has been tried without proper effect.'[37] 'Much more lasting good will be done here,' an officer wrote in Uganda in 1898, 'by patient dissemination of such as "Baraza" news in the outer districts than by hasty vindication of authority and a free use of arrest parties—who, after all, frequently occasion vexatious stampedes.'[38] 'Constant worrying patrols, even in the pagan countries . . . will not do much good, and I am putting my foot down on both heavily,'[39] Sir Percy Girouard, Governor of Northern Nigeria, announced in 1907. Even so force was widely used. This is made clear by a glance through any history of the British Empire for the nineteenth century, with its Kaffir wars, Zulu wars, Ashanti wars, Matabele wars; its Mahratta wars, Sikh wars, Burmese wars. This list does not give a false impression. In the period between 1909 and 1918 during which British authority was extended over the Langi peoples of northern Uganda—a stateless society situation—there was only one year in which a punitive expedition was not sent to some point or other in the area. Very rarely is there mention of any war of colonial expansion in Kenya. But by looking in detail at such early British records relating to Kenya as survive, it would be possible to produce a map showing that there was hardly one important area in the length and breadth of modern Kenya which was not the scene at one time or another of a British military (or armed police) operation.[40]

It may be argued that these were only minor operations. So they were. But even if to the imperial power they were, to use

Professor Hancock's terms, 'little wars', to the colonial peoples they were 'big wars', upon which all their energies were concentrated, and which they lost.[41] Dr. Margaret Read has told the story of a warrior people, the Ngoni of Nyasaland, who suffered from one such expedition in 1898. Ngoni warriors took great pride in their carefully fashioned shields, which hitherto had even withstood bullets. On the day of the British attack 'the Ngoni warriors sprang out, holding their shields before them, and were met by a hail of fire from machine-guns. To their horror they found their invincible shields were no longer a protection. Many fell, the rest fled . . . "The Azungu war was too strong" is the way they invariably end this often repeated tale.'[42] If force was not directly used, the knowledge that it might be, and that if it was, the results could be very serious, was widespread. Professor Monica Wilson has reported why the Pondo of the eastern Cape did not fight the British at annexation in the 1890s: 'Rhodes mowed down a mealie field with machine guns before the eyes of the paramount of eastern Pondoland and his councillors and explained that their fate would be similar if they did not submit.'[43]

They submitted. And so did other colonial peoples who, even if they did not suffer directly themselves, saw their neighbours suffer, and submitted before similar things happened to them. The best policy, the young Lugard put it, was to 'thrash them first, conciliate them afterwards; and by this method our prestige with the native tribes would be certainly greatly increased, and subsequent troubles with them would be less likely'. 'No doubt,' he wrote again thirteen years later when he was High Commissioner of Northern Nigeria, 'the policy of trying to make omelettes without breaking eggs has the cordial support of the section generally known as "Exeter Hall" in England. It is not the way our Raj has been established in India or elsewhere.' 'These people,' a British Commissioner in East Africa declared in 1897, 'must learn submission by the bullet—it is the only school . . . to have peace you must first teach obedience and the only tutor who impresses the lesson properly is the sword.'[44]

Imperial powers used force more often than they have been prepared to admit. They made it their business, moreover, to gather into their own hands all the coercive powers which they could. The confiscation of weapons, and the promulgation of various Arms Acts were crucial to the maintenance of imperial authority the world over. Moreover, for the most part they were very circumspect about the way they handled their native police and native troops. In East Africa native police were never employed in the tribal areas from which they came; only in the areas of distant tribes. 'The right principle,' Lord Grey remarked in 1896, speaking of Southern Rhodesia, 'is that followed by Caesar when he kept England quiet with a legion raised from the Danube and the Danube quiet with a British legion.'[45] In India—at all events after the crisis of 1857—no Indian, only British, troops were ever armed with field guns; whilst the British were always especially solicitous of the Punjabis, and particularly of the Sikhs amongst them, because of their importance to the recruitment and composition of the British-controlled Indian Army.[46]

And yet for all this, one of the most important characteristics of imperial authorities was that although they very frequently used force they also brought 'peace' as well. Indeed, in many colonial areas one of the reasons for the security of imperial authority was the fact that it was the imperial power which first brought a widespread peace. The *Pax* was of first importance. A British officer who served in Nigeria told how he once encountered an old, old woman 'leaning on her stick and gazing intently. Suddenly she began to speak: "Never before since the day I was born have my eyes seen the white man. Soon I must die, by reason of many years; therefore I am come to look upon you that, before death, I may know the appearance of white men." Then, with hands joined and bending almost to the ground, she continued "Salutations and blessings and peace! for in my young days we knew nothing but fear, peril and continual fighting. White men alone have brought safety and peace to our land. Therefore am I glad to have looked upon your face before I die." '[47] The one thing imperial authorities always stamped upon was breaches of the peace. Many people had a keen interest in the maintenance of peace, and if the peacemaker was successful in his purpose, they had an interest in supporting him. If one looks, for example, at the continual, bitter complaints of the Kikuyu of Kenya at the loss of their lands to European settlers, it is very striking how these were periodically relieved by such remarks as: 'We thoroughly appreciate the protection which we have obtained from Government and the peace wherein we now live...'[48] There can be no doubt, too, that the effects of the new *Pax* were frequently considerable. Before the advent of the British, the Kikuyu had lived in closely sealed homesteads, established within a carefully maintained forest fringe, with some of their menfolk on continuous watch on neighbouring hilltops. Upon the establishment of *Pax Britannica* all this was done away with: there were no more sentries, no more close homestead defences, and the forest fringe was steadily cut away.[49]

Force then, and peace were prime foundations of imperial authority. But there were various other important considerations as well. For example, although it is very probable that most colonial people would have much preferred to remain independent, it is difficult to avoid the impression that very few of them began by thinking that they had any inherent *right* to be independent. On the contrary, many of them recognised the legitimacy of the right of conquest,[50] and many of them lived within traditions which accepted the role of a satellite as fully legitimate as well.

It is, moreover, of considerable importance that in the early stages the demands and operations of most imperial governments were very limited. They would not tolerate breaches of the peace; but they did not, to begin with, make many other demands (they did not always at the outset even make tax demands), and it was only bit by bit that they extended their actual control.[51] Colonial peoples therefore, sometimes hardly realised that they had become subject to imperial authority, until it was altogether too late for them to do very much about it.

Equally, if British imperial rulers did not actually create for themselves the upper reaches which they themselves occupied of the stratified political structures that were generally to be found (as was usually the case in Africa), they themselves normally only held its upper levels.[52] This was certainly the case in India. It even meant (as Frykenberg has shown very dramatically for Gunter District in the first half of the nineteenth century)[53] that the answer to the question 'who ruled India during the British period?' was sometimes not so much 'the British', but rather 'the Indian subordinate bureaucracy' (just as in Africa it was sometimes said that it was not so much the District Commissioner who ruled his District as the District Commissioner's interpreter). If there were occasions, then, when British officials were very obtrusive, there were many other times when they were for a long while of no immediate consequence at all to a great many people.

As, moreover, a new generation grew up, so they knew no other order. To overthrow the imperial authority would clearly require a very considerable effort. It might besides, have all sorts of unforeseen and even disastrous consequences. So long as the *status quo* was not too patently oppressive, therefore, colonial peoples tended, until stirred from their lethargies, to accept it.

In particular there were always some indigenous peoples in a colonial society who had a vested interest in its maintenance. In the first place there were those who were enjoying the profits of steady pursuits—perhaps teachers, perhaps traders, perhaps even peasants. But as has often been pointed out, there were in addition always some indigenous peoples in an imperial situation who were directly dependent for their positions of prestige, and for their jobs, upon the patronage of the imperial power; and in the nature of things these constituted yet another support for imperial authority. They are sometimes spoken of as the collaborating classes. Within limits this is a useful concept. Sophisticatedly used it has to take cognisance, however, both of the fact that some of those so identified also showed themselves to be the most single-minded and successful of the opponents of imperial authority;[54] and of the fact that it suggests that there were some *non*-collaborating classes as well. But who, precisely, were these? It is a mistake to assume that those who were not openly associated with the imperial rulers can be considered as having been directly opposed to them. It was rarely so simple.

In this connection some of Gluckman's work is especially illuminating. It is now many years since he insisted not only that the Africans and their white rulers in the Zululand he studied belonged to a single 'social situation', but that the very paradoxes in this situation were part of its essence.[55] More recently he has refined the analysis further by insisting in the first place that even when people have been in open conflict with each other they may well have had common interests which they have been very careful to maintain (just as during a strike certain essential services may be kept going because the strikers see these, in either the short or the long run, as important to themselves). 'The crucial purpose of my terminology,' he then goes on, 'is to emphasise that it is essential to distinguish between "consensus", as agreement on values and goals, and structural "cohesion", as defining the extent to which the structure of a particular social field is maintained in something like continuous pattern by a variety of factors, such as outright force . . . and/or the cross-linking of individuals within the total field in terms of a variety of associations and values which prevent most persons from becoming wholeheartedly loyal to one bond and hostile to all other bonds. Consensus and cohesion are therefore to some extent independent of each other.'[56] Or in other words—in considering the present issue—even when one is affirming the absence of 'consensus', one may well feel bound to point to the presence of widespread structural 'cohesion'. Certainly it is from this standpoint that one can most appreciate the frustration of colonial nationalists, who have felt themselves stifled by and caught up in the socio-political cobwebs which the imperial rulers spun and dominated.

This brings us (as it brought Gluckman) to consider the imperial bureaucracy.[57] It was generally a very powerful bureaucracy. In the first place, until the rise of nationalist parties, it alone had its fingers upon a widespread administrative network. It alone controlled not only the military and the police, but the post office, the railways, the telegraph; tampering with these was always something which it watched extremely closely. Secondly, most imperial bureaucracies were not plagued as most traditional states have been, by succession wars: smooth continuity of personnel was very often something very new in the areas which became subject to Empire. And thirdly, it was the tradition of imperial bureaucracies that its members should trust each other implicitly (and personal rivalries were generally kept strictly under control). They usually, therefore, presented a united front to their subjects, which was never very easily undermined. What is more, the best imperial bureaucracies (by contrast perhaps with some metropolitan bureaucracies) at the same time deliberately encouraged initiative in their lower ranks. In the Indian Civil Service, for instance, a young man was given a vast area to rule over at a very early age; if he ran into trouble his superior was expected to back him against all comers (even though he might afterwards dress him down severely in private). Thus was nurtured the famous self-confidence, which should not be in the least underestimated: in Africa, for instance, the disdain of colonial administrators for social and cosmic forces, such as those before which many African peoples bowed, was a potent source of political power for imperial authority. Thus, if imperial authority depended a great deal upon coercion, it owed a great deal to its competence, rationality, and selfconfidence as well.

There is an additional sense in which this seems very often to have been important. Mannoni in his important book about Madagascar, *Prospero and Caliban*, sought to demonstrate that whereas European man possessed an inferiority complex, Malagasy man had what he called a dependence complex;

> 'It is clear that the dependence relationship contains no element of comparison or self-appraisal, no effort to "situate" oneself otherwise than within that special order of things which is in the system of dependence. This is true, of course, only so long as the feeling of security guaranteed by it remains intact. This is what distinguishes it radically from the attitudes which go to make up the inferiority complex. . . . The point I have tried to bring out is that the Malagache in course of colonisation transfers to his coloniser feelings of dependence the prototype of which is to be found in the effective bond between father and son. In the European these attachments are usually sublimated or liquidated in the course of growth, but in the Malagache they persist without any marked change and are preserved in the structure of society and in the cult of the dead.'[58]

There is no need to accept such views *au pied de la lettre* without more consideration and research. But few with any familiarity with a colonial territory would be ready to affirm that Mannoni was wide of the mark. Many, indeed, have come close to feeling that in this and in a number of other respects, there was a great deal in what he had to say. There is, for instance, the testimony of Professor Evans-Pritchard who studied, among others, two peoples of the southern Sudan—the Azande who possessed a state system, where 'the premise of inequality' applied, and the Nuer, a stateless society where there was no such premise. 'Azande,' he once said, 'treated me as a superior, Nuer as an equal.'[59] Again, there is the striking fact that throughout the first twenty years of its history many prominent leaders of the Indian National Congress regularly and loudly proclaimed the merits of 'the Empire on which the sun never set'.[60] (It was against the very widespread acceptance of this spirit of subordination to the British amongst their countrymen that Gandhi and other Indian nationalist leaders directed so many of their efforts.)[61] It is highly probable that in imperial situations one and two, dependence complexes were widely prevalent. If they were absent in imperial situation type three—and all these things have still to be properly demonstrated one way or the other—the likelihood is that because of the smallness of scale of the peoples composing them, the imperial administrator was more frequently credited there with spectacular powers than in the other two.

It looks, then, as if imperial authority depended upon

1. the gathering in of the threads of legitimacy where these existed;
2. the support for it of traditionally legitimate, if newly established, indigenous political authorities;
3. force; and a monopoly of coercive powers;
4. the establishment of a *Pax*; and the establishment of a new order offering a larger-scale existence;
5. (very often) upon the slow extension and remoteness of imperial authority, which prevented the colonial people from understanding what was happening until it was too late;
6. the vested interest that a number, sometimes a very large number, of local peoples had, for one reason or another, in the maintenance of the imperial regime;
7. the considerable strength and effectiveness of the imperial bureaucracy; and
8. upon the charismatic qualities which, at all events in the early years, imperial rulers possessed for many colonial peoples.

Some of the most striking testimonies of what transpired come from none other than that 'founder of modern India', the great Bengali figure, Raja Ram Mohan Roy (1772–1833). 'Thanks to the Supreme Disposer of the events of this universe,' he declared in 1823, 'for having unexpectedly delivered this country from the long-continued tyranny of its former Rulers, and placed it under the government of the English—a nation who not only are blessed with the enjoyment of civil and political liberty, but also interest themselves in promoting liberty and social happiness, as well as free inquiry into literary and religious subjects, among those nations to which their influence extends.' Ten years later he was to add: 'Finding them generally more intelligent, more steady and moderate in their conduct, I gave up my [earlier] prejudices against them, and became inclined in their favour feeling persuaded that their rule, though a foreign yoke, would lead most speedily and surely to the amelioration of the native inhabitants.'[62]

When, as an historian, one turns to a specific instance what does one find? By 1896, after seven years of upheavals of various kinds, most of the kingdoms of southern Uganda had become subject to British imperial authority. These kingdoms contained perhaps three million people. At this period there were never more than twenty-five British officials in the country at any one time. One accordingly asks the question: how did these twenty-five men establish their authority over three million people? The answer is, by a combination, on the one hand, of what was, in local circumstances, an extreme exercise in coercion, and on the other—again taking local circumstances into account—an unusual degree of skill, self-confidence and creativity. If one phrases this in terms of P. H. Partridge's discussion of 'Power'[63] (where 'power' is the most inclusive term within which one can distinguish between two poles—the pole of 'influence' and the pole of 'domination'—with a point of especial importance between them 'at which a *conflict situation* between the person exercising power and the person over whom it is exercised begins to manifest itself'), then one must say that imperial authority generally seems to have straddled the whole scale. But this is illuminating: for to some people—colonial nationalists, for example—an imperial situation was essentially a conflict situation, whilst others—imperial bureaucrats, for example—regularly denied this. Anyone who has lived in a colonial territory knows that it contained serious elements of conflict, but equally that this was not the whole story; and it looks as though only a careful analysis of each specific instance would enable one to draw up an accurate balance sheet. But a summary conclusion would be that at the outset imperial powers generally combined the roles of master and gunman (the exponents of Partridge's two poles of influence and domination) to an extreme degree; and that what happened when a colonial territory ceased to be a colonial territory was a shrinkage from the two extremes. The master lost his magic and the gunman dropped his gun. There is the striking case here of the Dutch in Indonesia where one can come close to dating the moments when each occurred. The Dutch 'lost their magic' when they were defeated by the Japanese in 1942. They finally 'dropped their gun' after the failure of their second military action against the Republic of Indonesia in 1949. If it is not quite so easy to date these developments for the British in India, or elsewhere, that in itself is instructive.[64]

The Intensity of Power

There can be no more than a brief discussion here of the third topic: the significance of Partridge's notion of the 'intensity of Power' for an imperial historian. 'What is called for,' he has written, 'is a great deal of analysis . . . and the substitution of more manageable concepts for the portmanteau concept of power.'[65]

From my own work on the story of the establishment of British authority over the kingdoms of southern Uganda, it has become fairly clear that British authority extended over them in a fairly regular manner. As it has turned out this had nothing to do, however, with whether or not a British sphere of influence, or a British protectorate, had been formally declared. In 1896, for instance, the British Protectorate of Uganda was formally extended over the kingdoms in the west and south-west of what became Uganda by a Proclamation under the British Foreign Jurisdiction Act of 1890, which was published in the London Gazette. Two of these kingdoms, however, had already been under British control for the previous two years; another group of them was not to be under British control for a further two years; and yet another group not for a further fifteen years. The language of the constitutional lawyers has therefore been of no use to me. Nor has that of the students of colonial administration: the issue here is not, for example, 'direct' as against 'indirect' rule. So I have had to go fending for myself. In due course I turned to the dictionary, but this was not much help either. I have been forced, therefore, to be somewhat arbitrary in my use of words.

The problems are these. First, it has been important to draw a sharp distinction between periods in which British officials who visited the Uganda kingdoms acknowledged the political authority of those kingdoms over their actions, and periods in which they refused to do this any longer. This roughly coincided, as it happened, with the difference between periods when because of the state of negotiations about the Partition of Africa away in Europe, this portion of Africa was or was not thought by British officials to be 'red on the map'. I have called the first period one of Impact; the second one of Domination.

Impact was of two different kinds. First, it was what I would call Influence—a very tenuous impact, but clearly recognisable even so. It was represented in this instance by Sir John Kirk, a remarkable British Consul-General at Zanzibar, who carried on a considerable correspondence with chiefs and rulers in the East African interior who were anxious to maintain contact with him, and for whom his name had become a by-word for distant power.[66]

When influence became more marked I have called it Sway, exemplified by the Zanzibar proverb 'when they pipe in Zanzibar, they dance upon the lakes'. The best example that I know of comes from the kingdom of Nkore in south-western Uganda in 1896. At that time there were no British officials in Nkore, and Nkore was in no sense under British authority. The leaders of Nkore, however, who were involved in a succession war, sent envoys to the British in Buganda to make sure that their views on the succession were made plain before the war was allowed to reach its climax. Here was a direct and tangible impact upon some crucial events within an African kingdom. There had not as yet been any move by the British to establish their authority over the kingdom, yet the leading men in that kingdom seem to have been acutely aware of the potentialities of British power for events in their kingdom, and were taking these fully into account in settling their internal problems. Such was Sway.

It was only after this, when the British had taken some decisive action which established that in the last resort they were the overlords and that their authority was present, that one could say that the foundations of British Domination had been laid. But here it has been necessary to make a good many further distinctions. First of all, there tended to be a stage during which the British made no direct interference in the workings of the native kingdoms, but when they no longer accepted the authority of those kingdoms over their own doings. I have called this—rather arbitrarily perhaps—a period of British Ascendancy. Thereafter British Domination developed in two distinct steps and in two distinct ways. First there would be *ad hoc* interference in the internal affairs of the kingdom. Let me quote here the orders given to one British officer in Uganda in July 1894: 'You will interfere as little as possible in local affairs, but should any case be brought before you for decision you will settle it yourself.'[67] I call this Predominance. Later there was often a step forward into regular interference with the internal affairs of the kingdom: 'I am running the show with the two Katikiros and Kago'[68] (the names of some of the senior chiefs), another administrator wrote in 1899. I call this Control.

It has been necessary, however, to distinguish between those kingdoms where British authority was readily accepted by its ruler and chiefs (for reasons touched upon earlier), and those where such authority was only very grudgingly accepted, generally after a colonial war had been fought and lost. Here, it was once more necessary to distinguish between *ad hoc* interference and regular interference. I call these two phases Mastery and Dictation. One kingdom, Bunyoro, for reasons which must be traced upon another occasion, passed between 1894 and 1902 through periods of British Ascendancy, Mastery, Dictation, and then across to Control.

There are two points to be made in conclusion. First, these distinctions are probably more useful as types rather than periods: in other words they periodically co-existed. Over land alienation the imperial regime could be 'dictatorial', while over succession law it may merely have been 'predominant', whilst at the same time over marriage law it may only have been 'ascendant'. Secondly, it is doubtful whether this particular scheme could be applied without adjustment to other situations. From some consideration of the story of the establishment of British authority both in India (and specifically in Bengal, the Peshwa's dominions, Sind and the Punjab) and elsewhere (for example in Malaya and in Fiji),[69] it is fairly certain that a careful characterisation of the successive stages through which British imperial authority passed during the early years of contact is not only very illuminating but is emphatically required. It is both possible and desirable, for example, to distinguish precisely between the position and power of the East India Company in Bengal[70] as it existed before the expulsion of the Factory from Calcutta in 1756; after its return in January 1757; in the sequel to the Battle of Plassey in June 1757; as a consequence of the supersession of Mir Jafar by Mir Kasim in 1760; as a result of the Battle of Buxar, the Treaty of Allahabad, and the procurement of the Diwani of Bengal in 1764–5; in the wake of Warren Hasting's decision in 1772 that the Company should 'stand forth as Dewan'; and finally in the aftermath of Cornwallis's administrative reforms of the 1790s. It is clear, however, that the salient characteristics of each of these stages differed significantly from those encountered in the history of Uganda. Analyses in terms of the 'intensity' of power that was exercised by the invading imperial agents is nevertheless called for in discussing such sequences, even if it seems difficult at present to notch up any single all-purpose tally.

NOTES

1. For the purposes of this chapter 'imperial authority' and 'colonial authority' are synonymous.
2. E.g. Robert I. Rotberg and Ali A. Mazrui, ed., *Protest and Power in Black Africa*, New York 1970.
3. P. Woodruff, *The Men who Ruled India: The Guardians*, London, 1954, p. 300. Gandhi used to put the issue thus: 'We in India may in a moment realize that one hundred thousand Englishmen [his estimate of their numbers in India] need not frighten three hundred

million human beings', 'The Doctrine of the Sword', *Young India*, 11 August 1920. The point is the same.

4. E.g. the report at the height of the Civil Disobedience Movement by the Inspector-General of Police in the United Provinces, R. J. S. Dodd, 3 September 1930, National Archives of India, Home Political, 259 of 1930: 'One pleasing and notable feature is the improved self-respect and self-assurance of the ordinary constable. He knows he has done his job well, he is proud of it and he feels that in any case Government is behind him. Recruits are readily available: as one Superintendent said, "I have to drive them away with a stick." On August 1 there were 123 vacancies in a force of 33,000—a record never yet reached since the Force was started.' It should be added that there were 57,000 British troops in India in 1931, India Office Records, L/M12/17.
5. Percival Spear, 'A Third Force in India 1920–47: a study in political analysis', in C. H. Philips and M. D. Wainwright, *The Partition of India: Policies and Perspectives, 1935–1947*, London, 1970, pp. 490–503.
6. For some beginnings see C. A. Bayly, 'Local Control in Indian Towns: the case of Allahabad 1880–1920', and F. C. R. Robinson, 'Consultation and Control: the United Provinces' Government and its Allies 1860–1906', *Modern Asian Studies,* 5, 1971, pp. 289–312, 313–36.
7. Percival Spear, *Twilight of the Mughals*, Cambridge, 1951, Ch. III is especially good on this. See also more generally his *India: a modern History*, Ann Arbor, 1961, Part III.
8. There is a useful account of the Sind story in Robert A Huttenback, *British Relations with Sind, 1799–1843*, California, 1962.
9. The prime authority on all this is still B. H. Baden-Powell, *The Land Systems of British India*, 3 vols., Oxford, 1892.
10. Biographers of Rhodes rarely resist this story, e.g. S. G. Millin, *Rhodes*, London, 1936, Ch. XXXVII, 'Bayete!' See, more generally, T. O. Ranger, *Revolt in Southern Rhodesia 1896–97*, London, 1967.
11. J. B. Kelly, *Britain and the Persian Gulf 1795–1880*, Oxford, 1968; B. C. Busch, *Britain and the Persian Gulf 1894–1914*, California, 1967.
12. The classic statement of the doctrine of Paramountcy with regard to the Indian States is Reading to Nizam of Hyderabad, 27 March 1926. For this and other documents illustrating the position see C. H. Philips, *The Evolution of India and Pakistan 1858 to 1947: Select Documents,* London, 1962, p. 415 sqq. See also for useful summaries (and bibliography), Terence Creagh Coen, *The Indian Political Service. A Study in Indirect Rule*, London, 1971.
13. Earl of Cromer, *Modern Egypt,* London, 1908, Vol. II, pp. 270–1, 280 sqq. Cf. 'the position of the Consul-General was anomalous, the highest authority in Egypt, but possessing no more legal authority than any other Consul-General: the position of the

British troops was anomalous, not employed by the Government of Egypt—accidentally present, yet supporting the whole structure; the position of the British officials was utterly anomalous—legally servants of the Khedive, in practice taking their orders from the Consul General'. Lord Lloyd, *Egypt Since Cromer*, London, 1933, Vol. 1, p. 37.

14. D. A. Low and R. C. Pratt, *Buganda and British Overrule 1900–1955*, London, 1960.
15. 'The prestige and influence of the Chiefs can be best upheld by letting the peasantry see that . . . there are not two sets of Rulers—the British and the Native—working either separately or in co-operation, but a single Government in which Native Chiefs have clearly defined duties', F. D. Lugard, *Political Memoranda; Revision of Instructions to Political Officers on Subjects Chiefly Political and Administrative*, London, 1906, 3rd ed., with a new introduction by A. H. M. Kirk-Greene, Frank Cass, London, 1970. p. 161.
16. Margery Perham, *Lugard: The Years of Authority 1898–1945*, London, 1960, pp. 128–9. See also D. J. Muffett, *Concerning Brave Captains,* London, 1964; A. H. M. Kirk-Greene, *The Principles of Native Administration in Nigeria: Selected Documents, 1900–1947*, Oxford, 1965; I. F. Nicolson, *The Administration of Nigeria 1900–1960*, Oxford, 1969; R. A. Adeleye, *Power and Diplomacy in Northern Nigeria 1804–1906*, London, 1971.
17. L. W. Hollingsworth, *Zanzibar under the Foreign Office*, London, 1953.
18. E. Sadka, 'The State Councils in Perak and Selangor, 1877–1895', in K. G. Tregonning, *Papers on Malayan History*, Singapore, 1962, esp. pp. 90–2.
19. Wilson to Sadler, 21 August 1902, Buganda Residency Archives, 'General' 1902.
20. Thruston to Ternan, 30 June 1897, Entebbe Secretariat Archives, A4/8.
21. Kirk to Anderson, 22 Nov. 1892, Foreign Office Confidential Print, 6362, no. 214.
22. Berkeley to Salisbury, 8 Dec. 1896, and enclosures, F.O. 2/93.
23. Percival Spear, *Oxford History of India*, Part III (various editions) will provide details of this.
24. P. M. Mutibwa, 'The Malagasy and Europeans: a study of Madagascar's foreign policy 1861–1895', D.Phil. thesis, University of Sussex, 1969, Chs. VII–IX.
25. Paula Brown, 'From Anarchy to Satrapy', *American Anthropologist*, 1963, Vol. 65, pp. 5–6.
26. M. Fortes and E. E. Evans-Pritchard, *African Political Systems*, London, 1949, p. 5. Cf. John Middleton and David Tait, *Tribes without Rulers*, London, 1958.
27. Here, and elsewhere, see J. A. Barnes, 'Indigenous Politics and Colonial Administration with special reference to Australia,'

Comparative Studies in Society and History, Vol. 2, 1960, pp. 133–49.

28. For an interesting comparison between the Nuer of the southern Sudan and the Gusii of Kenya, see Robert A. LeVine, 'The Internalization of Political Values in Stateless Societies', *Human Organization*, Vol. 19, 1960, pp. 51–8.
29. *Reports relating to the administration of the East African Protectorates*, Cd. 2740 (1905).
30. E.g. C. U. Aitchison, *Collection of Treaties, Engagements and Sunnuds relating to India*, 10 vols., Calcutta, 1892; *Laws of the Uganda Protectorate, Vol. VI, Native Agreements and Buganda Native Laws*, Entebbe, 1936.
31. E.g. V. P. Menon, *The Story of the Integration of the Indian States*, London, 1956; *Report of the Uganda Relationships Committee 1961 under the Chairmanship of the Right Honourable the Earl of Munster, P.C., K.B.E.*, Entebbe, 1961.
32. It is, for instance, plain that—using Weber's terms—the legal and rational element in the political authority of the independent states within the Commonwealth varies considerably, see Chapter 6 below.
33. For a fascinating example, see H. E. Lambert, *The use of indigenous authorities in tribal administration: studies of the Meru of Kenya Colony,* Communications, School of African Studies, Capetown, no. 16, 1947.
34. J. Maquet, *The Premise of Inequality in Ruanda,* London, 1961.
35. For an outline account see my Chapter II, 'Uganda: the establishment of the Protectorate 1894–1919', in V. T. Harlow and E. M. Chilver, *History of East Africa,* Vol. II, Oxford, 1966. For very close parallels in Bengal in the 1750s see B. K. Gupta, *Sirajuddallah and the East India Company 1756–1757,* Leiden, 1962, and other accounts of the British conquest of Bengal in that and the next decade.
36. D. A. Low, *Buganda in Modern History*, London and California, 1971, esp. Ch. III.
37. Revenue Despatch to Madras, 15 May 1805, quoted T. H. Beaglehole, *Thomas Munro and the Development of Administrative Policy in Madras, 1792–1818,* Cambridge, 1966, p. 65.
38. Wilson to Johnston, 10 Dec. 1900, Entebbe Secretariat Archives, A12/1.
39. Girouard to Elgin, 30 May 1907, Public Record Office, London, C.O. 446/63, quoted by Mary Bull in Kenneth Robinson and Frederick Madden, *Essays in Imperial Government*, Oxford, 1963, p. 59. See also Girouard's, *Memoranda for Provincial and District Commissioners*, Nairobi, 1910, pp. 15–18, 'Instructions for the Control of "Expeditions and Patrols" '.
40. During the reign of King Edward VII, 1902–10, thirty-four 'clasps', each to commemorate a (fairly considerable) British expedition somewhere in East, Central or West Africa, were issued

for attachment to the Africa General Service Medal, H. Moyse-Bartlett, *The King's African Rifles*, Aldershot, 1956, p. 698. See also D. A. Low, 'British East Africa: the establishment of British Rule, 1895–1912', Harlow and Chilver, *History of East Africa*, II, Ch. 1.

41. W. K. Hancock, *Four Studies in War and Peace in this Century*, Cambridge, 1962, Ch. 1.
42. Magaret Read, 'Tradition and Prestige among the Ngoni', *Africa*, Vol. 9, 1936, p. 475.
43. Monica Hunter, *Reaction to Conquest*, 2nd ed., London, 1961, p. 412.
44. F. D. Lugard, 'The Fight against the Slave Traders on Nyasa', *Contemporary Review*, 1889, p. 343, quoted H. A. C. Cairns *Prelude to Imperialism*, London, 1965, p. 43; Lugard to Burdon, 17 April 1902, Nigerian Archives Kaduna SNP 7/3/40, quoted R. A. Adeleye, *Power and Diplomacy in Northern Nigeria 1804–1906*, London, 1971, p. 257; Hardinge to Salisbury, 24 April 1897, F.O. 107/3.
45. Grey to his wife, 23 March 1896, GR1/1/1, quoted Ranger, *Revolt in Southern Rhodesia*, p. 119. For another example see Robert O. Collins, *Land Beyond the Rivers, The Southern Sudan 1898–1918*, Yale, 1971, p. 173.
46. E.g. Glancy to Linlithgow, 4 March 1942, Linlithgow to Amery, 6 March 1942, Nos. 236, 246, in Nicholas Mansergh, *India, The Transfer of Power 1942–7*, Vol. 1, London, 1970.
47. P. A. Talbot, *Tribes of the Niger Delta*, London, 1932, reprinted Frank Cass, London, 1967, p. 329. I owe this reference to Dr. Cherry Gertzel.
48. This occurs in the midst of a long list of complaints recorded by Beech, Memo on 'The Kikuyu Point of View', Dagoretti Political Record Book, 1908–12, Vol. i, D.C.'s Office, Kiambu, Kenya (now in the Kenya National Archives).
49. W. S. and K. Routledge, *With a Prehistoric People. The Akikuyu of British East Africa*, London, 1910, reprinted Frank Cass, London, 1968, pp. 7, 329.
50. E.g. 'Whatever the rights and wrongs of the attack on Kano and Sokoto may be the British were the instrument of destiny and were fulfilling the will of God', Alhaji Sir Ahmadu Bello, Sardauna of Sokoto, *My Life*, Cambridge, 1962, p. 19.
51. A. W. Southall, *Alur Society*, Cambridge, 1953, p. 283: see also Ch. IX, and pt. III passim.
52. For further thoughts upon all this see Chapter 6 below.
53. R. E. Frykenberg, *Guntur District 1788–1848, A History of Local Influence and Central Authority in South India*, Oxford, 1965.
54. Cf. the introduction to D. A. Low, *The Mind of Buganda*, London and California, 1971.
55. 'Analysis of a social situation in modern Zululand', *Bantu Studies*,

Vol. 14, 1949, pp. 1–30, 147–74; *Custom and Conflict in Africa,* Oxford, 1955.

56. 'Interhierarchical roles: professional and party ethics in tribal areas in south and central Africa', in Marc J. Swartz, (ed.), *Local-Level Politics,* London, 1969, pp. 69–94, and references there cited. See also Frykenberg, *Guntur District*, esp. Ch. XVI.
57. E.g. Woodruff, *The Men who ruled India*, passim; R. Heussler, *Yesterday's Rulers: the Making of the British Colonial Service*, Syracuse, 1963.
58. O. Mannoni, *Prospero and Caliban, The Psychology of Colonization*, London, 1956, pp. 83, 158. For a wider application of these ideas see Philip Mason, *Prospero's Magic*, London, 1962.
59. E. E. Evans-Pritchard, *The Nuer,* Oxford, 1940, p. 15.
60. E.g. the remarkable speech in April 1905 by G. S. Khaparde, President of the Central Provinces and Berar Provincial Conference, National Archives of India, Home Public, 217–227A, October 1906.
61. E.g. M. K. Gandhi, *Non-Violent Resistance*, New York edition, 1961, passim.
62. 'Final Appeal to the Christian Public in Defence of the Precepts of Jesus', *English Works*, Pt. 7, pp. 177–8; *Athenaeum*, 5 Oct. 1833, p. 666, quoted S. N. Hay, 'Western Indigenous Elements in Modern Indian Thought', in Marius B. Jansen, *Changing Japanese Attitudes towards Modernization*, Princeton, 1965, p. 319.
63. Cf. P. H. Partridge, 'Some Notes on the Concept of Power', *Political Studies*, XI, (1963), pp. 107–25.
64. G. M. Kahin, *Nationalism and Revolution in Indonesia*, Ithaca, 1952. For more on the British story see Chapter 5 below.
65. Op. cit., pp. 124–5.
66. R. Coupland, *The Exploration of East Africa 1886–1890,* London, 1939, passim.
67. Colvile to Spire, 15 July 1894, Spire Papers.
68. Wilson to Lugard, 22 March 1899, Lugard Papers.
69. E.g. Huttenback, *British Relations with Sind*; C. D. Cowan, *Nineteenth Century Malaya, the origins of British Political Control*, London, 1961; David Routledge, 'Pre-cession Government in Fiji', Ph.D. thesis, Australian National University, 1966.
70. There is some interesting material on this in Abdul Majed Khan, *The Transition in Bengal 1756–1775, a study of Saiyid Muhammad Reza Khan*, Cambridge, 1969.

2

Empire and Social Engineering

In the mid twentieth century 'development' has become a blessed word. With the world's population growing apace; with the gap widening between the resources available to the world's rich and the world's poor; with some increase in our sensitivity to the misery in which so many of our fellow human-beings subsist, the sophisticated organisation of development has now become amongst the most urgent of our moral imperatives. It is high time: the matter is urgent.

Momentarily, however, there is something to be said for reminding ourselves that there is a long intellectual history to our present concerns. Myrdal's recent fulminations against India's caste system are no more than an echoing of earlier diatribes.[1] The latter-day argument over what kind of education is most suitable for developing countries looks disappointingly thin beside Mountstuart Elphinstone's ruminations of a century and a half ago.[2] It is very plain that the intellectual history of 'development' in recent times—for such an historian may be allowed to affirm there has been—has many of the switchback characteristics of an earlier debate.[3] Though this earlier story is generally ignored,[4] it is in a number of respects singularly pertinent. Intellectualising upon India's ills, for example, is not an invention of the twentieth century. As long ago as 1784 an elaborate summary of some of the formulations already in existence was drawn up for the British Prime Minister, William Pitt;[5] and in a further review in 1793 it was firmly stated that India posed 'the greatest question in commercial and political economy, that has occurred in the annals of civil society'.[6] A hundred and eighty years later that would still pass as a fair dictum on the issues involved in Indian 'planning'.

To trace out this earlier story in any really satisfactory manner would require many times the space available here. Curiously the earlier history of Dutch thinking on this topic has been presented in brief compass more than once already.[7] There have been some admirable contributions to our understanding of the British story.[8] But they are not often pieced together, and there are still major lacunae. Given our present concerns, there plainly ought to be as much investigation of Western thinking about societal change in the non-Western world as about the purport of imperial expansionism there. All that can be offered here is an attempt at a preliminary sketch of what the British story appears to have contained.

There are five preliminary points to make. By 'social engineering' is meant here governmental action designed to secure, maintain, or restore the good life. In the course of time the currently preferred definition of what constitutes the good life has changed, and also the orthodox way to achieve it (though not, as one might think, always in tandem). In the last decade or so Western economists have had their orthodoxies here. Given the 'stagnation of real income and mounting inflation' in country *x* (they have been wont to declare) it has become clear that if it 'is to become a genuinely unified and prosperous nation, a take-off into visible economic growth cannot be delayed much longer'.[9] It is one implication of the story to be told here that it was only recenly that the problems came to be formulated in this way; and another that before very long such a formulation may well find itself relegated to a dusty niche along with all of its predecessors. Maoists, presumably, would already say that that would be to treat it much too kindly.

Secondly, it must be emphasised that the thinking about social engineering which will be referred to here, though concerned with, indeed directed at, in the main India and Africa, was that of British man, and not Indian or African man. Thirdly, not only is there no space to do justice to a good many of the very important cross-currents,[10] it will not be possible either to avoid blurring some of the sharp differences between some of the men discussed. Fourthly, it must not be thought that questions of social engineering can be divorced from questions of political authority. It would be possible to provide a host of examples of their intimate connection. But that would be another story. And fifthly, so would the *effects* of the policies to be discussed here: no general statement upon these can be offered here.

Taking, then, the two centuries of British thinking upon what the 1793 document called 'the greatest question in... political economy that has occurred in the annals of civil society,' there seem to be three distinguishable stages. These may be referred to successively as the Great Debate, the Settled View, and the Development Fever.

The Great Debate

The first lasted for just about a century, from around 1760 to around 1860. Its major focus was India.[11] It arose for one quite simple reason. During the course of that century, the British acquired for the first time a vast empire over a numerous, variegated, non-Western people with its own non-Western culture(s), and they soon found themselves asking those simple questions with intractable answers: 'What shall we do with it?' 'What *ought* we to do with it for its own good and for ours?'[12]

The first answer came from Robert Clive, Britain's Cortes in Bengal. In his view there should be as little interference as possible with the indigenous political system, and *a fortiori* with its social. 'When we first embraced the political system now established,' he was later to write, 'it was with diffidence: when we entered on the correction of abuses and the punishment of misconduct, it was with reluctance.'[13] For all the difference between him and Warren Hastings, his greatest successor in the supreme post in Bengal, they were agreed on this. They were of course at one here with Voltaire and other intellectuals of their time. 'The people of this country,' Hastings declared, 'do not require our aid to furnish them with a rule for their conduct, or a standard for their property.' 'We have endeavoured to adapt our Regulations to the Manners and Understanding of the People, and Exigencies of the Country, adhering, as closely as we are able, to their Ancient Usages and Institutions.'[14] This, of course, was to be a theme which was to be regularly reiterated, At its most imaginative, it gave rise—not least under Hastings's own patronage—to the great development of Western oriental scholarship which is associated with such names as Sir William Jones[15] and the anglicised German Max Müller. At its least imaginative it became the 'do-nothing-except-curb-the-most-scandalous-abuses' policy of the Political Department of the Government of India when dealing with the Indian princely states.[16]

However, even at a very early stage it did not pass unchallenged. It was not so much the principle of non-interference itself that was first called into question. Rather, it was the licence it seemer to allow the servants of the East India Company, and not least Clive and Warren Hastings themselves, to behave in India as extortionate 'Asian despots' were alleged to do. The memorable encounter in the Bengal Council between Warren Hastings and Philip Francis in the 1770s (which proved to be but the Indian preliminary to Hastings' subsequent impeachment trial in London) centred upon Francis's determination to cleanse what he saw as an augean stable.[17]

The most substantial issue between the two men concerned the revenue of Bengal. Revenue, or more particularly, land revenue, was a major focus of attention during the first century of British rule in any discussion of British policy in India[18]—a fixed point which had no counterpart in Africa. It was not just that in India the ruler, whoever he might be, procured the bulk of the finances necessary for government from payments made in respect of land held. The payment to a superior of land revenue was the single most important symbol of that superior's political authority. Moreover the structuring of the means by which land revenue was to be transmitted to the British administration became one of the chief methods which the British employed for laying the foundations of the good life, which their dominion, as they saw it, was at least in part designed to procure.

In the belief that he was fulfilling the 'original principles' of land revenue collection in Bengal, Hastings had auctioned it out to the highest bidders. But in consequence there were great abuses, upon which Francis quickly seized. There were two central points to Francis's subsequent campaign against Hastings. First, Francis took an *a priori* stand. 'To establish,' he once wrote, 'any proposition whatsoever we are constantly obliged to go back to first elements, and so deduce the argument step by step to a regular conclusion.'[19] To this kind of approach—which was to rear its head repeatedly—Hastings replied with the perennial impatience of the experienced administrator: 'More used to the practice of business than to speculation,' he riposted, 'I beg to be excused from discussing these propositions as general and abstract questions. I wish to confine them merely to the revenue of Bengal.'[20] The first round of the great debate was thus joined on an issue which persisted. Secondly, the 'first elements' to which Francis appealed were, surprising as it may seem, those of the cosmopolitan-minded French Physiocrats. And here we have the first clear demonstration of an attempted application to the non-western British Empire of a budget of nostrums which had originally been fashioned within a purely European intellectual milieu.[21] Mirabeau the elder wrote a vigorous *Dissertation concerning the Landed Property of Bengal,* and the domiciled Frenchman Henry Patullo wrote a formidable *Essay upon the Cultivation of the Lands and Improvements of Bengal.*[22] Francis stood intellectually with these men.

For the physiocrats land, not commerce, was the source of all wealth. For all the distinctiveness of their doctrines, moreover, they would have agreed with the mercantilist Alexander Dow: 'An established idea of property is the source of all industry among individuals and of course the foundation of public prosperity'.[23] Francis's own gloss on this ran as follows: 'The scheme of every regular government requires that the mass of the people should labour, and that the few should be supported by the labours of the many, who receive their retribution in the peace, protection, and security which accompanies just authority and regular subordination.'[24] In his view, it was in the correct structuring of the land revenue system that the constitution 'of the perfect social order' (the good life', as it is termed here) was to be found. The effect of the introduction of such notions into British thinking about India was immense.

It was not, however, until a decade after Francis's time that Cornwallis (on being appointed Governor-General of Bengal) put Francis's ideas into operation. The result was the so-called Permanent Settlement of Bengal of 1793, a pact for the payment of land revenue, fixed in perpetuity, between the British and those zamindars of Bengal whom the British recognized as the landlords, in the English sense, of Bengal. In addition, however, to being the inheritor of the physiocratic doctrine, Cornwallis was also an English Whig gentleman. 'I can assure you,' he thus told his superiors, 'that it will be of the utmost importance... that the principal landlords... should be restored to such circumstances as to enable them to support their families with decency and to give a liberal education to their children . . . that a regular foundation of ranks may be supported which is nowhere more necessary than in this country for preserving order in civil society.'[25] On a later occasion he expressed his hopes for the new arrangements in this way: 'Landed property will acquire a value hitherto unknown in Hindustan and the large capitals possessed by many of the natives in Calcutta . . . will be appropriated to the more useful purposes of . . . improving lands.'[26] Improving landlords, that is, of an English type would, he believed, be the agents of the economic prosperity of Bengal and of the security of its 'civil society'. (A century later this became the credo of the proponents of White Settlement in Africa).

Cornwallis was an English Whig in another sense as well. He believed most vehemently that the misgovernment of Bengal, for which the East India Company had by this time become notorious, could only be mended by a rigid application of the classical Whig doctrine of the division of powers. He accordingly set about removing from the hands of the Company's Collectors of Revenue all their judicial powers. These he had transferred to the hands of quite separate and greater officials, the District Judges and Magistrates. These men were to be the embodiment of the Whig system, empowered to administer "impartially" the impersonal law of Cornwallis's Code of Regulations against anyone—not least, the British Collectors themselves—who might be tempted to interfere with the sacred institution of land ownership. Odd as it may seem, neither Cornwallis nor Philip Francis would have acknowledged that he was seeking to effect a wholesale revolution in Indian society.[27] Their chief aim in their own eyes was to save Indian society from the rapacity of the

Company's servants. But they had, of course, set on foot a great deal else besides.[28]

Yet the Cornwallis system had no sooner become the Company's orthodoxy than it came to be challenged all along the line. The counter-attack was first mounted by Thomas Munro, who both before and after 1800 secured a great deal of formative experience whilst bringing areas inland from Madras under British rule for the first time.[29] Munro went on to be a Special Commissioner in Madras between 1814 and 1818, and then Governor of Madras in the 1820s. His ruminations upon his experience as a working district officer made him as impatient as Hastings had been with all those constructions which were not rooted in Indian experience. 'It is too much regulation,' he fumed, 'that ruins everything. Englishmen are as great fanatics in politics as Mahomedans in religion. They suppose that no country can be saved without English institutions. The natives of this country have enough of their own to answer every useful object of internal administration, and if we maintain and protect them our work will in a very few months settle itself.'[30] He was strongly opposed in particular to Cornwallis's institution of the separation of powers between Collector and Magistrate. 'Revenue and judicial and where practicable military powers also should be exercised by the same person,' one of his contemporaries wrote in 1820. 'Union, not division, should be the order of our rule. Confidence [in the integrity of British officials] not distrust should be the engine to work with.'[31] To Munro, indeed, and to those who stood with him—Elphinstone, Malcolm, Metcalfe, John Lawrence, and in due course a host of others—the District Officer should be the father of his people, their protector and guiding hand, to whom they could turn at any hour of the day or night, and at whose instance the good life could be brought gradually nearer without any notion (to quote Munro) that it could 'be suddenly improved by any contrivance of ours'.[32] Under the influence of the Munro school, as it came to be called, the new pattern, which was to last in the British Empire till the end (and has periodically reared its head subsequently), under which the District Officer possessed both executive and judicial powers, not least for the purposes of social engineering, came to be established practice.

But it was not just over 'regulation' and the separation of powers that Munro and his associates were opposed to the Cornwallis system. They were opposed as well to his zamindari or landlord system. Munro, for a start, had no time for the south India poligars who would have been the beneficiaries of a zamindari settlement there. He took a romantic, paternalist delight in the ordinary Indian peasantry, and in his view the unit of cultivation should be small, for only thus could be raised up 'a crowd of men of small, but of independent property, who, when they are certain that they will themselves enjoy the benefits of every extraordinary exertion of labour, work with a spirit of activity which would in vain be expected from the tenants and servants of great landholders'.[33] This doctrine, too, of course, was to have a very long life. It is to be found indeed in the Report of the East Africa Royal Commission 1953–55; in Kenyatta's post-independence Kenya; in the writings of Charan Singh, the ideologue since Independence of the ruling groups in Uttar Pradesh; and even, with a sigh of near despair, in Gunnar Myrdal's *Asian Drama*.[34] In Munro's day it led most immediately to the so-called ryotwari settlements in Madras and Bombay, and to the formation of settlement policies all over North India (not, let it be said, always without protracted argument: between 1770 and 1870 it is not very difficult to count ten distinct changes of course on land settlement policy in the area now covered by the large north Indian state of Uttar Pradesh).[35] In the thinking of the Munro school the improving peasant, rather than the landlord, was to be the hope of India's future.

We must beware, however, of exaggerating the extent of the switch from Hastings via Francis to Cornwallis, and then from Cornwallis to Munro, for the differences between them were as nothing to the differences between all of them and three other schools of British thinking about India during this first century. All of these earlier figures, for example, would have agreed with Malcolm—one of Munro's most important associates—when he wrote in the 1820's that 'All that Government can do is, by maintaining the internal peace of the country, and by adapting its principles to the various feelings, habits and character of its inhabitants, to give time for the slow and silent operation of the desired improvement, with a constant impression that every attempt to accelerate this end will be attended with the danger of its defeat.'[36] Some of them might think that there were things wrong with Indian society, but none of them went so far as to say it was in a state of degradation. Already, however, there was ranged on the other side a phalanx of men in influential positions concerning India, who had none of their tenderness towards 'the habits . . . of its inhabitants', and who believed that these were indeed utterly deplorable.

This second phalanx belonged to those three schools which were called respectively, evangelical, liberal, and utilitarian. As it happened, those of their number who were concerned with India included the foremost exponents of the day of each of these three points of view; and in sharp contrast to those whom we have so far considered, they all believed that the ordering of Indian society as it stood was appalling to the point of perversity. It needed, they believed, a radical transformation, which it was Britain's duty to effect. As a major figure from each of these schools put it, Indian society was marked by a 'general corruption of manners and sunk in misery'; 'sunk in the lowest depths of slavery and superstition'; comprised 'the most enslaved portion of the human race'.[37]

The prime evangelical figure was Charles Grant, a man who for four decades served the Company, first in India and then in London.[38] He had therefore, a great deal of Indian experience, yet his diagnosis of India's condition was diametrically opposite to that of Hastings or Munro. 'We cannot avoid recognizing in the people of Hindustan,' he had written in a very influential pamphlet first produced in 1792, 'a race of men lamentably degenerate and base; retaining but a feeble sense of moral obligation; yet obstinate in their disregard of what they know to be right, governed by malevolent and licentious passions, strongly exemplifying the effects produced on society by a great and general corruption of manners.'[39] Grant's proposed solution was in the first place the introduction to India of Christian missionaries, who when he first wrote, were being excluded by the Company in accordance with his opponents' regard for Indian feelings. 'Were Indians,' Grant asked, to be offered the 'Divine principles which have raised us in the scale of being', or were they to be left in 'error and ignorance'?[40] His own answer was clear. 'The pre-eminent excellence of the morality which the Gospel teaches and the superior efficacy of its divine system taken in all its parts, in meliorating the condition of human society, cannot be denied by those who are unwilling to admit to higher claims; and on this ground alone the dissemination of it must be beneficial to mankind.'[41]

In England he became a prominent member of the remarkable Clapham Sect, and from its leadership enlisted in his support none other than William Wilberforce himself—in 'that greatest of all causes', as Wilberforce himself was to call the conversion of India to Christianity, 'for I really place it before Abolition'.[42] Together, in 1813, they managed to secure an entrée for Christian missionaries into the Company's territories, and in the process showed themselves to be full-throated anglicists. Wilberforce, for instance, addressed the House of Commons in 1813 in these terms: 'Are we so little aware of the vast superiority even of European laws and institutions, and far more of British institutions, over those of Asia, as not to be prepared to predict with confidence, that the Indian community which should have exchanged its dark and bloody superstitions for the genial influence of Christian light and truth, would have experienced such an increase of civil order and security, of social pleasures and domestic comforts [the 'good life', that is] as to be desirous of preserving the blessings it should have acquired.'[43] Back in his day Hastings had spoken of 'reconciling the people of England to the nature of Hindustan'.[44] The evangelicals argued that one should work in precisely the opposite direction.

In so doing they joined hands with those liberals who believed that Western education was an urgent requirement for India, since it would 'silently undermine . . . the fabric of error'[45]—indeed, for the evangelicals education was often a prior requirement. Both not only believed in the pre-eminent efficacy of Western education. They were agreed as well upon the nature of the ills which it would put to rights. The key figure here was the liberal historian and politician, Thomas Babington Macaulay: and the key statement of his position is that famous passage in his Minute on Education written in 1835 in which he finalised the triumph of the 'anglicist' position over the so-called 'orientalist' doctrine which hitherto had enjoyed such a strong position in British thinking about India since the days of Warren Hastings:

> 'The question now before us [Macaulay declared] is simply whether, when it is in our power to teach [the English] language, we shall teach languages in which . . . there are no books on any subject which deserve to be compared to our own . . . whether when we can patronize sound philosophy and true history, we shall countenance, at the public expense, medical doctrines which would disgrace an English farrier . . . history, abounding with kings thirty feet high, and reigns thirty thousand years long —and geography made up of seas of treacle and rivers of butter.'[46]

Macaulay stood as far from those who saw India as 'a polished and civilised nation'[47] as Grant and Wilberforce, and they and their like could accordingly work closely together.

His closest association with India followed his appointment as Law Member of the Governor-General's Council in Calcutta in 1834.[48] Whilst there he laid the foundation for the three great Indian legal codes, and it was through this enterprise that he was linked with much the most formidable reforming figure of the day so far as India was concerned, James Mill.

It is still somewhat surprising that outside the cognoscenti it is still not generally known that both James Mill, and his better known son John Stuart, for many years earned their living as senior bureaucrats in the India Office in London.[49] James Mill joined the Company's executive in 1819, and was head of the office as chief Examiner between 1830 and his death in 1836. John Stuart joined soon after his father and remained with the Company until its demise in 1858. He did not, it seems, have the impact upon Indian affairs that his father had had. He seems to have been concerned for much of his time on business concerning the Indian princes (though the influence of that upon his *Essay on Representative*

Government is still to be assessed). In his day, however, James Mill was the towering figure in Indian policy-making. As he himself once put it, his daily lot was 'the very essence of the internal government of 60 millions of people'.[50] Since he was the most fervent of the lieutenants of Jeremy Bentham, and of his doctrine that it was man's duty to procure the greatest happiness of the greatest number, it was through him that the pure milk of the utilitarian word came to be spilled over India.

Historians have had little difficulty in recognising the influence of Bentham's Utilitarianism upon English governmental reform in the 1830s and 1840s. But its influence upon India was far greater. It is difficult indeed to think of any school of philosophy whose immediate impact upon government policy has been quite so direct as that which the arch-utilitarians exercised over British policy in India in the second, third and fourth decades of the nineteenth century. As Bentham himself once put it—and without overmuch exaggeration—'Mill will be the living executive, and I shall be the dead legislative of British India' (and he added very perceptively: 'Twenty years after I am dead I shall be a despot').[51]

James Mill shared with Charles Grant the view that a 'hideous state of society' existed in India, 'dissembling, treacherous, mendacious, to an excess which surpasses even the usual measure of Indian society'—to quote just one of his phrases. And he agreed about its cause—'that by a division of the people into castes, and the prejudices which the detestable views of the Brahmans raised to separate them, a degrading and pernicious system of subordination was established among the Hindus'.[52] But in one crucial respect Mill differed from both Grant and Macaulay. Though a supporter of popular education, he did not believe that education on its own was of much use. His own focus was upon the much larger structures within society. 'The form of government is one,' he had written, 'the nature of the laws for the administration of justice is the other of the two circumstances by which the condition of the people in all countries is chiefly determined'; and 'of these two primary causes no result to a greater degree ensures the happiness of the people than the mode of providing for the pecuniary wants of the government'. What, therefore, Mill had in mind was a revolution in Indian society carried through by the operation of 'good' government, 'just' laws and a 'scientific' system of taxation. 'Clearness, certainty, promptitude, cheapness' in their administration would, he believed, effect 'a complete deliverance'.[53] By such means would individual energy be released from the tyranny of priests and aristocrats, so that India would be set upon the path of 'improvement'—that blessed early Victorian panacea—towards that individualist, competitive society which, following, among others, Adam Smith, he believed to be the acme of an advanced civilisation.

A central feature of Mill's thinking lay in his opposition to Cornwallis-style zamindari settlements, and to the parasitic society which these appeared to him to produce. Here his most startling suggestion was that, basing itself on pre-existing practice, the British state in India should stand forth as the landlord of India, with each peasant holding directly from it as tenant. In this way, Mill believed, his friend Ricardo's doctrine of rent could more particularly be made to apply. According to this, rent was the difference between that which the worst and the best land could produce from the same investment of human and capital resources; it could be appropriated by the landlord without affecting either the rate of profit or wages, or the price of produce, and without producing any deleterious effect on the economy: indeed, quite the contrary, for in this way a surplus could be procured from which the cost of measures to improve its well-being could be met. In Ricardo's theory there was for Mill a scientific basis for land revenue policy in India; and by adapting Munro's ryotwari system to it, he sought to turn Munro's originally rather conservative-minded programme in a much more reformist direction. In so doing he fashioned a dogma about land revenue policy which was to dominate British thinking until the end of the nineteenth century.

It is important to remember that Mill was no novice in Indian affairs. He had already completed a laborious investigation of them before he ever went to the India Office, as the six volumes of his *History of British India* bear witness. He was thus able to call upon not just a considered dogma but upon a vast store of knowledge about India; and in drafting his great policy-forming dispatches to Calcutta he was able to set on foot (as Eric Stokes has put it in his splendid book *English Utilitarians and India*) 'the establishment of a strong central government possessed of exclusive legislative authority for the whole of British India, the embodiment of all law in a set of scientific codes, an entire reorganisation and expansion of the judicial system, a complete overhaul and reshaping of the administrative service, the survey and registration of all landholdings, and a scientific assessment of the land revenue based on detailed statistics of agricultural production', all to the end, in Mill's own words, that the government should 'best minister the public wealth and happiness' of the people of India.[54]

All of this is very familiar to those conversant with the literature upon British India. It should be added that much of it was applied by the Colebrooke-Cameron reforms to Ceylon as well;[55] and that much of it was reinforced by the thinking that stemmed from Adam Smith and the other Scots thinkers of the eighteenth century and their successors.[56] It still needs to be stressed, however, that this great burst of energy did not come to an end in the mid 1830s. In the first place, for the next quarter of a century the Government of India was still engaged upon implementing many of the reforms which were proposed (they became the very ground and being of the British government of India, and in many respects later on of British Governments in Africa as well); and in the second place there was that special burst of creative energy which came with the appointment to the Governor-Generalship of India in 1848, at the age of thirty-five, of the Marquis of Dalhousie. With Dalhousie's appointment, in the words of Percival Spear, change was 'accelerated to full throttle'. The Punjab was finally conquered. So were parts of Burma. Wherever possible, native states not yet incorporated into British India were annexed. Educational policy was reinvigorated from top to bottom. Social reform legislation, including a Hindu Widows Remarriage Act, was pushed through. A public works department was created. Canals were extended; so were a host of major roads. The telegraph was introduced; a great network of railways was planned, and the first lines laid. The spirit in which all this was done can be gauged from Sir Charles Trevelyan's statement in 1853 that 'now we have served our noviciate; we know on every point what is required for the benefit of India to make it a great and flourishing country; and the time for giving effect to this knowledge has arrived, and I expect that the next 20 years will be a period of great improvement in India'[57], and then more particularly from Dalhousie's own publicly expressed hope that his Indian railways network would develop 'upon a scale commensurate with the magnitude of the interests that are involved, and with the vast and various benefits, political, commercial, and social which that great measure of public improvement would unquestionably produce'. There were, he once said, 'three great engines of social improvement', railways, uniform postage, and the electric telegraph.[58] In Spear's other phrase, Dalhousie substituted the watering-can of his predecessors with a hose-pipe.[59]

The Settled View

But for a whole complex of reasons, upon Dalhousie's departure (an exhausted man who died before he was fifty), these accents were not to be heard again for another century. One of the reasons, of course, was that within a year of his departure, the great upheaval of 1857 had occurred. It is no part of the present purpose to say anything very much about 1857. We may note, however, that within a year of its suppression, the historian, J. W. Kaye, at this time one of the Secretaries in the India Office in London, was to be found saying publicly that: "The prime object . . . of all our [present] efforts is the tranquilization of the public mind . . . until we have restored the national confidence in the non-aggressive spirit of the British Government'.[60] The same point was made a little later on by Fitzjames Stephen (of whom more in a moment) when he avowed that the events of 1857 had led to 'the renunciation of the attempt to effect an impossible compromise between the Asiatic and European view of things, legal, military and administrative. The effect of the

Mutiny on the statute book was unmistakable.'[61] The great period of confident reformation was certainly over; little more was to be heard of social reform in India at British hands; landlordist land settlements edged their way back into being; and within decades that scholarly British Governor Sir Alfred Lyall was concluding his second volume of *Asiatic Studies* with the comment, 'All that the English need do is to keep the peace and clear the way'.[62]

What had happened was that the great debate had come pretty abruptly to an end, and the settled view had taken its place. It should be emphasised that this does not mean that nothing more of a creative kind was done:[63] more railways were built, so were canals, so were universities. But it does mean that very little more was now heard of that argument upon fundamental issues which had distinguished the great debate. Its marks were scattered across the face of India. Never again, however, were the shifts in British thinking about India to oscillate so violently; and for all the impact of Mill, the future now lay with the heirs of Munro. There were, it is true, a few deviants in the ranks of the British, but they were ardently despised; and, by the time the century was out, that portentous viceroy, Curzon, was pronouncing: 'If I were asked to sum it up in a single word, I would say "Efficiency". That has been our gospel, the key-note of our administration.'[64] Not 'Improvement', the word Grant and Macaulay and Mill and Dalhousie, even Munro, had all cried (let alone the later 'Development'), but 'Efficiency'. That was the word.

And to what end?

The seminal statement here is from Fitzjames Stephen, Law Member of the Viceroy's Council between 1869 and 1872. In his notable book, *Liberty, Equality and Fraternity,* which was published in 1873, Fitzjames Stephen vigorously attacked John Stuart Mill for betraying the utilitarian creed. In contra-distinction to Mill, happiness, Stephen insisted, not liberty, was the true end of man according to Bentham, the master. And four years later Stephen drew the corollary for India in a letter to *The Times*:

'The British Power in India [he wrote] is like a vast bridge over which an enormous multitude of human beings are passing, and will (I trust) for ages to come continue to pass, from a dreary land, in which brute violence in its roughest form had worked its will for centuries . . . on their way to a country . . . which is at least orderly, peaceful, and industrious . . . The bridge was not built without desperate struggles. A mere handful of our countrymen guard the entrance . . . Strike away its piers and it will fall . . . One of its piers is military power: the other is justice . . . so long as the masterful wills which make up military force are directed to the object which I have defined as constituting justice, I should have no fear, for even if we fail . . . we fail with honour, and if we succeed we shall have performed the greatest feat of strength, skill and courage in the whole history of the world'.[65]

This is not the place to try and situate this statement, and all that went with it, in its full context. We may, perhaps, note that whereas the two most popular textbooks on the history of early Victorian England are called respectively *The Age of Reform* and *The Age of Improvement*,[66] reform and improvement are not thought to be appropriate words for the later period. In it, so the Cambridge historians are telling us, there was an increased emphasis on efficiency in administrative and political circles in Britain;[67] a marked shift intellectually from philosophical radicalism to social evolutionism;[68] and a deep split in the ranks of intellectual liberals (not least in Cambridge itself) precisely along the lines of the conflict between Stephen and Mill which proved to be the forerunner to the liberal unionist split with Gladstone over Home Rule for Ireland.[69] There was also the move towards Neo-Classicism in economics—the so-called 'marginal revolution'—which 'manifested itself in a tendency to concentrate attention on allocation rather than development',[70] and in which 'the economic order was viewed as an organic unit, the components of which were virtually interdependent'.[71] And then there was Darwin, and all the racism which justified itself by reference to him. There was, moreover, Social Darwinism—although it seems important to remember that 'in the spectrum of opinion that went under the name of Social Darwinism, almost every variety of belief was included'. It is Walter Bagehot's version which is relevant here, published in 1867 under the title

Physics and Politics. Claiming that he was applying 'Natural Selection' to 'Political Society', Bagehot stressed 'the efficacy of the tight early polity . . . and the strict early law on the creation of corporate characters'. What was required, he affirmed, was 'a cake of custom'. 'That this regime forbids free thought is not an evil; or rather, though an evil, it is the necessary basis for the greatest good; it is necessary for making the world of civilisation, and hardening the soft fibre of early man.'[72] The congruence between Bagehot's general statements and Stephen's, not least about India, is exact.

Such ideas found expression in British policy in India at the viceregal level more particularly in Lytton. Despite the Ripon viceroyalty which followed, they also conditioned most of his successors, Conservative and Liberal Unionist alike.[73] They found their way as well into the major British text book on India, John Strachey's *India,* written by one of Lytton's close associates, published in 1880, constantly reprinted thereafterwards, and in fact dedicated to Stephen. In one way and another, therefore, Stephen's thinking, buttressed by Social Evolutionism and Cultural Relativism, by some brands of Social Darwinism, and reinforced by Neo-Classical Economics, became a central part of British imperial thinking in the second half of the nineteenth century. It was, moreover, to have a very long life: even in the 1950s Lord Hailey (the greatest Indian Civil Servant of the twentieth century, before he turned his attention to Africa) could still write that India did not attain independence 'as the result of a judgement regarding the political capacity of her politicians or her people', but because it was 'not practicable . . . to defer [it] any longer'.[74] In Africa there were comparable attitudes. For instance there are well authenticated stories of a District Commissioner in Kenya who migrated to South Africa in 1960 because he was convinced to the marrow of his being that the grant of independence to Kenya was an intolerable offence to the ordinary African population.[75] These are perhaps extreme examples, but it would be very unwise to doubt the presence of Stephen's doctrines in one form or another amongst administrators in both India and Africa, both before, and for a very long time after, he propounded it.

Perhaps the major tragedy of the end of the debate, and

of the shift to Stephen's point of view which took place just after mid-century, was that it occurred at the very moment when another ruling oligarchy in Asia, far from pulling in its horns like the ruling British oligarchy in India proceeded to do, was beginning to set out on an aggressively modernist course of its own. One has in mind here, of course, the Meiji oligarchy in Japan, which, to use Fitzjames Stephen's words, was in no doubt that it was perfectly possible—indeed that it was essential—to effect a 'compromise between the Asiatic and European view of things', and in a variety of ways set out to show how it could be done. Whatever one may think of some of the features of this occurrence in the long run, it resembled, in many vital ways, what Dalhousie had attempted to do in India, but which in the decades following his departure was no longer pursued there with anything like his zeal.[76]

Yet if Stephen's creed was the overriding dictum of the settled view, there was another and, for present purposes, an even more pertinent doctrine at another level. Again, it is in no way possible to enlarge upon the context in which it originated. It owed something to the German historical school and to all those intellectual shifts in Britain at mid-century to which we have just referred. Very specifically it owed a great deal, too, to Henry Maine, yet another of those Victoran intellectuals who was Law Member of the Government of India—in his case between 1862 and 1869. In a series of writings (of which *Ancient Law* was only the best known), Maine challenged the notion of abstract ideas which were divorced from the limitation of their actual historical origin in an institution or system of law, since he believed that in operation these could only have disastrous results. In particular, he thought the attempt to precipitate Indian society from status to contract in the manner Mill and Macaulay had purposed to do ought to be, if not abandoned, at least substantially curbed. According to Maine, 'the usages which a particular community is found to have adopted in its infancy and in its primitive seats are generally those which are on the whole best suited to promote its physical and moral well-being; and if they are retained in their integrity until new social wants have taught new practices, the upward march of society is certain'.[77]

Maine persistently lent his intellectual weight, moreover, to the claims of the authoritarian administrator. Even in his *Popular Government* (as a recent commentator has remarked) 'Maine gives us not so much the legal historian's mature judgement as the irritable official's conviction that politics can, and should, be reduced to administration'.[78]

One of Maine's disciples, Sir Raymond West, took up the central issue here. In a pamphlet called *Land and the Law in India*, published in Bombay in 1872, West argued: 'No policy can be enduring which does not find room under it for the national virtues and defects; and while we are striving to improve the moral and intellectual tone of the Hindus by the influence of new and wholesome ideas, we ought in some things to wait patiently for their fruition [the settled view?]. If our superciliousness prevents our doing this [a cut at Mill and Dalhousie], we may place ourselves on some mechanical success while we may in truth have been sowing the seeds of political disaster and of a dissolution of society.'[79] That phrase, 'the dissolution of society', became the new bogey—just as the 'hideous state of society' had been for the whole of a previous generation. West, we must remember, was not writing from an armchair. As Chief Justice of Bombay it was clear to him that the atomising effects of the ryotwari system in Bombay, operating under the Ricardian doctrine of rent, had been substantial. When coupled with the workings of the legal system which Mill and Macaulay had fashioned with such confidence, it had already brought about changes in the rural balance, more particularly between the peasant cultivator and the money lender, which he thought to be reprehensible. To West, and to men like him, such developments, far from producing happiness and prosperity for the people of India, as Mill had argued that they would, were producing nothing less than the dissolution of society. There had long been clear signs of this in Bengal, and in the North West Provinces.[80] By mid-century, as Dr. Spear has outlined in an admirable passage in *Twilight of the Moguls*, the cohesion of rural society around Delhi had already been gravely damaged by the Mill system.[81] During the upheaval of 1857 itself, there had been serious attacks on moneylenders and other commercial castes who had been appropriating land and extorting interest on a much greater scale than ever before—all of which suggested there was something seriously wrong with the existing system. Practical experience and the ruminations of the idealogues both pointed, howsoever hesitantly, in the same direction.[82]

There was some talk in British circles during the 1860s about amending the law so as to curb the most extortionate activities of the merchant castes. But nothing eventuated, until in 1875 there were serious anti-moneylending riots in Maharashtra, the so-called Deccan Riots of 1875, which eventually led to new legislation being enacted, the Deccan Agriculturalists Relief Act of 1879—a vital imperial landmark which made moneylending bonds subject to judicial scrutiny as they had never been before. In the event, this proved to be but the first step in a substantial reversal of Mill's majestic efforts to set free the energies of individuals in India through the equal operation of the law. Henceforward the emphasis was upon the need to conserve Indian society, rather than set it free—and the villain of the piece was deemed to be the moneylender, who, taking advantage of the backing he could claim from the 'impartial' administration of British courts, was not only able to impose high rates of interest upon his victims, but could foreclose on their mortgages so that their land fell into his hands.[83]

Two further developments in the direction set by the Deccan Act then followed. In the first place there was a protracted country-wide investigation into the extent of the alienation of land from the hands of peasant communities into the hands of what were called the non-agricultural castes, a development which is associated with the name of S. S. Thorburn. It culminated in the Punjab Land Alienation Act of 1900, which placed a further brake upon this practice in that province, to which it was first applied.[84]

The second development was in a similar direction. It was based upon a similarly protracted investigation, this time into the possibility of establishing a series of cooperative agricultural banks upon the Raffeisen model as it operated in Germany. This eventuated in the Cooperative Societies Act of 1904 and in the subsequent Cooperative Movement.[85] Both developments were explicitly designed to check what West had called the dissolution of society. And this concern, and to a remarkable degree this concern alone, came to dominate the socio-economic thinking of the Government of India. Sir Malcolm Hailey's last action as an Indian Governor in the 1930s was devoted to one more attempt to reduce peasant indebtedness in his provinces;[86] and in the settled view, the defence of Indian peasant society against the disruptive forces which Mill had deliberately sought to set loose upon it became for Hailey and his generation a dominant idea. Nowhere is this better illustrated than in the volumes of one of the three or four most interesting ICS men of the twentieth century, Sir Malcolm Darling. His most widely read book, *The Punjab Peasant in Prosperity and Debt,*[87] is replete with this view. It is also to be found in that of one of the other most interesting figures, Furnivall, in his strictures upon the effects of British rule on Burmese society in *Colonial Policy and Practice.*[88]

When one considers that the settled view was at no stage coupled, except in the western Punjab, with any major campaign of rural economic development in a country in which neither Cornwallis's belief that improving landlords would bring about a new era, nor Munro's belief that this would come from a land-holding peasantry, nor Mill's view that law would produce a new society in India, proved justified, one comes fairly close to some of the roots of India's economic problems in the mid-twentieth century. When in 1931 Sir Malcolm Hailey, a very great governor in his own way, found his charge, the United Provinces, scourged by the consequences of the world slump, what did he do? With consummate ability, he had rent throughout the province reduced, and had four million slips of paper issued to peasant-holders in which their individual reductions were set out in detail.[89] But he did not, it seems, say anything about a major programme of economic development. Hailey took great pride in what was called 'village uplift' (the programme associated with the name of F. L. Brayne). But by this was meant little more than pit latrines, Persian wheels, Hissar bulls and more education for village women.[90]

So far there has been little or no mention of Africa. But that is primarily because once the Indian story is set out.

the African story, to a greater extent than Africanists are sometimes aware, falls, in a number of respects very quickly into place. From the outset there was a marked tendency to call Africans 'savages'; but at the end of the eighteenth century there were plenty to dub them 'noble'. The whole ideology of the anti-slavery movement rested, moreover, upon the rejection of polygenetic ideas, and stood upon the belief that Africans were men like other men.[91] Certainly they had their critics; but these could be vehemently rebutted, in tones which are reminiscent of Clive and Warren Hastings. 'It is now proved beyond reach of controversy', the Sierra Leone Company proclaimed, for example, in 1808, 'that the African does not labour under the intellectual inferiority which had been so long imputed to him; that he is capable of comprehending and fulfilling every civil and social obligation ...'[92] There were those, moreover, who spoke of African questions much as Munro had of Indian. 'The success of our administration on the Gold Coast,' an 'African' merchant and a Member of Parliament told the West Africa Committee in 1842, 'may fairly be ascribed to this that the officers in command at the various forts had the wisdom to take the native laws and customs as their rules, extracting from them, and bringing forward, that basis of justice which will always be found in the laws of the most debased tribes, and throwing into the background the cruelties and absurdities which, in a negro, as in a European code of laws, are corruptions only".[93]

Nevertheless, as for India, there were also those who doubted the validity of this approach. It was no less a person than Wilberforce who stated (in 1807 in a pamphlet in which he was thinking chiefly of Africa) that 'we are well warranted, by the experience of all ages, in laying it down as an incontrovertible position—that the arts and sciences, knowledge, and civilisation, have never been found to be a native growth of any country; but that they have ever been communicated from one nation to another, from the more to the less civilised'.[94] And it was his associates, who, following through this line of thought, and coming to believe that the slave trade was not the only reason for Africa's ills, increasingly emphasised the need to transmit to it 'Christianity and Civilisation'. 'A nobler achievement now awaits ...,' the other great abolitionist Thomas Fowell Buxton wrote in 1839. 'It may be that . . . a thousand nations now steeped in wretchedness, in brutal ignorance, in devouring superstition . . . shall, under British tuition emerge from their debasement, enjoy a long line of blessings—education, agriculture, commerce, peace, industry, and the wealth that springs from it; and far above all, shall willingly receive that religion which, . . . opens the way to an eternal futurity of happiness.'[95]

All this is directly reminiscent of the British debate about India, and does not seem to add anything very new to it.

If there was a difference of emphasis it stemmed from the difference between a continent where the British did not exercise political control and one where they did. As regards Africa it was not possible, as it was for India, for anyone to think that administrative diktat could bring about a new order. Because of this, and because of the rhetoric which declared that 'legitimate' trade was the most likely slayer of the 'illegitimate' slave trade, Buxton and his like argued the case for 'commerce'. Never, however, quite able to suppress their doubts about its reliability as an agent for good, they argued as well for the installation in Africa of 'managerial cadres of white colonists . . . [who would] speed up the process of culture change'. From this ensued such ventures as Buxton's ill-starred Niger expedition in 1852, David Livingstone's plans for a settlement in the Zambezi region a few years later, Baker and Gordon's championship of the Egyptian thrusts up the Nile in the 1860s and 1870s, and a host of similar—and universally abortive—schemes.[96]

By the 'sixties, however, there was as much recoil in British thinking about Africa as we have noted that there was over India; and hardly surprisingly it used the same rationale. 'While the goal was still conversion to Western culture,' Professor Curtin, the foremost commentator upon all of this, has written, 'it was to be achieved by changing African culture slowly, under African authority, and not by substituting British authority and British institutions.'[97] In the second half of the nineteenth century, the British in India never proposed to go to quite these lengths—they were already too heavily involved in India. Nevertheless, the close parallels between the various post mid-century changes of course do suggest that it is important not to overstress the particular impact of 1857 on British thinking about India. And from other evidence it soon becomes patent that the change of course just after mid-century was a very widespread phenomenon indeed. One can see it exemplified in West Africa in the late nineteenth-century missionaries' criticism of Bishop Crowther, the first Anglican African Bishop, and in the post-Crowther reaction which ensued.[98] In South Africa it was exemplified by the switch from the 'civilisation by mingling' policies of Sir George Grey (Governor of the Cape 1854-61) via the intermediate position of his influential Secretary for Native Affairs, Theophilus Shepstone, to the Cape of Good Hope's *Commission on Native Laws and Customs* of 1883. 'The result of the enquiries so prosecuted,' this reported, '. . . will be found clearly to demonstrate that many of the existing Kafir laws and customs are so interwoven with the social conditions and ordinary institutions of the native population . . . that any premature or violent attempt to break them down or sweep them away would be mischievous and dangerous to the highest degree . . . We consider it would, therefore, be most inexpedient wholly to supersede the native system by the application of Colonial Law in its entirety'—an exemplary statement of the settled view if there ever was one.[99] The same sentiments were expressed by Sir Arthur Gordon (Lord Stanmore) during his memorable Governorship of Fiji (1875-80). And they were expressed by Sir Evelyn Baring (Lord Cromer), Britain's uniquely influential Consul-General in Egypt. 'I have been proceeding steadily on the principle of Burke's maxim,' he wrote at the end of his time there, 'that the main thing for a reformer to decide is what not to reform, and I am strongly impressed with the idea that the time when a reform is taken in hand is quite as important as the merits of the case itself.' The British administrators in Egypt, so their most substantial historian has written,

> 'certainly did see themselves as transformers of traditional Egyptian society. They realized that the impact of the West, under a system of colonial rule, would decisively alter that society's basic institutions and values . . . These men, however, generally did not believe in the universality of western ideas and institutions. Unlike earlier generations of colonial reformers,

such as the Benthamites in India, they did not believe that they could make Egyptian society over in the image of England. Indeed, they felt that basic changes in values and mentality would have to spring from the Egyptian peoples themselves and that the most that colonial rulers could do was to prepare the material and economic conditions for such changes'.[100]

It is tempting, no doubt, to believe that Joseph Chamberlain struck a rather different note in the 1890s. 'What is wanted for Uganda,' he once proclaimed, 'is what Birmingham has got—an improvement scheme.' Uganda, however, never got—never in fact looked like getting—an improvement scheme; and for all Chamberlain's talk about developing the 'imperial estates', when he became Colonial Secretary in 1895 his actual achievements never came within striking distance of his rhetoric.[101]

Mention of both Cromer and Chamberlain reminds us, however, of the public works programmes which they and many others made it their business to promote. There can be no doubt that the building of railways and other such development were a marked feature of the period of the settled view and that this suggests some qualification to it. After millenia of nothing swifter than the horse and, at best, horse-drawn vehicles, and in the days before both motor and air transport, railways were of course an astonishing technological advance; and in the age of the Trans-Siberian, the Canadian Pacific, the Union Pacific, the Berlin-Baghdad and the Trans-Australian railways, the world's foremost power, Britain, was not likely to be backward in laying them down in out of the way places, whatever its prevalent social theories might be. In any event, as the Romans knew, good communications were often vital to the maintenance of imperial authority; and of the strategic importance of imperial railways in both India and Africa there can be no doubt. Irrigation works too, in India and in Egypt alike, had for millenia been symbols of imperial power; and any self-respecting imperial power was likely to take steps to improve them, if only to keep the subject peoples fed. Like railways, irrigation works, moreover, had the great merit of being likely to pay their own way. Indeed, in many instances they were vital to securing that modicum of economic activity without which there would be no basis for government revenue. Perhaps one should cast into the reckoning as well the relative autonomy of the engineering profession and the accompanying prestige which made it something of a law to itself: but having done so, the facts remain. First, in some ways perhaps the more notable consideration is that there were not more railways built—'Cape to Cairo' was not, to mention only one. Secondly, there were certainly some elements of a contradiction with some of the current social theory, as the most notable social theorists seem to have recognised.[102] But the third and in this context the most important fact of all, is that the prevalence of public works programmes is a vital reminder that the settled view was never an ideology of stagnation. All its exponents believed in 'progress', howsoever much they were concerned about its disruptive effects; and if much of their social theory focused on the latter, railway building, and irrigation works, were a prime expression of the former—of Britain's call to her 'civilising mission'.

When in the 1880s and 1890s the British did become heavily involved in tropical Africa, some of the arguments which were used clearly bore—as one would expect—the post-Darwinian stamp. 'The Negro,' Sir Harry Johnston, for instance, wrote in 1890, 'seems to require the intervention of some superior race before he can be roused to any definite advance from the low stage of human development in which he has contentedly remained for many thousand years.' They bore as well the stamp of the settled view. The African explorer, Cameron (an ardent 'African' imperialist if ever there was one), argued that 'with regard to education and civilisation, we must be satisfied to work gradually and not attempt to force our European customs and manners upon a people who are at present unfitted for them'.[103] And the truth was that upon such issues there was really no 'African' debate which was separate from the one over India. With the Partition, indeed, British policies towards African societies took the great majority of their basic ideas from the settled view already generated in India.

There is one feature of the Indian story which, because of its consequences for Africa, deserves further exploration. Cornwallis's zamindari settlements, and Munroe and his successors' ryotwari settlements, had not produced, as each of them in his own way avowed that they would, an economic revolution. If there were marketable non-industrial goods coming from within the British Empire in Africa or Asia, these were either being produced for the most part on European plantations or were the natural products of West Africa's forests: by the time the British secured their share of Africa, that is, 'natives', not least in India, had nowhere shown that they could carry out an economic transformation. But White Settlers had done so—in the Americas, in Australasia, and in South Africa. Casting one's mind back to the late nineteenth century—by reading, for example, Charles Dilke's *Greater Britain*—one can understand very quickly why it was that Rhodes was the great British hero of the day, and why it was that White Settlement in Africa, wherever it seemed possible to mount it, seemed to so many Englishmen to provide the only hope for the creation of a money economy and a transformation of society where there had been none before. Over large parts of Bantu Africa, this was to involve the proletarianisation of the African population. The only role which the new European-dominated society offered to Bantu Africans was that of a labouring proletariat—in most places an agricultural one, in some an industrial one. There were those, moreover, who sought to advance a justification for this. 'The native,' one of the arch-apologists, Elspeth Huxley, was to put it, 'must be taught that work was the solid basis of prosperity, that you cannot in the long-run get something for nothing, that to enjoy the fruits of civilization you must also cultivate the tree that bears them.'[104] 'I am prepared to state definitely,' the Governor of what was shortly to become Kenya said in 1917, 'that we desire to make of the native a useful citizen, and that we consider the best means of doing so is to induce him to work for a period of his life for the European.'[105] This was social engineering, settler-style, of an order which even Francis and Cornwallis had not contemplated.

The irony of it was that in the crucial decades between 1891 and 1911, when White Settlement was being launched in the Rhodesias and in Kenya, the Ghana cocoa farmers were showing what could be done by an African peasant population where land was available, as generally in Africa it was. In 1891 the Gold Coast exported 80 pounds of cocoa beans: in 1911, 88 million pounds, which was equal to 46 per cent of its total exports. The rise, moreover, in gross domestic product in the Gold Coast in the intervening two decades seems to have been of the order of 7.6 per annum.[106] The result was that as early as 1906 a Governor of Uganda was talking about introducing what he called 'West Coast Policies' into his East Coast protectorate; and 'Grow More Crop' campaigns regularly became a feature of British governments in Africa thereafter—in Tanganyika for example during the 1930s.[107] But by 1906, it was already too late in Kenya, which did not get its 'West Coast Policy' till the Swynnerton Plan in the 1950s.[108] And also, more generally, as Cyril Ehrlich has shown most strikingly for Uganda, and Christopher Wrigley for Nigeria, 'West Coast Policies' very often became stifled by the demands of Curzon-type 'Efficiency', and by socio-economic policies designed to protect the peasant from the machinations of others;[109] or in other words, by both aspects of the settled view which we have noted in India.

At this stage of the argument, the correspondence between the other feature of the settled view and Britain's most distinctive policy in Africa, Indirect Rule, hardly needs emphasising. One of the most remarkable high priests of the newly emerging doctrine of indirect rule in Africa at the very end of the nineteenth century was the remarkable West African woman traveller Mary Kingsley. 'I hold,' she once wrote in a typical passage 'that one of the most awful crimes one nation can commit on another is destroying the image of Justice, which in an institution is represented more truly by the people by whom the institution is being developed than in any alien institution of Justice; it is a thing adapted to its environment. This form of murder by a nation I see being done in the destruction of what is good in the laws and institutions of native races.' This may seem novel in a West African context; but it is pure Raymond West; pure Henry Maine; the settled view all over. Like Stephen railing against 'some few anglicized Bengali babus', moreover, Mary Kingsley could not stand, 'seedy demoralized natives'. Furthermore, existing British practice in West Africa, she wrote in 1898, 'necessarily destroys native society . . . and has not in it the power to reorganize'.[110] This might have been Sir Richard Temple, Governor of Bombay, arguing for the Deccan Agriculturalist Relief Bill of 1879.

The son of Sir Richard Temple of Bombay, Charles Temple, was Lieutenant-Governor of Northern Nigeria between 1914 and 1917, and became the chief exponent of the most extreme form of the doctrine of indirect rule. He spoke of 'the active harm which contact with our civilization will certainly cause' and expressed himself emphatically in favour of full Government support for the Emirs and Chiefs of Nigeria 'to an ever-increasing extent'.[111]

But the doyen of the indirect rulers was, of course, Lugard, and in him the settled view reappeared too. 'The danger,' he wrote in his classic statement, *The Dual Mandate in Tropical Africa,* 'of going too fast with native races is even more likely to lead to disappointment, if not to disaster, than the danger of not going fast enough'. 'The advent of Europeans cannot fail to have a disintegrating effect on tribal institutions, and on the conditions of native life.' The 'decay of tribal authority has unfortunately too often been accentuated by the tendency of British officers to deal directly with petty chiefs, and to ignore . . . the principal chief. It has been increased . . . by the influx of alien natives who, when it suited them, set at naught the native authority, and refused to pay the tribute which the chiefs were given no means of enforcing, or acquiring lands which they held in defiance of native customary tenure'. 'In brief,' he wrote, 'tribal cohesion [is the watchword] of our policy in regard to these backward races.'[112] Adapted to the conditions of African society, this was what men such as West, Temple, Thornburn, and Darling spent their lives saying in India. And so it went on. In 1934 the most substantial commentator on latter-day indirect rule, Margery Perham, wrote that 'the great task of indirect rule is to hold the ring'[113]—precisely the metaphor which Sir Alfred Lyall had employed about British rule in India half a century before.

If there was a difference, perhaps it was this: in India the actions which the British took to prevent 'the dissolution of society' were essentially curative, in Africa preventive.

It was probably this difference which enabled the British

administrators in Africa, beginning with Lugard, to explore more fully the methods by which tribal society might be changed from within than was ever attempted in India. The method first chosen in Africa was to educate the chiefs 'in the duties of rulers according to a civilised standard'.[114] There were of course developments within the doctrine of indirect rule,[115] and there were variations in its application to such widely different areas of Africa as the Sudan, Tanganyika, and Northern Rhodesia. Its most vigorous proponents recognised, moreover, 'that it is not by mere non-interference that tribal institutions can be carried over in working order from the old into the new Africa, but by vigorous leadership and continuous administrative education'. Even so, their emphasis was upon Africans becoming 'members of the civilised world, not as individuals, but as communities', and they specifically claimed that 'we have corrected the nineteenth-century complacency about the universal superiority of our own ideas and institutions, and instead of enervating by over-paternalism have begun to work self-government from the bottom upwards'.[116] Accordingly, for all the differences within the Indirect Rule school, it is somewhat difficult to see them as very much more than a set of variations upon a single theme.

At first sight there were some imperial rulers in the interwar period who look to have been different—Guggisberg, for instance, Governor of the Gold Coast between 1919 and 1927. But his Ten Year Development Plan (so his biographer tells us) was concerned with infrastructure rather than development; it was always his hope 'that an African way of life could prevail unsullied by Bogus European institutions'; whilst the model for his pride and joy, Achimota College, was clearly the Tuskegee Institution, Alabama—a striking case of cultural relativism, if ever there was one![117] Few, moreover, were more relativist at this time than some of the most 'progressive' thinkers of the day: none more so indeed than Malinowski and the functional anthropologists who were frequently to the fore at this period.[118] We have it as well on the authority of Sir Andrew Cohen (a major figure in the most recent period) that in the Colonial Office he knew in the 1930s, there was still more insistence 'on safeguarding African society than on helping Africans to develop and stimulating the inertia which tended to prevail among the people of many parts of Africa'. He recalled one critic who dubbed it all the 'woad' policy.[119]

The Development Fever

As twilight fell on the British Empire a great change did, however, come eventually. Its characteristic note was struck in Britain itself when the Macmillan Committee on Finance and Industry stated in 1931 that 'we may well have reached the stage when an era of conscious and deliberate management must succeed the era of undirected natural evolution'.[120] It is noteworthy that it was mostly too late to influence British rule in India. The British had been there for the best part of two centuries, but it was not until a decade after they had left that they put up the money for the steel works at Durgapur—although the Tatas had begun to build theirs at Jamshedpur half a century previously.[121] During the mid 1930s there were some preliminary indications of the development fever that was soon to come. The Government of the United Provinces, for instance, made some hesitant gestures towards what was called Rural Development. In 1938 the Indian National Congress established a National Planning Committee under Nehru's chairmanship; and during the second world war the Government of India took some further steps.[122] There is striking evidence, however, of the continuing novelty of 'planning' at this time in some words of Dr. Harold Mann, the Government of India's prime witness before the Royal Commission on Indian Agriculture in 1927, fairly certainly the outstanding Indian agricultural official of his day, and a notable social scientist as well. Reviewing in 1944 *A Plan for the Economic Development of India* which some Bombay businessmen had produced, Mann declared:

> 'Here for the first time in my experience, were a group of men who saw that the rapid raising of the standard of life of the people of India was possible, that, in order to accomplish it it was necessary to make a very large investment of capital and that the scheme to accomplish it was worthy of being placed on the first priority list of matters to be dealt with by the national government of India when this is formed. These conceptions themselves form a great advance.'[123]

Mann was writing in wartime, and within four years of the ending of the British Raj in India. Change, however, was now once again being noised abroad. One can hear the hinges turning in some articles which Margery Perham, a key figure in all of this, wrote for *The Times* in March 1942:

> 'A revision of the time factor is needed for all aspects of our colonial policy. Some of its principles and methods were laid down in the leisurely days of the last century and the first decade of this . . . we developed towards our backward charges a paternalism that could hardly conceive of their coming of age. We established at the top standards of administrative purity that we could not bear to see diluted by too much possibly clumsy and corrupt native participation. With our cult of "thorough" ["Efficiency", Curzon called it] and our belief that human institutions are not made but grow [remember Maine!] we set ourselves to bring change by gradual development from the old order rather than through the rapid imposition of the new [we adopted, that is, "the settled view"]. Some of these were merits in their day, and have not become defects overnight. But since modern inventions and administrative methods have changed the whole tempo of human affairs, they, too, need revision.'

The Times leader upon her articles was somewhat more forthright. To bring 'the social and political life of colonial territories . . . into a healthy relation with the more advanced countries,' the leader writer declared, 'is a task which demands careful and deliberate planning.'[124] The development fever was catching on.[125]

Once again, it is really not feasible to trace the origins of this further change of course in any detail. But clearly it owed much to the new thinking generated by the world slump, to Keynesian economics (with its novel emphasis upon the need for a managed economy), to American anti-imperialism, to the example of the Russian five-year plans, to the spirit accompanying the establishment of the welfare state in Britain, and no doubt to much else besides.[126] The seminal moments came in Britain, first with the passage of the Colonial Development and Welfare Act of 1940 (an idea originally stimulated by West Indian distress), and then with Creech Jones's occupancy of the Colonial Secretaryship after the war with the older Sir Hilton Poynton and the young Andrew Cohen at his side. Men once more thought that a supreme effort could and should be made to change societies overseas, and were less concerned than before that they might damage what Margery Perham had called as late as 1937 'the whole delicate cooperative pattern of primitive life'.[127] Once again the vehement accents of Dalhousie came to be heard in Government House. In their crucial Local Government despatch of 1947, Creech Jones and Cohen emphasised the vital necessity for the development of the political education, not so much of the chiefs (as the indirect rulers had insisted) as of the people. Local government reform, they went on, was aimed at securing African cooperation 'in the programmes of political, social and economic advancement on which we have now embarked'. The purpose of these was to eliminate the existing 'static policy'. 'Development or progress,' Creech Jones added, 'planned and inter-related change and improvement in all fields, economic, social, and political, are the keynotes of our present policy.'[128] There ensued what may now be called the 'second colonial occupation' of Africa.[129]

The details cannot be pursued here. Adlai Stevenson dubbed it 'the moral commitment to humanity'. But there are perhaps two last points to be made. First, the main emphasis was not immediately upon economic development. To begin with, 'welfare' was seen as the main component of 'development'. It involved more education, more community development, more health services, more water resources, and a good deal of local government reform. Professional economists with all their paraphernalia did not begin to move wholesale into the business until the late 1950s.

Secondly, we must turn once again to India. For there is clearly more to the origins of British development policy in Africa and the Colonies in the 1940s than has just been suggested, once it is placed alongside Nehru's move towards a planning commission and the first Indian Plan: and *mutatis mutandis,* more to the roots of Nehru's development policy than Nehru's socialism or Indian hunger.[130] Though separate, these various developments were clearly parallel. As before, it seems important to allow for the possibility that there may be tides in the affairs of men.

NOTES

1. Gunnar Myrdal, *Asian Drama,* London, 1968, e.g. p. 763 sqq.
2. R. Jolly (ed.), *Education in Africa,* Nairobi, 1969; cf. Ravinder Kumar, *Western India in the Nineteenth Century,* London, 1968, pp. 48–56 and references there cited.
3. See, for example, Paul Streeten and Michael Lipton (ed.), *The Crisis of Indian Planning,* London, 1968, and Colin Leys (ed.), *Politics and Change in Developing Countries,* Cambridge, 1969, passim.
4. Though not by Professor W. J. Barber; see his *A History of Economic Thought,* Harmondsworth, 1967.
5. 'Abstract of the Several Plans transmitted relative to the future Government of Bengal and the other British Settlements in India', John Rylands Library, Eng. Mss., 215 and 235, quoted R. Guha, *A Rule of Property for Bengal: An Essay on the Idea of Permanent Settlement,* Paris, 1963, p. 21 and Appendix pp. 201-7.
6. John Bruce, *Historical View of Plans for the Government of British India . . .,* London, 1793, p. 44.
7. J. S. Furnivall, *Netherlands India,* Cambridge, 1944; J. S. Furnivall, *Colonial Policy and Practice,* Cambridge, 1948; Clifford Geertz, *Agricultural Involution: The Process of Ecological Change in Indonesia,* Berkeley, 1966. For something of the French story, see Raymond F. Betts, *Assimilation and Association in French Colonial Theory 1890–1914*, New York, 1961.
8. Especially Eric Stokes, *The English Utilitarians and India,* Oxford, 1959.
9. Benjamin Higgins in Geertz, op. cit., p. xv.
10. For example see the early nineteenth-century 'heterodoxy' of Richard Jones, Rev. W. Whewell (ed.), *Literary Remains, consisting of lectures and tracts on Political Economy of the late Rev. Richard Jones,* London, 1859; and R. Jones, *Peasant Rents: an essay on the distribution of wealth and on the sources of taxation,* London, 1831.
11. The broadest survey is in G. R. Bearce, *British Attitudes towards India 1784–1858*, Oxford, 1961.
12. See, for example, Vincent T. Harlow, *The Founding of the Second British Empire,* Vol. II, London, 1964, p. 19.
13. K. K. Sinha, *Fort William—India House Correspondence,* Vol. V, Public Department 1767–9, New Delhi, 1949.
14. Hastings to Lord Mansfield, 25 August 1774, G. R. Gleig, *Life of Warren Hastings,* London, 1930, Vol. I, p. 401; Hastings to Court of Directors, 3 Nov 1772, G. W. Forrest, *Selections from the State Papers of the Governors-General of India: Warren Hastings*, London, 1910, Vol. II, p. 277.
15. David Kopf, *British Orientalism and the Bengal Renaissance,*

Berkeley, 1969; S. N. Mukherjee, *Sir William Jones: A Study in eighteenth-century British attitudes to India,* Cambridge, 1968.

16. C. H. Philips, *The Evolution of India and Pakistan,* Oxford, 1962, p. 415 sqq. contains a series of relevant documents.
17. Sophia Weitzmann, *Warren Hastings and Philip Francis*, Manchester, 1929; P. J. Marshall, *The Impeachment of Warren Hastings,* Oxford, 1965; Harlow, *Second British Empire,* II, Chs. II and III.
18. The classic study is B. H. Baden-Powell, *The Land Systems of British India,* 3 vols., Oxford, 1892.
19. Francis to Ellis, 22 Feb 1775, India Office Library, Francis Mss. 47 (36) 51, quoted Guha, *Rule of Property,* p. 95.
20. R. C. Dutt (ed.), *Sir Philip Francis's Minutes on the subject of a Permanent Settlement for Bengal, Behar and Orissa,* Calcutta, 1901, p. 128 quoted Guha, loc. cit. p. 95.
21. For a recent critique of 'Economic Models and their usefulness for Planning in South Asia' see Appendix 3 by Paul Streeten in Myrdal, *Asian Drama,* Volume III.
22. London, 1772.
23. Alexander Dow, *The History of Hindostan,* Vol. III, London, 1772, p. cxviii, quoted Guha p. 39.
24. Dutt, *Francis's Minutes,* p. 116, quoted Guha, p. 109.
25. Charles Ross, *Correspondence of Charles, First Marquis Cornwallis*, 2nd Edn., Vol. I, London, 1959, p. 554, quoted Guha p. 171.
26. General letters to Court of Directors, 12 April 1920, Revenue Department, Vol. 7, quoted Guha p. 172.
27. Stokes, *Utilitarians,* p. 8.
28. In addition to Guha, loc. cit., pp. 167-173, see A. Aspinall, *Cornwallis in Bengal*, Manchester, 1931, and Harlow, *Second British Empire,* II, pp. 205-24.
29. T. H. Beaglehole, *Thomas Munro and the development of administrative policy in Madras 1792–1818,* Cambridge, 1966.
30. Munro to Elphinstone, 12 May 1818, G. R. Gleig, *The Life of Major-General Sir Thomas Munro,* London, 1830, Vol. III, p. 252.
31. Metcalfe, 29 June 1920, J. W. Kaye, *Selections from the Papers of Lord Metcalfe,* London, 1955, p. 150, quoted Stokes p. 22.
32. Minute by Munro, 31 Dec. 1924, Gleig, *Munro,* III, p. 381, quoted Stokes p. 19.
33. Munro to Read, 5 Sept. 1797, J. W. B. Dykes, *Salem an Indian Collectorate,* London, 1853, p. 71, quoted Beaglehole, *Munro,* p. 28.
34. *East Africa Royal Commission 1953–1955 Report Cmd 9475*; J. Kenyatta, *Harambee*, Nairobi, 1964, Ch.7; Charan Singh, *Agrarian Revolution in Uttar Pradesh,* Bombay, 1958; Charan Singh, *Joint Farming X-Rayed*: *The Problem and its Solution,* Bombay, 1959; Myrdal, *Asian Drama,* p. 1380.

35. W. C. Neale, *Economic Change in Rural India, Land Tenure and Reform in Uttar Pradesh, 1800-1955,* London, 1962; S. C. Gupta, *Agrarian Relations and Early British Rule in India,* London, 1963; Jagdish Raj, *The Mutiny and British Land Policy in North India 1856–68*, London, 1965.
36. Sir J. Malcolm, *The Political History of India,* London, 1826, Vol. II, p. 183.
37. Charles Grant, *Observations on the State of Society among the Asiatic Subjects of Great Britain . . .* British Parliamentary Papers, 1813, x, p. 71; Macaulay's speech in the House of Commons, 10 July 1833, *The Complete Works of Lord Macaulay,* 1898 ed., Vol. XI, p. 583; James Mill, *History of British India,* 2nd ed., London, 1920, Vol. II, p. 167, see Stokes, pp. 31, 45, 54.
38. Ainslee T. Embree, *Charles Grant and British Rule in India,* London, 1962.
39. Grant, *Observations*, p. 71.
40. Ibid, p. 77, quoted Embree p. 151.
41. Grant, *Observations,* p. 99.
42. See the references in Stokes, p. 28.
43. *Substance of the Speeches of William Wilberforce Esq. on the Clause in the East India Bill . . .*, London, 1813, p. 93, quoted Stokes, p. 35.
44. Quoted by C. H. Philips, 'British Historical Writing on India', *The Listener,* LIV, 8 Dec. 1955, p. 985, quoted Embree p. 143.
45. Quoted Stokes, p. 32.
46. Quoted G. O. Trevelyan, *The Life and Letters of Lord Macaulay*, London, 1931, Vol. I, p. 291. For a very informative account of the 'anglicist' vs. 'orientalist' controversy, which paralleled so much that is discussed here, see Kopf, *British Orientalism and the Bengal Renaissance.*
47. Q. Cranford, *Sketches Chiefly Relating to the Historical Learning and Manners of the Hindoos,* London, 1790, I, pp, 71-4, quoted Embree, p. 148.
48. Stokes, *Utilitarians,* p. 184 sqq.
49. Ibid, passim. See also Donald Winch, *Classical Political Economy and Colonies,* London, 1965, p. 160.
50. Mill to Dumont, R. Sraffa, *The Works of David Ricardo,* Vol. VIII, Cambridge, 1951-2, p. 40, quoted Stokes, p. 48.
51. J. Bowring (ed.), *The Works of Jeremy Bentham,* London, 1943, Vol. X, p. 490.
52. Mill, *British India,* Vol. II, pp. 195, 166-7, quoted Stokes, pp. 53-4.
53. Ibid, I, p. 47; V, pp. 474, 521. Stokes, pp. 56, 146.
54. Stokes, pp. 81-139, 78, 65. See also William J. Barber, 'James Mill and the theory of economic policy in India', *The History of Political Economy,* 1, 1, Spring 1969, pp. 85-100.
55. G. C. Mendis, ed., *The Colebrooke-Cameron Papers, Documents*

on British Colonial Policy in Ceylon 1796–1833, 2 vols., Oxford, 1956.

56. A helpful resumé is in Donald Winch, *Classical Political and Economy*, London, 1965, esp. Ch II. See also K. N. Chaudhuri (ed.), *The Economic Development of India under the East India Company, 1814–58*, Cambridge 1971.
57. Evidence, 21 June 1853, *Second Report of the Select Committee of the House of Lords*, 1853, p. 153.
58. Dalhousie's Railway minute, 20 April 1853, quoted M. N. Das, *Studies in the Economic and Social Development of Modern India 1848–56*, Calcutta, 1959, pp. 79–80; and Bearce, *British Attitudes,* p. 220.
59. The two quotations from Percival Spear in this paragraph are from his *India: a Modern History,* Ann Arbor, 1967. For Dalhousie see ibid, Ch. XXIV, and Das, op. cit. A new, full-scale study of Dalhousie is now rather badly required.
60. J. W. Kaye, *Christianity in India,* London, 1859, pp. 488-9, quoted Thomas R. Metcalf, *The Aftermath of Revolt, 1857–1870*, Princeton, 1964 (which should be consulted more generally).
61. Quoted Stokes, p. 269.
62. First series, 2nd ed., London, 1907, p. 325.
63. The general picture is helpfully delineated in Chapter 12 on 'The Development of Dependencies', and especially in its final section on 'Some reasons for the cautious attitude towards development' (with its statement, p. 469, that 'the policy of development was not then a positive one') in R. Hyam, *Elgin and Churchill at the Colonial Office 1905–08*, London, 1968. One has only to read Stokes on Mill at the India Office, and think of Sir Andrew Cohen later on at the Ministry of Overseas Development, to sense the great differences in emphasis.
64. Sir T. Raleigh (ed.), *Lord Curzon in India 1889–1905*, London, 1906, p. 564.
65. Stephen to *The Times,* 4 Jan. 1878.
66. By E. L. Woodward, Oxford, 1938, and Asa Briggs, London, 1959, respectively.
67. E.g. Oliver Macdonagh, 'The Nineteenth-Century Revolution in Government: a reappraisal', *Historical Journal,* I, i. 1958, pp. 52–67; and G. R. Searle, *The Quest for National Efficiency,* Oxford, 1971.
68. J. W. Burrow, *Evolution and Society, a Study in Victorian Social Theory,* Cambridge, 1966.
69. John Roach, 'Liberalism and the Victorian Intelligentsia', *Cambridge Historical Journal,* Vol. XIII, 1, 1957.
70. Lord Robbins, *The Theory of Economic Development in the History of Economic Thought*, London, 1968, p. 14.
71. Barber, *History of Economic Thought,* p. 215. (This, and the previously quoted volume provide useful surveys for the whole period discussed here).

72. Gertrude Himmelfarb, *Darwin and the Darwinian Revolution*, London, 1959.
73. R. J. Moore, *Liberalism and Indian Politics 1872-1922,* London, 1966.
74. See his foreword to Hugh Tinker, *The Foundations of Local Self-Government in India, Pakistan and Burma,* London, 1954, p. xv.
75. Personal report from Mr. Alan Simmance.
76. W. G. Beasley, *The Modern History of Japan,* London, 1963.
77. Maine, *Ancient Law*, Oxford, 1954 edition, p. 15, quoted Burrow, op. cit.
78. Burrow, p. 174.
79. Government of India, *Selections from Papers on Indebtedness and Land Transfers,* Vol. I, quoted Kumar, *Western India,* pp. 198-9.
80. N. K. Sinha, *Economic History of Bengal,* Calcutta, 1956; B. S. Cohn, 'The Initial British Impact on India', *Journal of Asian Studies,* XIX, 4 Aug. 1960, pp. 418-31.
81. Cambridge, 1951, Ch. V. See also Metcalf, *Aftermath of Revolt*, pp. 65, 204 sqq.
82. Cf. here, of course, the discussion amongst historians of Britain which ensued upon the publication of Oliver Macdonagh, *A Pattern of Government 1800-60; the Passenger Acts and their Enforcement,* London, 1861. For a parallel story of responsive administration see B. M. Bhatia, *Famines in India*, London, 1963.
83. On all this see Kumar, *Western India in the Nineteenth Century,* Chs. V, VI, VII, and Bhatia, loc. cit.
84. The fullest account is in P. H. M. van den Dungen, *The Punjab Tradition. Influence and Authority in Nineteenth-Century India,* London, 1972; see also Norman G. Barrier, *The Punjab Alienation of Land Bill of 1900,* Duke University, 1966. S. S. Thornburn's published work was *Musalmans and Money-lenders in the Punjab,* London, 1886.
85. Kumar, *Western India,* Ch. VII. See also I. J. Catanach, *Rural Credit in Western India,* California, 1970; and his "Democracy and the Rural Cooperative Movement', *Proceedings of the Second International Economic History Conference 1962,* Paris, 1965, pp. 353-361.
86. This is clear from a preliminary glance at the Hailey Papers in the India Office Library.
87. 2nd ed., London, 1928.
88. Cambridge, 1948.
89. Hailey Papers, India Office Library, Mss. Eur. E. 220/29.
90. S. S. Nehru, *Current Problems,* 2nd ed., Lucknow, 1933, pp. 26 sqq. F. L. Brayne, *The Remaking of Village India,* London, 1929; F. L. Brayne, *Better Villages,* London, 1937.

91. Philip D. Curtin, *The Image of Africa,* London, 1965, pp. 49 sqq., 229 sqq. (This should be consulted more generally.)
92. *Report of the Sierra Leone Company 1808,* p. 13, quoted ibid, p. 139.
93. Evidence before the West Africa Committee, 27 July 1942, *British Parliamentary Papers,* 1842, XI (551), p. 713, quoted Curtin, p. 475.
94. W. Wilberforce, *A Letter on the Abolition of the Slave Trade,* London, 1807, p. 74, quoted Curtin, p. 252.
95. T. F. Buxton, *The African Slave Trade and its Remedy*, 2nd ed. 1840, reprinted Frank Cass, London, 1967, p. 528.
96. Curtin, *Image of Africa,* p. 272, and Ch. 12; see also R. Coupland, *Kirk on the Zambezi,* Oxford, 1928; Richard Gray, *A History of the Southern Sudan 1839-1889,* Oxford, 1961.
97. *Image of Africa,* pp. 476.
98. J. F. A. Ajayi, *Christian Missions in Nigeria 1841-1891. The Making of a New Elite,* London, 1965, Chs. 7 and 8.
99. Capetown 1883, p. 20. I am indebted to Dr. Rodney Davenport for this reference. For Grey see J. Rutherford, *Sir George Grey: A Study in Colonial Government,* London, 1961; for Shepstone see J. R. Sullivan, *The Native Policy of Sir Theophilus Shepstone,* Johannesburg, 1928.
100. R. L. Tignor, *Modernization and British Colonial Rule in Egypt, 1882–1914*, Princeton, 1966, pp. 396–7. For the quotation from Cromer to Grey, 8 March 1907, Cromer Papers, Vol. 13, p. 54, I am much indebted to Dr. Ronald Hyam. For Gordon see J. K. Chapman, *The Career of Sir Arthur Hamilton Gordon, first Lord Stanmore, 1829-1812,* London, 1964.
101. Joseph Chamberlain, *Foreign and Colonial Speeches,* London, 1897, p. 136; J. L. Garvin, *The Life of Joseph Chamberlain,* Vol. III, London, 1934. pp. 19-20; for his failure see pp. 175-7. The view I have expressed seems to be confirmed in S. B. Saul, 'The Economic Significance of Constructive Imperialism,' *Journal of Economic History,* XVII, June 1952, 2, pp. 173-192, and in H. A. Will, 'Colonial Policy and Economic Development in the British West Indies, 1895-1903', *Economic History Review,* XXIII, 1, 1970, pp. 129-147.
102. I am indebted to my colleague John Burrow for drawing my attention to a passage in which Herbert Spencer noted that 'within a generation the social organism has passed . . . to a stage like that of a warm-blooded creature with an efficient vascular system and a developed nervous apparatus', but that 'manifestly this . . . has aided the growth of both the industrial organisation and the militant organisation', *Principles of Sociology,* London, 1876- , pp. 144-5.
103. H. H. Johnston, 'The Development of Tropical Africa under British Auspices', *Fortnightly Review,* Nov. 1890, p. 705, and V. L. Cameron, *Across Africa,* p. 540, quoted H. A. L. Cairns,

Prelude to Imperialism: British Reactions to Central African Society 1840-1890, London, 1965 pp. 190, 212-13. (This study should be consulted more generally.)

104. Elspeth Huxley, *White Man's Country,* Vol. I, London, 1935, p. 223. A 'Machakos settler' wrote to *The Leader of British East Africa,* 28 Oct. 1916: '. . . either through possessing wealth in the shape of cattle or through laziness acquired by their women-folk doing all the manual work required throughout the past centuries, these Akamba men are at present time indolent, useless members of the community and the only course open to us settlers to train them in the way to go, and to teach them to work and to put them on the path to civilization and advancement, is to take them from their reserve, cattle and children and to teach them to understand and trust the white man'.

105. Sir Henry Belfield, *Proceedings of the East Africa Protectorate Legislative Council,* 1st Session 1917, p. 3.

106. R. Szereszewski, *Structural Changes in the Economy of Ghana, 1891-1911,* London, 1965; Polly Hill, *The Migrant Cocoa-Farmers of Southern Ghana,* Cambridge, 1963.

107. H. H. Bell, *Glimpses of a Governor's Life,* London, 1946 Part II; Ralph A. Austen, *Northwest Tanzania under German and British Rule*, London, 1968, pp. 221, 240–1.

108. R. J. M. Swynnerton, *A Plan to Intensify the Development of African Agriculture in Kenya,* Nairobi, 1954. It should be said that, in accord with the argument in the last few pages of this chapter, 'development' began to be spoken of in a new way in Kenya during the 1940s by some people in the Administration, though by no means by all.

109. C. Ehrlich, 'Some social and economic implications of paternalism in Uganda', *Journal of African History,* p. 275 sqq.; C. C. Wrigley, 'Economic and Social Development', in J. F. Ade Ajayi and Ian Espie, ed., *A Thousand Years of West African History,* Ibadan, 1965, pp. 423 sqq.

110. Mary H. Kingsley, *West African Studies,* 2nd ed., London, 1901; 3rd ed., with a new introduction by John E. Flint, Frank Cass, London, 1964. pp. 332, 326, 306. It is worth noting that she spent her intellectually formative years in Cambridge in the 1880s and early 1890s, see Roach 'Liberalism and the Victorian Intelligentsia'.

111. A. H. M. Kirk-Greene, *The Principles of Native Administration in Nigeria, Select Documents 1900-1947,* London, 1965, pp. 50, 57 (quoting C. L. Temple, *Native Races and the Rulers,* Cape Town, 1918). 2nd ed., with a new introduction by Mervyn Hiskett, Frank Cass, London, 1968.

112. Ibid, pp. 155, 166, 167 (quoting F. D. Lugard, *The Dual Mandate in British Tropical Africa,* London, 1922; 5th ed., with a new introduction by Margery Perham, 1965.)

113. M. F. Perham, 'A restatement of Indirect Rule', *Africa,* VII, 3, July 1934, pp. 331.
114. Lugard's *Political Memoranda,* 1918, quoted Kirk-Greene, p. 96.
115. See especially Sir Donald Cameron, *My Tanganyika Service and some Nigerian,* London, 1939; 2nd ed., with a new introduction by R. Heussler, Frank Cass, London, 1972, and Kirk-Greene passim.
116. Margery Perham, *Colonial Sequence 1930-1949,* London, 1967, pp. 81, 65, 145-6. See also Ralph A. Austen, 'The Official Mind of Indirect Rule: British Policy in Tanganyika, 1916–1939', Prosser Gifford and W. R. Louis, *Britain and Germany in Africa,* New Haven, 1967, pp. 577-606.
117. R. E. Wraith, *Guggisberg,* London, 1967, pp. 256, 262, 260, 138 sqq.
118. *Methods of Study of Culture Contact in Africa,* Mem. XV, International African Institute, 1935.
119. Sir Andrew Cohen, *British Policy in Changing Africa,* London, 1959, pp. 18-19.
120. *Report of Committee on Finance and Industry* (1931), Cmd. 3897, p. 5, quoted Donald Winch, *Economics and Policy,* London, 1969.
121. F. R. Harris, *Jamsetji Nusserwanji Tata,* Bombay, 1958, Chs. VIII-X.
122. A. H. Hanson, *The Process of Planning: A Study of India's Five Year Plans 1950-1964,* London, 1966, esp. Ch. II and references there quoted (and elsewhere passim).
123. H. H. Mann, *The Social Framework of Agriculture,* Bombay, 1967, p. 295 (and the Introduction). For anyone who is interested in the genesis of the 'Bombay' plan, there are relevant papers in the Thakurdas Mss. in the Nehru Memorial Museum, New Delhi.
124. Perham, *Colonial Sequence,* pp. 226-7, 232.
125. J. M. Lee, *Colonial Government and Good Government*, Oxford, 1967. For an admirable account of how the change may be traced in the history of one British colony see Cyril Ehrlich, 'The Uganda Economy, 1903-1945', in Vincent Harlow and E. M. Chilver, *History of East Africa,* Vol. II, Oxford, 1965, esp. pp. 469-75.
126. Some parts of the story are set out in my colleague Donald Winch's *Economics and Policy*, in W. K. Hancock, *Survey of British Commonwealth Affairs*, Vol. II, Problems of Economic Policy 1918–1939, Part II, London 1942, p. 268, and in Vincent Harlow, 'The Historian and British Colonial History', an Inaugural Lecture 1950, Oxford, 1951, p. 23. For intimations in the 1920s of things to come, see E. A. Brett, 'Development Policy in East Africa between the wars', unpublished Ph.D. London University, 1966, especially Chapter 3.

127. Perham, *Colonial Sequence 1930-1949,* p. 165.
128. Kirk-Greene, *Native Administration,* pp. 238-48 reprints the crucial public documents.
129. See the introductory chapter by D. A. Low and J. M. Lonsdale in Low and Smith, *History of East Africa,* III, Oxford (forthcoming).
130. Those who read Lee, *Colonial Development and Good Government,* should also read Hanson, *The Process of Planning,* and vice versa. [I regret that Elizabeth Whitcombe's *Agrarian Conditions in Northern India, Vol. 1, The United Provinces under British Rule*, California 1972, was published too late to be used in writing the middle section of this chapter.]

3

Empire and Traditional Rulership

As the Mughal empire fell apart in India in the mid eighteenth century, a number of formerly subordinate polities thrust themselves forward into increasing independency. Amongst these was Oudh (comprising the area around Lucknow in the upper Ganges valley) whose Nawab, a former imperial official, soon assumed the status of a traditional ruler. Of the others, none was more successful than the British East India Company. In time the destinies of these two became intertwined. In the late eighteenth and during the first few years of the nineteenth century, the East India Company came to annex some of the outer areas of Oudh to its own dominions. Until the mid-nineteenth century, however, the core of Oudh remained an Indian native state, in treaty relations with the British, but with its independence still substantially intact.

During the intervening period, there was within Oudh itself, however, a replication—at the next level 'down' as it were—of the developments which had overtaken the Mughal empire in the previous century. Some of the Nawabs of Oudh were able men; but others were effete and ineffective rulers, who soon found themselves challenged from below by the 'Barons of Oudh', the so-called Talukdars of Oudh, many of whom possessed a substantial, localised, traditional authority. Their growth to independence can be readily indicated. In 1800, there were said to be seventeen private fortresses in Oudh; by 1849, 246.[1] The rapaciousness of the talukdars and their violent conflicts with the Nawab's nazims (the Nawabs revenue agents) became notorious.[2]

In 1856 that reforming British Viceroy, Lord Dalhousie, finally decided to annex Oudh to British India, and in so doing made it very plain that he wished the institutions of traditional rulership which existed there to be expunged altogether. The Nawab of Oudh—since Lord Hastings' day the British had called him 'King'—was deposed and deported; and Dalhousie gave instructions that in the land settlement which followed there was to be no 'interposition of middlemen, as Talookdars, Farmers of the revenue and suchlike'.[3] The talukdars of Oudh had seen their counterparts largely expunged by the British from those outer areas of Oudh which the British annexed half a century earlier, and there could scarcely be much doubt that there would shortly be a showdown for them with the British. They appear, however, to have decided that the moment of annexation was not itself an appropriate one for testing their strength; and in the event Dalhousie's settlement instructions were not carried out to the letter. But enough talukdars lost enough of their villages to make them profoundly apprehensive for the future—so that when in 1857, the year after annexation, the sepoy mutiny broke out to the westward, many of them very soon grasped the opportunity it presented for making one final bid to preserve their former hard-won independency. By the end of 1857 the Indian Revolt had become, in north central India, a major civil rebellion—in Oudh, with the talukdars much to the fore in its leadership.

By September 1857, however, thanks to the maintenance of their position in the Punjab, the British had been able to storm their way back into Delhi, the original nodal point of the revolt, and early in the new year were poised to recover their whole position in the upper Ganges valley. Their prime objective was now the final relief of the beleaguered British garrison in the old capital of Oudh, Lucknow; and on 8 February 1858 the British Commander-in-Chief, Sir Colin Campbell, met Lord Canning, Dalhousie's successor as Viceroy, in Allahabad to discuss their future moves. In the preceding months various efforts had been made to wean the talukdars over to the British side, but with no success, and Canning had now decided that the time had come for him to deliver the *coup de grâce* against them. The two men thereupon discussed the terms of a proclamation (which was to be ready for publication as soon as Lucknow had been finally relieved), in which the Viceroy was to declare that the lands of those talukdars who had joined the revolt—and by this time that was the great majority of them—were to be forfeited.[4]

But when Sir James Outram, the British Chief Commissioner in Oudh, received the Viceroy's draft proclamation he was greatly perturbed. When the talukdars heard of it they would be impelled, he felt, into 'a desperate and prolonged resistance' which the British could ill afford to face. He accordingly begged the Viceroy to reconsider his decision. Canning was reluctant to do so. Like the sepoys, the talukdars, he believed, had to be taught that armed rebellion against the British would not be tolerated. He agreed, however, that Outram could use his discretion to emphasise 'the indulgence of the Government": and in the end the so-called Oudh Proclamation which Outram then isued on 14 March 1858—the day of the major British victory in the streets of Lucknow—eventually included a promise to those talukdars who gave 'their support in the restoration of peace and order': 'The Governor-General will be ready to view liberally,' ran a new clause, 'the claims which they may thus acquire to a restoration of their former rights.'

There was little immediate response to this new offer. But with the British army anxious to avoid an extensive campaign for the re-establishment of its control over the rural areas of Oudh, strenuous efforts were made during the summer months of 1858 to draw the attention of the talukdars to it. These gradually succeeded. By October 1858 two-thirds of the talukdars had submitted; and by the end of the year most of the others. They remained suspicious, however, of the ultimate intentions of the British, and in an effort to ease their hesitations a new British Chief Commissioner in Oudh suggested in 1859 that they should be given sanads (that is formal imperial deeds) guaranteeing them the tenure of their lands. By this time a settlement with the talukdars of Oudh had become a central point in the plans of the British for the restoration of their authority in the upper Ganges valley, and the suggestion was readily accepted. In October 1859 Canning indeed, for all his earlier animadversions at Allahabad eighteen months previously, presided over a durbar in Lucknow at which 169 sanads were presented to the assembled talukdars.

The Canning settlement, as it came to be called, required that the talukdars should abandon their former posture as overmighty subjects: their fortresses were pulled down, their cannon confiscated, and their private armies disarmed. But the sharpest minds amongst them soon discovered that within the terms of the Canning settlement there lay an opportunity to secure a new role for themselves, which, if they were skilful, could maintain for them a good deal of that local importance which (as one British officer was to put it in 1865) was still 'their present ambition'. Since Oudh was annexed to British India they could not expect to be treated as native princes. Some of them were given judicial and executive powers; but there was no precedent in recent British Indian history for their becoming subordinate administrative agents of the British. The one role offered to them was that of landlords. Within the terms, however, which this allowed, there was just a chance that if they kept their elbows sharp and used them deftly they might be able to hold on to a great deal of that 'local importance' for which, during the last decades of the Nawabi, so many of them had fought so strenuously. With this end in view, several of them set out to work assiduously, and for the most part successfully. There were three key figures. In the first place, there was the Maharajah of Balrampur, the talukdar with the largest estate, and one of the few who had remained 'loyal' to the British throughout 1857-58; he brought respectability to the campaign. Then there was Maharajah Man Singh, a former Nawabi nazim who had turned talukdar on his own account: a man who showed both in his cautious slither into revolt in 1857, and in his vehement efforts after 1859 to see that no claims by any of his own subordinates were sustained against him, that he was determined to hold on to as much of his hard-won gains as he could; it was he who brought resolution to the talukdar's recovery campaign. And, thirdly, there was Babu Dakhinaranjan Mukherji, the one Bengali amongst them, and the man who showed them the best way to proceed. He himself was already a member of the influential Bengali landlords lobby, the British India Association of Calcutta. He soon set about creating an Oudh counterpart to this, the British India Association of Lucknow, of which he himself became Secretary, Man Singh Vice-President, and, for twenty years, Balrampur President. Together these three men, in association with a whole new 'school' of British officials, created the machinery which made sure that the 176 talukdars who were eventually given sanads possessed every ounce of privilege which was in any way available to those who were leading landlords in British India. As a consequence, the Talukdars of Oudh succeeded not just in weathering their mid-century crisis, but in turning themselves into the most powerful Indian community in any part of British India: it was estimated in 1881 that 77 per cent of the population of Oudh were tenants-at-will of its landed aristocracy—pre-eminently the talukdars of Oudh.[5]

First Crisis

This complex story merits consideration both because it provides some of the keys to the later discussion, and because, more immediately, it illustrates a number of the preliminary points to be made. Traditional authority was defined by Max Weber as 'resting on an established belief in the sanctity of immemorial traditions and the legitimacy of the status of those exercising authority under them'. Traditional rulership has in its day taken innumerable forms. The increasingly sophisticated work on African kingdoms is revealing some of the range.[6] At the moment there are few parallels in Indian studies to these African studies, but the 'little kingdoms' of India, of which many of the Oudh talukdars were fairly typical examples, are clearly examples of a fairly widespread phenomenon. With the spread of British imperial rule they, and their varied counterparts in India, in parts of south-east Asia, and in a number of widely dispersed areas in Africa, became subject to British imperial authority, and in the process faced what may be called their first crisis.

It should be emphasised that it was a major crisis, and for two particular reasons. First, having asserted their control over peoples with traditional rulership, the British—and no doubt other imperial conquerors too—almost always had a clear choice between two alternative means of proceeding. They could either supersede a pre-existing political authority, as in Oudh they did the Nawab, or they could superimpose their authority over a pre-existing political authority which they maintained in existence under their aegis—as in Oudh they eventually did to the talukdars. Because these two alternative possibilities were almost always open to an imperial power, the first crisis for a traditional rulership upon being subordinated was nothing less than a desperate matter of life and death. All the more so (and this is the second reason why the first crisis was so substantial) because the British at all events do not seem to have had any persistent preference between the two choices which were almost always open to them. Sometimes they were Malcolms who were anxious to preserve traditional rulership; sometimes they were Metcalfes who were opposed to so doing; and sometimes they were Cannings—who changed their minds.[7]

In the event, indeed, it becomes exceedingly difficult to discern any precise set of reasons why the fortunes of one traditional rulership, or one set of traditional rulerships, when subjected to British empire-builders ran in one direction, while others ran in another.

Consider some of the contrasts here—with those rulerships that survived their annexation by the British being mentioned first: amongst the Marathas of central India, for example, the contrast between Baroda and Indore, on the one hand, and Nagpur and the Peshwa's dominions, on the other; in north-western India between the erstwhile Punjabi province of Kashmir and Punjab proper; or, elsewhere, between the fate of the Nizam of Hyderabad and the Nawab of Bengal, or the fate of the talukdars of Oudh and the talukdars of Agra. Consider as well the contrasts in Africa between the fate of the Basuto kingdom and the Zulu kingdom, between the Barotse kingdom and the Ndebele, between the sultanate of Sokoto and the kingdom of Ashanti: and elsewhere between the Arab sultanate of Zanzibar and the Burmese kingdom of Ava.[8]

It is no doubt tempting to try to suggest that the British destroyed rulership which in their thinking had become notorious for their violent rapaciousness. This would fit the Punjab in the 1840s, the Zulu kingdom in the 1870s, and Lobengula's Ndebele in the 1890s. But the case of the talukdars of Oudh gives it no support, nor that of the Ngoni of central Africa. Both were notoriously predatory; but both sets of rulerships survived.

What, however, of the evil reputation of the ruler? Is there not some explication to be found here? Certainly this was a consideration in the case of the Nawab of Oudh, as in that of a Nawab or two in Bengal a century previously; or in Africa in respect of both the Asantehene of Ashanti and the Oba of Benin in the middle 1890s.[9] But here there are some striking cases from Uganda which must give us pause. By 1890 the evil reputation in British circles of Kabaka Mwanga of Buganda, who had had a bishop murdered in 1885 and a number of Christian converts burnt alive in 1886, was certainly no less than that of Mukama Kabarega of the adjacent kingdom of Bunyoro, a man who had regularly clashed with most of his European visitors since the early 1860s and had won himself a bad press as a consequence. At first, however, Captain Lugard, the first British agent, supported Mwanga while attacking Kabarega; while later on, after a series of violent conflicts with both of them, both rulers were deported. Both kingdoms, however, survived![10]

What then of Britain's economic interests? Was there not some regularity in their influence? Bengal in the mid-eighteenth century, Malabar in the late eighteenth century, Sind in the early nineteenth century, or the classic case of Jaja's Opobo in the Niger delta half a century later in 1887, suggest that there might be.[11] But Sir George Goldie's dictum as President of the Royal Niger Company in 1898 that 'the general policy of ruling on African principles through native rulers must be followed for the present'—not to mention the policy which actually followed from this—makes it impossible to hold even this variable steady.[12]

It seems, indeed, well-nigh impossible to advance any systemised set of explanations for the contrasts of fate which one notices. On fairly close examination, moreover, it really does appear to have been touch and go for traditional rulerships in their first crisis (with the British at all events) on a very great number of occasions. Oudh illustrates this. Not only did its king disappear while its talukdars survived; had either Dalhousie's instructions of 1856 or Canning's first draft of his Oudh proclamation of 1858 (as originally discussed with General Campbell at Allahabad on 8 February 1858) been fully carried out as originally intended, it is most unlikely that the talukdars of Oudh would have weathered their first crisis. For the peculiar multiplex of reasons that have been briefly sketched out, they did. And if their behaviour suggests that between 1856 and 1860 they thought there was little they could do but play a series of hunches at roughly six monthly intervals, a review of the available comparisons suggests they were right. It is in these terms that the first crisis of traditional rulership confronted by empire was intensely real for all of those involved in it.

Even so, there are some suggestions to be offered to those who would explore such episodes further, which go beyond the notion that in the end one comes back to the specifics of the case: a truth indeed, but not necessarily the only one. In so doing it may be helpful to try to develop the argument a little further by taking into consideration two other 'first crises,' both of them, as it happens, from Africa: one from Uganda, the other from northern Nigeria.

In the 1870s, the larger Uganda kingdoms in east central Africa had a dress rehearsal of their first crisis when they confronted the Egyptians and their associates coming south up the Nile. This initial encounter revealed several characteristic features of the later full drama. First, the response of neighbouring kingdoms was noticeably different. Bunyoro was at once uncertain of itself and prone to fall into conflict with the Egyptians, while Buganda, under its redoubtable Kabaka Mutesa I, played an astonishingly steady hand throughout: when an Egyptian force appeared upon its territory it quietly forced it to withdraw by withholding food supplies. (Once more the specifics of the case warrant close attention.) But, secondly, it is clear that few in the area had much compunction about securing the support of alien intruders in advancing the causes they had at heart within their own kingdoms. Some northern traders, moreover, found it possible to intrigue in a Bunyoro war of succession for a candidate who, had he succeeded to the throne, would have become their protégé.[13] These considerations open up a number of further analytical possibilities.

By the time the major crisis came to the northern Lake Victoria region in the 1890s, a new and much more volatile Kabaka had succeeded in Buganda. In 1885 he had showed his mettle by ordering the murder of an Anglican bishop, who was advancing towards his country with a sizeable caravan, because he saw in him a threat to the integrity of his kingdom. In 1888, however, there was a revolution in Buganda; not just a rebellion and the installation of a new ruler, but in many respects a real political revolution, from the midst of which there sprang a powerful group—specifically of armed Christian converts and more particularly of some Protestants—who were anxious to secure external assistance for their internal ambitions and seemingly displayed no hesitation in seeking it wherever they could. When the young Captain Lugard advanced toward Buganda in 1890, he accordingly found himself (far from being murdered, as poor Bishop Hannington had been five years before) actually welcomed by the revolutionary Christians, and more specifically by the leaders of the Protestants. There were many vicissitudes in the ensuing years. At one point Lugard in direct alliance with the Protestants fought the Kabaka, who thereafter, however, submitted to him. At another, in 1898, a British Foreign Office official suggested that the Kabakaship should be done away with altogether. Lord Salisbury, however, the British Prime Minister, swiftly suppressed the idea. And in the end the essential ingredient in the eventual resolution of Buganda's first crisis was the creation of an alliance between the British and this group of Christian converts within the kingdom who had their own interests to pursue, and who saw nothing illegitimate in securing any outside help they could to advance them.[14]

The spread of British dominion, and the nature of the first crisis in the other Uganda kingdoms, characteristically revealed two further considerations. First, there was usually rivalry, if not indeed open conflict, between those who were equally legitimate successors to the thrones of these kingdoms. If the existing holders delayed at all in seeking accommodation with the British, the British usually managed to back one of their rivals against them, and, by using armed support, they could almost always secure the quite legitimate succession of a candidate to the throne who was henceforward beholden to them. Furthermore, once the immediate advantages of co-operating with the British had become clear, even some of those who might have considered resisting them were soon tempted to make their submission.[15]

When one turns next to northern Nigeria, all these possibilities seem to have been in operation there too. As in the case of the Uganda kingdoms, there was never much likelihood of the British actually erasing the Nigerian rulerships from the map (as they erased, for example, the Ndebele kingdom). But this does not mean there was no real 'first crisis' for the emirates. The ease with which a few well-timed marches by British-led troops reduced the once great Fulani empire (which had been founded by Usman dan Fodio's *jihad* in the early nineteenth century upon the remains of a series of previous Hausa kingdoms) should not blind us to the fact that the Fulani elite was not numerous, and that if the British had sought to expel it the Hausa majority beneath them would very probably not have objected. The structure of political authority here, moreover, was to an unusual degree so well founded that if the British had ejected the Fulani, the problems for the British in establishing their administration would not have been substantially aggravated. For a start they could, as in Katsina, have restored the exiled Hausa dynasties, as some of the British Residents suggested.

The choices were clearly there, and the Sultan of Sokoto drew attention to them when he threw down a terse verbal challenge to Lugard, the first British agent. When Lugard became High Commissioner for Northern Nigeria in 1900, however, he already had Goldie's dictum behind him (as already quoted and now endorsed by the Selborne Committee of 1898 on the administration of Nigeria), the viewpoint expressed by Mary Kingsley (as mentioned in the last chapter), and his own successful experience in Uganda, to guide him, and he promptly decided that the Emirates should be maintained.[16]

In addition to the use of British-led force—and the technique here was now finely honed, as the dramatic capture of the great city of Kano after a few hours' fighting suggests (the vast market was opened three days later)—the three characteristics which were noted in the discussion of Uganda's first crisis were repeated. First, some emirs (the Emir of Zaria, for instance), like the Baganda Christians, seized the opportunity of the British advent to call in the new world to redress, as they desired it, the balance of the old. Secondly, hostile emirs were readily replaced by alternate candidates who were equally legitimate candidates for the post but were prepared to acknowledge British supremacy. Such was the fate of the Emir of Kano, and even of the pre-eminent Sultan of Sokoto. Indeed, in the first nine years after Lugard's appointment, seventeen emirs were treated in this way. And, thirdly, their replacements, and most of the remaining emirs as well, however hostile they might feel towards the British at heart, soon concluded (like Maharajah Man Singh and the Talukdars of Oudh before them) that discretion was the better part of valour. When the most serious early threat to the British erupted—the Satiru revolt of 1906—the new Sultan of Sokoto backed the British against it.[17]

These two further examples of first crises taken from Africa thus extend the earlier discussion which was based largely on India. First, they indicate that there were sometimes factions within traditional rulerships that saw personal advantage in linking their fortunes to the alien invader: to revert to India, there is evidence of this in Bengal in the 1750s, and in the Punjab in the 1840s.[18] Secondly, it was often possible for empire-builders to replace a hostile ruler by a more amenable rival who was at the same time a fully legitimate candidate for the throne. We have considered some African examples.[19] But this was plainly the game of the Frenchman Dupleix in the early eighteenth century. Clive and his successors played it in Bengal a few years later; and there is the intriguing variation on this theme in Britain's failure on two successive occasions during the nineteenth century to play it successfully in Afghanistan to suggest how regular a ploy it had become by then in their hands.[20] And then, thirdly, there were sometimes elements within the traditional rulership which, although inherently hostile to the alien order, often, like the talukdars of Oudh in the course of 1858, came to feel that a time had come when to compound with one's 'adversary whilst he was in the way' was the only sensible course for an intelligent man to pursue. One of the most striking cases of this comes from India in the decision of so many Chitpavan Brahmins to work with the British in the decades after the annexation of Poona in 1818, despite the British destruction of the kingdom of the Peshwa.[21] These three groups may be categorised as 'the door-openers', 'the alternates', and 'the canny'. From the cases we have considered, it looks as if it might be said that the presence of all three was a necessary condition of the ability of a traditional rulership to survive the first crisis. But, let it be emphasised, not a sufficient condition.[22] If Canning had been more resolute with Sir James Outram, or another man had been Chief Commissioner of Oudh in 1858 (a man in the Metcalfe rather than the Malcolm tradition—John Lawrence for example), it is difficult to believe that the talukdars would have survived, certainly not in the form they did. Uncertainty always seems to have remained, chiefly, as we have said, because of the two alternatives which were almost always open to the British—between which they persistently oscillated. It may be in the end indeed that we should see the particular predilection of the particular British officer who was primarily responsible as being the really critical variable affecting the outcome. In Oudh's case, not, as the talukdars thought, Canning, but Outram.

Perhaps that is to take the analysis here far enough. There are, however, three further considerations which a glance at a fairly wide selection of first crises suggests. In the first place, where pre-existing political authorities were maintained, albeit in a subordinate position, they were generally required to adapt to roles that were at least marginally different from those they had enjoyed in the past: the talukdars of Oudh, for instance, were required to go through that very English-looking transmutation from overmighty subjects to landed aristocracy. This was a peculiar variant upon a very common theme: in Uganda, some minor rulers were expected to transform themselves into bureaucrats.[23] Secondly, it is striking how frequently the establishment of British authority over a traditional rulership seems to have required two successive displays of force. One can think here, in India, of the battles of Plassey and of Buxar in Bengal; of the second and third Maratha wars in the Deccan; of the two Sikh wars in the Punjab; and, in Africa, of the Ndebele war in 1893 and the Ndebele revolt of 1896; of the first battle of Mengo in Buganda in 1892 and the suppression of Kabaka Mwanga's revolt in 1897–99; and of the forcible annexation of Ashanti, together with Prempeh's deportation, in 1895, and of the Ashanti revolt of 1900.[24] Oudh here is a case in point. Indeed, its original story bears a very close resemblance to that of Ashanti. In both instances the British annexed the country uninvited and forcibly deported the overruler. In both, a revolt erupted subsequently (rather more quickly in Oudh, since the sepoy mutiny provided an early occasion for it), and it was only when the British had used very much greater force on a second occasion that the previously subordinate but, in both cases, recently more independent, sets of local rulers who remained, finally submitted to British imperial control. It should be emphasised that these two-act dramas were by no means universal; they were nevertheless not infrequent. (And, let it be added that one gets no help here in determining why some traditional rulerships survived the first crisis and others did not; there are cases—Buganda, for example—where a two-act conflict occurred but the rulership survived.)

The third point here is this. It looks as if, during the last hundred years of the British empire, the importance of the outcome of the first crisis was of very substantial moment. Whilst 'doctrines of lapse' persisted in India, this had not quite been the case there. For decades, as we have seen, the core of Oudh had remained an Indian native state with a British Resident. Even so, annexation to British India had come to it in 1856. And during this period there were similar shifts in the fate of several other Indian princely states. But with '1857', and what has been called the aristocratic reaction which followed it,[25] the arbitrary supersession of a pre-existing traditional rulership at a date long subsequent to its first crisis became a very rare occurrence in the British Empire. Indeed, it is difficult to think of examples from Africa—the lapse of the Sultanate of Witu on the death of the old sultan in 1923, and the dilution of the rulership of the Bamangwato following the Tshekedi and Seretse imbroglio in the 1950s are the only, marginal instances that come readily to mind.[26] The tendency ran the other way: in Mysore, for example, in India, where the so-called 'rendition' of power to the Maharajah occurred in 1881; or in Ashanti in Africa, where the Asantehene was restored in 1935, as the Oba of Benin had been in 1914, and, down south, Cetshwayo in Zululand in 1883.[27] The implication here is important. Those traditional rulerships that survived the first crisis, or the year 1860, whichever was the earlier, came to compose, as in an elimination contest, those rulerships which were left to face the second crisis, which came with the onset of national independence linked to the ballot box and to universal suffrage.

Second Crisis

I have suggested in Chapter 1 that during the interim period, when imperial authority was in full spate, it is possible to place traditional rulerships under British imperial authority upon a continuum whose poles relate to the degree to which, at one end, the extent of British control over their conduct of affairs was minimal, to the other at which it was maximal—from, as I put it, quasi-diplomatic connections at one end, to full administrative control at the other. When one turns, however, to consider why some traditional authorities brought subject to imperial domination showed little ability to survive the crisis of national independence—the 'second crisis' as it is termed here—while others seem to have weathered it, this scale is not of much help. At one end the Persian Gulf rulers have (so far!) survived, while all the Indian princes have by now gone to the wall, whereas at the other end the Malayan sultans remain and find from their number the Malayan head of state, while the Sultan of Zanzibar is a refugee in Britain. And, of those in the middle, the rulers of Uganda have been pensioned off, while the emirs of northern Nigeria remain.

It is probably very rash to argue the reasons why some traditional rulerships have, so far at least, managed to survive the 'second crisis', since the apparently successful may yet become its victims. But there seems enough of a contrast between the fate of the talukdars of Oudh, who went quickly to the wall, and the success of the emirs of northern Nigeria, who survived both the onset of ballot box politics and the first two military coups, at least to pose the question why there was so much difference. To this we may now turn; and if some allusion is also made to the Uganda kindoms, it will be because they provide some controls upon the suggestions to be offered. The variables are still highly mercurial. There were for example, 413 talukdars and only 38 emirs. But the population involved was not all that different—perhaps 20 millions in Oudh and 20 millions in northern Nigeria all told at the relevant periods. More important, it seems possible to postulate a much more persistent tendency in nationalist governments who have come to power through the ballot box, to be rid of traditional rulerships as soon as they are able than was ever displayed by the British. The comparisons to be made can only be very preliminary. But, for the moment, it may be that there is something to be said for seeking to probe the contrasts in fate between the traditional rulerships of Oudh, southern Uganda and northern Nigeria under a set of three headings, which may be called respectively 'administration', 'the enemy', and 'matters concerning the moral community'.

First, then, the talukdars of Oudh. Just as there was a distinguished phalanx of 'Indirect Rulers' amongst British administrators in Africa, so there was a distinguished 'Oudh School' of British administrators in India. The latter comprised a succession of those who worked in Oudh and came to venerate the talukdars, and the Canning settlement which buttressed them, as the great hope of India. In 1906, the year of Lugard's *Political Memoranda* on indirect rule in Northern Nigeria (so the comparison is not wholly fanciful), the last great figure of the Oudh school published its most explicit manifesto, Harcourt Butler's *Oudh Policy: the Policy of Sympathy*, in which he soliloquised (it was the year of the Calcutta Congress and Naoroji's 'Swaraj' speech there):

> 'How comes it that thoughtful men on all sides now are asking why the government of Oudh has been so strikingly successful? Where, they ask, in India can be found more true happiness and ease under British rule, more solid progress, more unquestioning loyalty? Where such smooth relations between the rulers and the ruled, between the party of order and the party of change? Where a like measure of agrarian peace? Where a more effective combination of old sanctions and young aspiration? What are the peculiar possessions of the province, what institutions, what particular foundations or superstructure, to which it owes its great and growing reputation?'

He was quick with the answer: 'The preservation of its landed aristocracy, the ancient, indigenous and cherished system of the country, as Lord Canning truly called it, is the secret of its strength.'[28] In the famous phrase, the right way to rule India, so the Oudh school believed, was through 'the natural leaders of the people'.

As it happened they themselves did nothing of the kind, as any comparison with the emirs' administration will quickly reveal. After 1857 a number of talukdars were given magisterial powers, and to that extent they acted somewhat like British Justices of the Peace.[29] But this did not last. They once held police powers too, but these seem to have been largely taken away from them by the end of the nineteenth century. In a revealing aside, Harcourt Butler himself declared: 'to the bulk of the people the British Government is the patwari, chaukidar and tahsili chaprassi'.[30] To the bulk of the population, that is, the *persona* of the British administration was felt to be directly present in the lowliest official. Butler might assert that the talukdars 'remain the executors and sole trustees of political power'; but he himself defined this to mean 'as local counsellors and the right-hand men of the local authority'.[31] So that whatever members of the Oudh school might assert in their more expansive moments, the talukdars under their dominion were not native princes, nor administrative chiefs, nor justices of the peace, nor administrative agents of the imperial power. They were—and this is precisely the point—simply landlords. The truth slipped out from Benett, the Oudh school's doyen: 'Where formerly three hundred native chiefs executed their commands through the first handful of stalwarts available for the purpose, twelve [British] deputy commissioners now carry out the orders of the courts and the administration.'[32]

There is a revealing account of what this involved from a village upon the largest talukdari estate, the Maharajah of Balrampur's, written by an American woman who spent a year there in the late 1920s. The Maharajah had his own tehsildar in the area, who was plainly a key figure—a bailiff, rent collector, and resolver of disputes. He had, moreover, subordinate agents, or thekedars, installed in each village under his charge. But Balrampur's was the largest estate in Oudh, and had special privileges and problems which gave its tehsildars more authority than others; and even here it seems to have been quite clear that a direct appeal to the European

Deputy Commissioner against a ruling by the estate tehsildar was by no means *ultra vires*. Installed, moreover, in the village police station was the local police sergeant, and he owed no allegiance to the Maharajah; he was directly responsible to British police officers.[33]

The underlying point is that Oudh was part of British India: it did not comprise a region of princely states. Histories of British India tend to discuss at some length the argument both before and after the end of the eighteenth century between Cornwallis's doctrine of the separation of powers between magistrates and collectors, and the rival view—of Shore, Munro, Mill and their followers—of the necessity for a single district officer with both revenue and judicial powers.[34] This, however, tends to cloak the crucial movement during the same period (which, admittedly, proceeded by fits and starts) from supervision of the native states' revenue and judicial administration by British officials, to the exercise of revenue and judicial functions (with the help of appointed Indian subordinates) by British officials themselves—a very different matter indeed. In due course, all assertions to the contrary notwithstanding, this direct British control was introduced into Oudh after annexation, and was exercised through British Deputy Commissioners, as Benett indeed explained. In one of his most pungent phrases he himself made the essential point: 'The Commissioner has supplanted not so much the Nazim as the Raja.'[35] Not so much the ruler's agent, that is, as the ruler himself. Specifically, this implied that although the talukdars had their estate officers, they did not head local governments.

For present purposes it is important to emphasise that they never really had. Few things here are more important to note than the limited development of patrimonial office—let alone bureaucratic office—under the talukdars in all the centuries in which their 'little kingdoms' had had some existence.[36] As Benett put it: 'formerly three hundred chiefs executed their commands through the first handful of stalwarts available for the purpose'. The Maharajah of Balrampur had his tehsildars, but the administrative tradition in which they stood was clearly very thin indeed. Talukdars, we may be clear, exercised political authority; in significant respects some of this became transformed into what might be called 'public' authority. But they did not command—and the distinction here must be pressed—either before or after the British annexation, any substantial governmental machine.[37] If they were 'natural leaders', they were not heads of governmental administrations, however small.

One important consequence of this was that once after 1860 their survival was guaranteed by British rule and British sanads, their role turned out to be a very undemanding one. It certainly was not a requirement that the occupant should, in the European sense, be well educated. Some of the talukdars saw that their sons underwent some degree of western education; but in 1934 the talukdars' own British India Association conceded the essential point when it remarked in an official publication that 'the kind of education which most of them have been in the habit of giving to their sons is not such as to enable them to enter [governmental] service by competitive examination'[38]

For all Man Singh's efforts, and the protestations of the Oudh school, the talukdars ended up, therefore, by being simply landlords; and with no hands upon any substantial administrative levers, and little Western education, they were in terms of their administrative reach very ill positioned to meet the second crisis when it came.

For all this, the landlords of the United Provinces, of whom the talukdars were a major part, did manage to win a majority of seats—admittedly on a very restricted franchise—to their local Legislative Council as late as 1926, and on an occasion, moreover, when there was really very little Congress boycott of the polls.[39] Even so, their 'enemy' soon proved to be far too formidable for them. For a start it was in their midst and all round: the merchants and the new professionals of the many towns and cities of the region. Moreover, these people were propelled towards a policy of landlord abolition (one can see this vividly spelt out in Jawaharlal Nehru's *Autobiography*)[40] by their experience of the peasant jacqueries in Oudh in the early 1920s. These were directed against those who were seen as the worst of the villains of the harsh landlord-dominated regime which the Canning settlement had brought into being.[41] By the early 1930s Congress in U.P.

under Jawaharlal Nehru's leadership had become, in consequence, much the most socially radical of all the provincial Congresses in India. And in two stages, and by perfectly 'legal' means, it broke the back of the talukdari regime in Oudh; first, by soundly defeating the landlords' National Agriculturalists' Parties at the provincial elections in 1937, and then by abolishing talukdari tenures in the U.P. Zamindari Abolition Act of 1950.[42] The talukdars' 'enemy' proved to be quite irresistible.

What of the moral community? On this the Oudh school, at all events, was repeatedly emphatic. Benett wrote:

> 'What made the Oudh barons so strong is that they were a necessary element in the religious system of the country. Their race had been set apart by immemorial tradition and the sanction of all sacred literature as the wielders and representatives of Hindu power. The Chattri ruler was as indispensable as the Brahman priest, and his might and magnificence were—and are—still gloried in by the people as the visible manifestation of their national prosperity... It is this fact which commands for him the unquestioning obedience, and it may almost be said the enthusiastic affection, of his subjects.'[43]

Even at this level of abstraction one can, however, trace a new shape to the thinking about the moral community in the general area in which Oudh stands as the nineteenth century changed to the twentieth: first, in the Hindu revival, symbolised perhaps by such places as the Kashi Vidyapeeth in Benares, at which Sampurnanand taught and Lal Bahadur gained his coveted title of Sastri[44]; and then more particularly—and the evidence for this is remarkably clear—by the preachings and journeyings of Gandhi.[45] If the talukdars once filled a cardinal role in the maintenance of the Hindu order, this was not a claim that could be widely advanced on their behalf by the time the second crisis came to press upon them.

Thus, in terms of the administration they did, or rather did not do, the strength of their enemy, and the loss of the status they seemed to have previously enjoyed within the moral community, the talukdars of Oudh were in a most feeble position when their second crisis came. In the event, between 1937 and 1951, the role of talukdars as such—as Dalhousie and Canning had planned on two occasions nearly a century before—was eradicated.[46]

What of the Uganda kingdoms? They belong at the point of balance, as the Kabaka of Buganda's appointment as President of Uganda in 1964 and the Uganda government's armed attack upon his palace two years later, illustrate.[47] In considering the Uganda kingdoms, it should be noted that in the aftermath of the late nineteenth century revolution in Buganda, the ruler's ministers and the 'native council' were as important to them as the ruler himself. The focus is upon Buganda, but it is important to realise as well the degree to which, during the British period, its institutions were replicated throughout the rest of the country. Within the kingdom structure the kingdom's government possessed extensive administrative and judicial powers—to a degree that the talukdars did not. It is notable, moreover, that in a survey of members of the 'native council' in 1956 the official members proved to be substantially better educated than the elected members. (Indeed the last of the Buganda chief ministers was a graduate of both London and Oxford Universities.) The extensive pre-colonial elaboration of patrimonial offices in Buganda gave traditional sanction, moreover, to the bureaucratic offices which developed during the British period;[48] while the fact that the relationship of the Buganda prototype with the British was regulated by a solemn treaty meant that the Uganda local governments were not just the district agents of the central government. In many respects they stood over against it.[49] But because of the treaty the central government's powers were somewhat limited, so that the British administration was careful to maintain separate subordinate administrative structures for those items —and for a long time they included health, agriculture, education and other developmental projects—which lay outside the treaty's limits. As one British officer put it in 1917: 'In all indirect matters of administration such as agricultural progress, dealings with non natives and Government laws not in conflict with the Uganda Agreement . . . the executive lies with the British Government.'[50] As a result, although the kingdoms possessed substantial administrative powers, their local control was not complete. They could hinder the central government's operations, but they could not ultimately frustrate it. Despite some changes from the 1930s onwards, these conditions persisted. They were deeply irksome to the radical central government under Dr. Obote, which governed Uganda after independence; and in destroying the palace of the Kabaka of Buganda in May 1966, he and his colleagues were explicitly destroying the dual system which had persisted hitherto. They had, however, to use *force majeure* to carry this through successfully.

If the administrative reach of the Uganda kingdoms thus placed them in an intermediate position, so did their relationship to the 'enemy'. Here the symbolic figures were Kabaka Mutesa II of Buganda and Dr. Obote. Obote came from the non-kingdom north of Uganda. His Uganda People's Congress began life as an undistinguished anti-Baganda party. But it never had the power of Nehru's Congress in U.P. in the 1930s. Whereas in 1937 the talukdars' National Agriculturists' Parties made very little showing in the elections in Oudh, and died thereafter, Buganda's *Kabaka Yekka* ('Kabaka only') party all but swept the board in Buganda in 1962. Obote accordingly chose to enter into an alliance with it rather than oppose it; and later in 1963 made Kabaka Mutest of Buganda the first President of Uganda. But thereafter he successively set about undermining Kabaka Yekka's parliamentary strength; and when by 1966 there were signs that Mutesa was taking an interest in the threats to Obote's position within his own party, Obote arrested five of his own colleagues, suspended the constitution—and President Mutesa with it—and shortly afterwards bombarded the Kabaka's palace. In the aftermath all the Uganda kingdoms were abolished.[51] In the end, therefore, their 'enemy' proved to be much more powerful than they were. But the relative strength of the two parties to the conflict was very much more evenly balanced than it ever was between the talukdars and Nehru's Congress; and it was only the centre's control of the armed forces that tipped the balance.

It was not very different here with 'matters concerning the moral community'. Buganda is the key once again. There was not much that was 'religious' about its sense of community. It turned, in the first place, upon the fact that its Kabaka was at once head of its exogamous clans and also head of its appointed hierarchy of administrative chiefs. But it derived as well from its attachment to a long tradition (relating to both the pre-colonial and to the colonial periods) of vehement resistance to any threat to the integrity of the country, that was coupled to a no less persistent tradition of opposition to inflexible attitudes to outside contacts. This combination was summed up by Kabaka Daudi Chwa (1897–1939) in a pamphlet which he called *Education, Civilisation and Foreignisation* (1935): he was opposed to the last, but in favour of the first two.[52] The second part of this complex was periodically very influential. Did not Mutesa II himself make at least two deals with Dr. Obote? When, in the end, therefore, Mutesa adopted a totally inflexible attitude towards Obote, some of his subjects (those who were members of Obote's Cabinet, and the 150 Baganda out of the country's top 200 civil servants, for example) understandably saw here not a vindication but something of a betrayal of the demands of the moral community which they all purported to serve. Certainly they never raised a finger to support Mutesa, and scarcely any of them acted as if they believed that the course he took represented the best interests of the Baganda people. Once again, the balance for the Uganda kingdoms' prototype turned out to be exceedingly fine.

Perhaps it is now possible to deal quite summarily with the northern Nigerian emirates, since the thrust of the argument will be apparent already.

First, the striking fact about the emirates under Indirect Rule is that, far from having no administrative responsibilities, or only some of those belonging to the now greatly enlarged range of Government business, as in the Uganda kingdoms, the 'native authorities' of northern Nigeria (as they were technically called) exercised all governmental duties at the local level; thanks to the flexibility of their constitutional position and their own practical response, all the new developmental ones in particular.[53] As even post independence commentators have put it, 'the Native Authorities virtually are the administration of the country'.[54] It is clearly important as well that the elaboration of patrimonial office in northern Nigeria had preceded both the British and Fulani. Its roots went much deeper than in Buganda, let alone in Oudh.[55] Moreover, since the native authorities were responsible for the full range of governmental activity at the local level, they took steps to secure competent officials from amongst their own kinsmen and associates—the ruling *sarakuna* class—to perform it: in this connection the opening of Katsina College in 1922 for 'young Mohammedan men of birth and standing', as the Governor put it in his inaugural speech, was especially important.[56] Not only did the northern Nigerian emirates, therefore, do all the work of government at the local level: they were the heirs to a long established governmental tradition; with a flexibility of response that was very unusual, they maintained it to the standard of the times; and every superior government placed over them was thereupon obliged to operate through them. No means existed by which they could be bypassed.[57] If there was a change with the advent of independence, it lay in the capture of the regional institutions by the existing local elite. Since no treaties had limited the British administration's competence, the fit between their administration and the native authorities had been closer than in Uganda. It now became closer still. 'Northernisation', it has been said, led, as independence came, to a marked 'concentration of political and administrative power in the hands of the narrow class of top Native Authority officials who were part and parcel of the traditional ruling oligarchy'.[58]

There was, of course, an 'enemy'. But in northern Nigeria it was, in the first place, confined to small isolated urban groups, frequently of alien southerners. By making full use of the varied resources of the Native Authorities (with which they had intimate personal connections), the Western educated northern elite successfully mobilised their powerful Northern Peoples Congress against the enemy within their gates.[59] (It transpires indeed, from the three situations we have considered, that the degree of successful adjustment to ballot-box politics was in direct proportion to the extent of the traditional authority's administrative reach.) But there was the 'enemy' to the south as well: the politicians of the two southern regions who had little patience with these conservative northerners. The numerical superiority, however, of the northern region over the two southern regions combined, and its separation from them in the constitution of federated Nigeria, held in check this greater enemy (which in any event was itself sharply divided), and, indeed, gave the Northern Peoples Congress the preponderant voice in the whole country (rather as if the Nationalist Agriculturalists' Parties of Agra and Oudh had dominated the whole of northern India through the period before and after Independence). To begin with at all events, the Nigerian military coups did not make much difference. Northern leaders were certainly murdered, but when the Colonels came to appoint a Military Governor of the Northern Region in 1966 they chose one of their number who was the son of the Emir of Katsina. He became chairman of the administrative council of the six states into which the north was then divided, and, although alongside their development there was some movement upwards of a largely new generation, the emirs all remained prominent and some of them important.[60]

As for matters concerning the moral community, just two words will suffice. In the emirates Islam was its guiding light; and the emirs remained its prime custodians. To quote a 1965 authority, each emir was 'the religious head of his people and the appellate court in all matters of custom and native law'.[61] He remained the head of the moral community.

'Power remains vested,' a critically minded Nigerian political scientist wrote in 1968, 'in the traditional authority of the North.'[62]

Thus, while under each head of the argument the talukdars showed weakness—and the combination of weakness in each of the three instances was evidently thoroughly debilitating—the Uganda kingdoms hung on a balance (wherein lies the fascination of their story), while the emirates of northern Nigeria showed strength at all points. This will not necessarily secure their position inviolate even in the immediate future: strength can ebb quickly. But perhaps it does go some distance to explain why, in the midst of the second crisis, they appear to have been so resilient whereas the talukdars as such were readily expunged and the Uganda kingdoms passed through an altogether uncertain period.[63]

Whether this analysis can be widely applied to other

instances must be left to others to determine. It looks, however, as if it can be applied to the collapse of the Sultanate of Zanzibar on the one hand and to the survival of the Malayan sultanates on the other. In Zanzibar the 'administrative reach' of 'His Highness' Government (manned at the top by British officials) was very extensive; while the administrative capacity of the Arabs in government service was without parallel in East Africa. For all the efforts, however, of nationalist-minded Arabs, like Ali Muhsin Barwani, 'the enemy' in the shape of the previously much subordinated Afro-Shirazi majority proved, under the leadership of Abeid Karume, to be much too formidable for them. At the same time for all the prestige of the long-lived Sultan Khalifa—and the various attempts to weld all Zanzibaris together as 'His Highness' Subjects' on the basis of their common allegiance to Islam—the fragility and superficiality of any common moral community between the dominant Arab minority and the subordinated Afro-Shirazi majority was very soon revealed in the period following his death. Frustrated by the structuring of the electoral system, the Afro-Shirazi revolution burst forth in January 1964. Sultan Khalifa's grandson fled from his sultanate, and the Sultan's Palace was quickly renamed 'the People's Palace'.[64]

In Malaya the governments of the States had likewise a very extensive administrative reach, and the Malay aristocracy was strongly entrenched within them. 'The enemy', in terms of those who were seen as the major threat to the position of the Malay majority in the peninsula, were, however (somewhat as in northern Nigeria) alien trading communities—in Malaya, primarily of Chinese though also of Indian origin. In such circumstances the cleavages which existed within Malay society did not open wide, and the sultans stood forth as the much revered symbols of the integrity of the society and culture of the Malay majority against the internal threats from outsiders which the energy and growing numbers of the immigré communities represented.[65] The Malayan sultanates accordingly survived.

Although it would be a very much larger task to provide even an outline account, it would appear that the analysis employed here could be profitably applied to the collapse of the Indian princely states as well.[66] The role of various Indian princes as heads of their local moral communities need not be denied.[67] It was no bulwark, however, against the energetic policy of independent India's remarkable States' Ministry under Sardar Patel and V. P. Menon. The Indian National Congress, moreover—and even at its instance the Indian States Peoples Congress—was always more than a match for the Indian princes; and their abolition provided an effectual political rallying cry at the national level.[68] But in considering their collapse in any greater detail it would be important, not merely to distinguish between some of the 'model' states, such as Travancore and Mysore, and the others,[69] but to consider the first head of the argument here, 'administration', rather more precisely than previously in its four different aspects, namely the extent of business covered, the depth of bureaucratic tradition, the articulation with the next level, and the competence of the bureaucracy.

There are two very last thoughts. First, it looks as if there is one feature of the outcome to a first crisis which has played a role—not necessarily decisive, but a role nevertheless—in the resolution of some second crises. If a traditional rulership, or even a political system conducted in its name, commanded in the aftermath of its first crisis an administration with a substantial administrative reach, then it seems to have been relatively well placed—other things being equal; and, of course, they not always were—to survive the second crisis. The second point is linked. For it ought perhaps to be noted that of the three heads of the later argument employed here only one—'administration' again—derived any part of its nature from the particular contact with Empire. Empire has had a good deal to do with the ability or otherwise of traditional rulerships which survived the first crisis to weather the second; but it should be remembered that there have almost always been other considerations besides.

NOTES

1. Jagdish Raj, *The Mutiny and British Land Policy in North India 1856–1868* London, 1965.
2. On Oudh, see A. L. Srivastava, *The First Two Nawabs of Oudh*, Agra, 1954; T. R. Metcalf, 'From Raja to Landlord: the Oudh

Talukdars, 1850–1870' in R. E. Frykenberg, *Land Control and Social Structure in Indian History*, Madison, 1969; C. A. Elliott. *The Chronicles of Oonao, a District of Oudh*, Allahabad, 1862; W. C. Benett, *A Report on the Family History of the Chief Clans of the Roy Bareilly District*, Lucknow, 1870; Pundit Bishambhar Nath Tholal, *History of the Sombansi Raj and the Estate of Partabgarh in Oudh*, Cawnpore, 1897; P. Carnegy, *Historical Sketch of Fyzabad Tehsil*, Lucknow, 1896; *Gazetteer of the Province of Oudh*, I, Lucknow, 1877, Introduction; P. D. Reeves, *Sleeman in Oudh*, Cambridge, 1971.

3. T. R. Metcalf, *The Aftermath of Revolt. India 1857–1870*, Princeton, 1964, p. 45.
4. On all this, and the next two paragraphs, see Michael Maclagan, *'Clemency' Canning*, London, 1962, passim, and especially Ch. 8.
5. Jagdish Raj, op. cit.; Metcalf, *Aftermath*, Ch. IV; Metcalf, 'Raja to Landlord' and his other essay, 'The Social Effects of British Land Policy in Oudh', in Frykenberg, *Land Control*, p. 142, sqq.
6. Max Weber, *The Theory of Social and Economic Organization*, paperback edition, New York, 1947; P. C. Lloyd, 'The Political Structure of African Kingdoms: An Exploratory Model' in Michael Banton (ed.), *Political Systems and the Distribution of Power*, London, 1965; Daryll Forde and P. M. Kaberry, *West African Kingdoms in the Nineteenth Century*, London, 1967; Jan Vansina, *Kingdoms of the Savanna*, Madison, 1966; and the bibliographies in all these last three items.
7. This is to pick up, of course, part of the argument of Chapter 1. For a summary of the contrast between Malcolm and Metcalfe, see Eric Stokes, *The English Utilitarians and India*, Oxford, 1959, pp. 18–19.
8. Most general histories relating to the British Empire will provide the essential facts here.
9. E.g. Brijen K. Gupta, *Sirajuddallah and the East India Company, 1756–1757, Background to the Foundation of British Power in India*, Leiden, 1962; William Tordoff, *Ashanti under the Prempehs 1888–1935*, Ch. 1; Alan Ryder, *Benin and the Europeans 1485–1897*, London, 1969, Ch. 7.
10. There is a summary account in D. A. Low and R. C. Pratt, *Buganda and British Overrule 1900–1955*, London, 1960, Ch. 1.
11. Gupta, loc. cit.; Pamela Nightingale, *Trade and Empire in Western India 1784–1806*, Cambridge, 1970; Robert A. Huttenback, *British Relations with Sind 1799–1843*, Berkeley, 1962; K. Onwuka Dike, *Trade and Politics in the Niger Delta 1830–1885*, Oxford, 1956, Ch. X; Roland Oliver, *Sir Harry Johnston and the Scramble for Africa*, London, 1957, Ch. 4.
12. J. E. Flint, *Sir George Goldie and the Making of Nigeria*, London, 1960, esp. p. 262; A. H. M. Kirk-Greene, *The Principles of Native Administration in Nigeria*, London, 1965, passim.
13. The classic account is still J. M. Gray, 'Mutesa of Buganda',

Uganda Journal, I, 1935, pp. 22–49; but see also D. A. Low, 'The Northern Interior, 1840–1884' in Roland Oliver and Gervase Mathew, *History of East Africa*, I, Oxford, 1965, p. 337 sqq.

14. D. A. Low, *Buganda in Modern History,* London and California, 1971, especially Chs. 1 and 3.
15. D. A. Low, 'Uganda: The Establishment of the Protectorate 1894–1919' in Vincent Harlow and E. M. Chilver, *History of East Africa*, II, Oxford, 1965.
16. D. M. Last, *The Sokoto Caliphate*, London, 1967; R. A. Adeleye, *Power and Diplomacy in Northern Nigeria 1804–1906,* London, 1969; H. A. S. Johnston, *The Fulani Empire of Sokoto*, London, 1967; M. G. Smith, *Government in Zarru 1800–1950,* London, 1960, Margery Perham, *Lugard. The Years of Authority 1898–1945*, London, 1960, Part 1; Robert Heussler, *The British in Northern Nigeria,* London, 1968, esp. Chs. 1 and 2.
17. Perham, loc. cit.; Smith, *Zazzau*, Ch. VI; D. J. M. Muffett, *Concerning Brave Captains*, London, 1964; Adeleye, op. cit.
18. Gupta, loc. cit.; Kushwant Singh, *The Sikhs*, London, 1953. For a further African example see Andrew Roberts, 'A Political History of the Bemba to 1900', Ph.D. thesis, University of Wisconsin, 1966, Ch. VII, and Henry S. Meebelo, *Reaction to Conquest. A Prelude to the Politics of Independence in Northern Zambia 1893–1939,* Manchester, 1971, Ch. II.
19. It should *not* be thought that this was an imperialist invention. For some remarkable pre-colonial examples of 'puppetry', if that is the suitably invidious term, see J. M. Gray, 'The Year of the Three Kings of Buganda', *Uganda Journal*, XIV, i. 1950, pp. 15–32; and Smith, *Zazzau*, passim.
20. H. H. Dodwell, *Clive and Dupleix*; J. A. Norris, *The First Afghan War 1838–1842*, Cambridge, 1967; D. P. Singhal, *India and Afghanistan*, Queensland, 1963.
21. Ravinder Kumar, *Western India in the Nineteenth Century*, London, 1968, esp. Chs. 1 and 2. For Gluckman's helpful insights into this situation see Chapter one above.
22. All three were present in Bengal—respectively, the Calcutta Hindu merchants, the sons of Mir Jafar, and the Hindu and Muslim zamindars, but the Nawabi of Bengal was overthrown.
23. Low, Oxford *History*, II, pp. 95 sqq.
24. These episodes are well known, but see, for example, Percival Spear, *India. A Modern History*, Ann Arbor, 1961, pp. 197, 200, 222, 224, 264–5; Khuswant Singh, loc cit., T. O. Ranger, *Revolt in Southern Rhodesia 1896–7,* London, 1967; Low and Pratt, loc. cit.; Tordoff, loc. cit.
25. Metcalf, *Aftermath*, passim.
26. I am indebted to Dr Richard Cashmore and Mr. Neil Parsons for reminding me of these.
27. C. H. Philips, *The Evolution of India and Pakistan, 1858–1947, Select Documents*, London, 1962, pp. 418–21, prints extracts from

the 'Instrument of Transfer' for Mysore. See also Metcalf, *Aftermath of Revolt*, pp. 227–37. For the African cases see Tordoff, *Ashanti*, Ch. XIV; Ryder, *Benin*, p. 294; Colin Webb, 'Great Britain and the Zulu People 1879–1887', in Leonard Thompson (ed.), *African Societies in Southern Africa*, London, 1969, p. 315.

28. S. H. Butler, *Oudh Policy, the policy of sympathy*, Allahabad, 1906, p. 28.
29. Metcalf, *Aftermath*, p. 154.
30. S. H. Butler, *Oudh Policy considered historically and with reference to the present political situation*, Allahabad, 1896, p. 69, footnote.
31. Sir Henry Davies, quoted ibid., p. 70.
32. [W. C. Benett], *Gazetteer of the Province of Oudh*, Vol. I, Lucknow, 1877, p. lxl.
33. Gertrude Emerson, *Voiceless India*, New York, 1930.
34. See the useful survey by B. B. Misra, 'The Evolution of the Office of Collector 1770-1947', *Indian Journal of Public Administration*, XL, 3, July-Sept. 1965, pp. 345-67.
35. Benett, *History . . . of the Roy Bareilly District*, p. 69.
36. On all this see Benett and other items listed in footnote 2 above.
37. I am here, and throughout, greatly indebted to the knowledge I have gained from my colleague, Dr. Peter Reeves. He must not be held responsible, however, for the thesis advanced here.
38. *Memorandum submitted by the British Indian Association of the Talukdars of Oudh to the Joint Select Committee London* [1934], p. 10. The most critical account of the talukdars is H. C. Irwin, *The Garden of India*, London, 1880.
39. P. D. Reeves, 'The Landlords' Response to Political Change in the the United Provinces of Agra and Oudh, India, 1921–1937', unpublished Ph.D. thesis, Australian National University, Ch. IV.
40. Jawaharlal Nehru, *Autobiography*, new ed., Bombay, 1962, Chs. VIII-XI; W. F. Crawley, 'Kisan Sabhas and Agrarian Revolt in the United Provinces 1920 to 1921', *Modern Asian Studies*, 5, 1971, pp. 95-109.
41. See the extracts from the Fauncefote report in *The Pioneer* (Lucknow), 17 May, 1922; also ibid, 4 Feb. 1921, 29 Mar. 1922.
42. P. D. Reeves, 'Landlords and Party Politics in the United Provinces, 1934-7', in D. A. Low (ed.), *Soundings in Modern South Asian History*, London and California, 1968.
43. Benett, *Oudh Gazeteer*, I, p. xliv.
44. D. R. Mankekar, *Lal Bahadur, A Political Biography*, Bombay, 1964, p. 49 sqq.
45. For information on early evidence of this I am indebted to Professor Ravinder Kumar for drawing my attention to a report by a European police officer called 'Kishan Sabha in Allahabad' in National Archives of India, Home Political Deposit Feb. 1921, No. 13.

46. For the variations in the ability of erstwhile talukdars to adjust to new roles after 'abolition', see T. R. Metcalf 'Landlords without Land: the U.P. Zamindars today', *Pacific Affairs,* XL, 1 and 2, 1967, pp. 5-18.
47. See generally here Low, *Buganda in Modern History,* esp. Chs. 3, 6 and 7.
48. Martin Southwold, *Bureaucracy and Chiefship in Buganda,* East African Studies, No. 9, Kampala, 1961.
49. Low and Pratt, loc. cit.
50. Quoted D. A. Low, *The Mind of Buganda,* London and California, 1971, p. 50.
51. *Buganda in Modern History,* Ch. 7, seeks to review both these and the events referred to at the end of the next paragraph.
52. *The Mind of Buganda* reprints the pamphlet, and presents these issues in fuller detail.
53. Kirk-Greene, loc. cit.; Margery Perham, *Native Administration in Nigeria*, London, 1937; Heussler, *British in Northern Nigeria,* I. F. Nicolson, *The Administration of Nigeria 1900-1960, Men, Methods and Myths,* London, 1969.
54. L. F. Blitz, *The Politics and administration of Nigerian Government,* London, 1965, p. 102. See also Heussler, esp. pp. 174-89.
55. The *locus classicus* is M. G. Smith's *Government in Zazzau.*
56. Alhaji Sir Ahmadu Bello, *My Life,* Cambridge, 1962, p. 28. This, and the titles mentioned in the remaining footnotes, should be consulted more generally as well.
57. Heussler, *British in Northern Nigeria,* p. 174 *et al.*
58. B. J. Dudley, *Politics and Parties in Northern Nigeria,* Frank Cass, London, 1968, p. 222.
59. Ibid., esp. Ch. IV.
60. Ibid., passim. See also on all of these matters C. S. Whitaker, *The Politics of Tradition, Continuity and Change in Northern Nigeria 1946–1966,* Princeton, 1969, and Sir Bryan Sharwood Smith *'But Always as Friends', Northern Nigeria and the Cameroons,* London, 1969. On the 'new generation', I am indebted to A. H. M. Kirk-Greene for kindly allowing me to see his mimeographed 'Qualification and the Accessibility of Office', since published in Arnold Rivkin (ed.), *Nations by Design,* New York, 1968. See also Heussler, pp. 189-90. For an example of information about the continuance of traditional rulership in northern Nigeria, see 'King of Bornu', *West Africa,* 16 November 1968, pp. 1341-3.
61. Blitz, *Nigerian Government,* p. 124. I cannot help feeling that amid all his no doubt justified aspersions upon the operations of the NPC and it leaders, Dr. Dudley in his *Politics and Parties* seriously underplays these matters. The issues are illuminatingly discussed in Murray Last, 'Aspects of Administration and dissent in Hausaland, 1800-1968', *Africa,* XL, 4, 1970, p. 345 sqq.

62. Dudley, loc. cit., p. 256.
63. For a preliminary, and inconclusive, estimate see Ch. 7 'The Creation of New States in the North', in S. K. Panter-Brick, *Nigerian Politics and Military Rule: Prelude to the Civil War*, London, 1970.
64. Michael Lofchie, *Zanzibar: Background to Revolution,* Princeton, 1965; Jhon Okello, *Revolution in Zanzibar,* Nairobi, 1967. I referred to Arab exclusiveness in a 'turnover' article in *The Times.*
65. Gordon P. Means, *Malaysian Politics,* London, 1971, esp. Chs. 1, 5, 8, 10, 12.
66. The starting point would be V. P. Menon, *The Story of the Integration of the Indian States,* London, 1956. But see the two articles by Lloyd I. and Suzanne Hoeber Rudolph, 'Rajputana under British Paramountcy: the failure of Indirect Rule', *Journal of Modern History,* 38, 2, June 1966, pp. 138-60; and 'The Political Modernisation of an Indian Feudal Order: an analysis of Rajput adaptation in Rajasthan', *Journal of Social Issues,* XXIV, 4, 1968, pp. 93-127. See also Urmila Phadnis, *Towards the Integration of the India States 1919–1947*, London, 1968, and Richard Sisson, *The Congress Party in Rajasthan,* California, 1972.
67. E.g. as exemplified in the appointment of the Sikh Maharajah of Patiala to the National Defence Council at the time of the Sino-Indian conflict in 1962. See also Myron Weiner (ed), *State Politics in India,* Princeton, 1968; and F. G. Bailey, *Politics and Social Change, Orissa in 1959,* California, 1963.
68. Mrs. Indira Gandhi employed it especially in the Indian national election of 1971.
69. Mr. Robin Jeffrey and Mr. James Manor are writing theses on Travancore and Mysore at the University of Sussex; for 'the others' there is nothing to match E. M. Forster's, *The Hill of Devi.*

4

Empire and Christianity

It will long since have been apparent that the present endeavour is an exceedingly ambitious one. But if it is tempting providence to try to offer some more general perspectives upon social engineering, or upon the fate of traditional rulerships, it is probably merely foolhardy to plunge into a discussion that touches religion, especially when some of the argument involves a comparison between the cultural characteristics of two very large sub-continents. There may well be those who will find parts of the discussion which follows—even perhaps the whole of it—thoroughly invidious. Very sincere apologies are offered to them in advance, since nothing invidious is in any way intended. The purpose is to try to provide some new illumination upon a series of associated topics which seem to have dimensions to them that are not always allowed for. The attempt may, of course, be deemed to have failed. It will nevertheless be essayed in a genuinely tentative spirit.

In 1919, on the north-west frontier of India, war broke out for the third time between the British and the Afghans. This time the invasion came primarily from the Afghans crossing the British frontier. Behind the invasion lay, in part at least, the preaching by Muslim Mullahs of the necessity of *jihad,* holy war, against the infidel.[1] There is a sense in which this would seem to have been the archetypal response of religious leaders to the phenomenon of a Western, and allegedly Christian, imperial power. It is notable that this archetypal response was not more common. Professor Ranger has provided, for example, a full and fascinating study of the manner in which the priests of the Shona and Ndebele organised and led the opposition to the British occupation of their country. And numerous other examples could be adduced.[2] But when such opposition with a firmly religious stratum to it arose, it sometimes seems to have had a new dimension to it as well. Certainly in Africa there is steadily increasing evidence of marked developments within African indigenous religions which were very largely in response to the threatening danger of an advancing imperial power from outside. Perhaps the classic case comes from the Nuer of the southern Sudan, who appear to have developed a whole new series of prophets to give them increased supernatural support against the 'Turks' and 'Khartoumers' coming down in the middle and late nineteenth century from the north;[3] but the Yakany cult in the area west of Lake Albert to the south,[4] or, equally classicly, the Maji-Maji movement in southern Tanzania in the first decade of the twentieth century,[5] represented no less clearly an indigenous religious development arising from a felt need to mobilise increased supernatural strength against the enormous danger that the advance of European empires represented. It begins to look as well as if the so-called Wahabi movement in nineteenth-century India possessed very similar characteristics.[6] There are examples, therefore, not only of existing religious leaders and religious bodies providing the driving force for resistance to empire but of new developments of a religious kind to this end as well.

And so it seems to have continued. There were both religious leaders and religious concerns close to the heart of the Indian revolt of 1857; patently in the Mahdist revolt in the Sudan; and in such outbreaks as that at Bulhoek in South Africa in 1921, or by Dini ya Misambwa in Kenya in 1950.[7] I for one shall never forget, moreover, the quite uncanny way in which at the two moments during the so-called 'Kabaka crisis' in the kingdom of Buganda in Uganda in 1953–5, at which there seemed, temporarily, to be a decreasing chance of the conflict between the British and the Baganda being satisfactorily resolved, a self-styled Muganda 'prophet', claiming to be 'Kibuka', the erstwhile Baganda God of War, made a public appearance—the second time after managing to escape from prison—preaching from some high point and attracting very considerable attention.[8] From all this, and from other evidence besides, it would seem fairly clear that for quite a number of those affected by it, 'Empire' was as much a religious as a political or economic or ideological problem.

It has to be said that this consideration has not always

received the attention it deserves. Take, for example, so much of the treatment by political scientists and historians (not to mention latter-day nationalists themselves) of nationalism. For many of them it has been first and last a secular matter. But was it?

Let us leave on one side the most obvious case to the contrary—Muslim nationalism in India—partly because it is so obvious,[9] but partly, too, because nowadays it is chiefly its non-religious, non-intellectual features which need to be explored most. Let us take instead the other side of the Indian story. As is well known, the national movement in India was first generated in those small, generally English-educated, elitist circles which grew up in nineteenth-century India in the so-called Presidency towns—Calcutta, Bombay and Madras. It looks, moreover, as if its strength can be correlated with the numbers of English-speaking university students that were to be found there. It is undeniable, however, that a central concern of so many of those who were of key importance to these 'new' nineteenth-century Indian elites was religious.[10]

The first major figure was Ram Mohan Roy (1774-1838). Learned in ten languages and a correspondent of Jeremy Bentham, he made substantial studies of Hinduism, Buddhism, Islam, and Christianity, as well as of the philosophy and science of the West. He became the leading figure in the intellectual ferment of Calcutta in the 1820s. Keenly impressed by many features of Christianity, he nevertheless remained a Hindu, yet, under the influence of Christian ideas, a reformist Hindu, best rememberd for his action in founding in 1828 the new religious order, or 'divine society', the Brahmo Samaj.[11] There followed several other such developments in elitist, proto-nationalist circles in India before the century was out, quite apart from the various off-shoots of the Brahmo Samaj itself. The greatest Indian intellectual figure of the second half of the nineteenth century, Ranade, apart from being involved in political movements like the Poona Sarvajanik Sabha and the Indian National Congress itself, and in social reform movements like the National Social Conference, was deeply involved as well in the western Indian counterpart of the Brahmo Samaj, the so-called Pratharna Samaj.[12] Concurrently, the Gujarati Brahmin Dayananda founded in

1875 the more militant Arya Samaj, which became between then and the end of the century the foremost vehicle for elitist nationalism in the Punjab and regions adjacent thereto.[13] And in the new century there developed—based this time upon Madras—the Theosophical Society (with which Jawaharlal Nehru seriously toyed as a young man), led by that redoubtable Indian nationalist, the Englishwoman Mrs. Annie Besant.[14]

One of the most important expressions of the importance of religion in the leadership of Indian nationalism is to be found in the career of the great Maharashtrian nationalist leader, Tilak. For him, indeed, British imperialism was intolerable precisely because of the threat to Hindu religion and to the social structure which was intimately associated with it. He spent much of his life as a politician and newspaper editor, but he was also a Sanskritist who wrote extensive commentaries upon some of the Hindu sacred books. For him, the link between religion and nationalism was direct.

> 'Hindu religion as such,' he once wrote, 'provides for a moral as well as a social tie. This being our definition we must go back to the past and see how it was worked out. During Vedic times India was a self-contained country. It was united as a great nation. That unity has disappeared bringing on us great degradation and it becomes the duty of the leaders to revive that union. A Hindu of this place is as much a Hindu as the one from Madras or Bombay . . . the wiser sentiments which move you are all the same. The study of the [Hindu religious] classics produce the same ideas throughout the country. Are not these our common heritage? If we lay stress on it forgetting all the minor differences that exist between different sects, then by the Grace of Providence we shall ere long be able to consolidate all the different sects into a mighty Hindu nation. This ought to be the ambition of every Hindu.'[15]

Tilak's opposite number as a vehement nationalist in Bengal, Aurobindo Ghose, was to an even greater degree concerned with religion;[16] while Tilak's contemporary and opponent, Gokhale, for all the greater secular bent of his mind, crowned his career by creating a secular brotherhood, the Servants of India Society, which appears to have been deliberately modelled on the ideas he had received of the workings of the Jesuits, and of the Cowley Fathers hard by him in his own city of Poona.[17] The clearest example, however, of an Indian nationalist leader who seems to have been as much preoccupied with religious issues as with the nationalist cause was, of course, Gandhi.[18]

Perhaps, as far as later African nationalists were concerned, their religious concerns were not, in general, quite so patent as they were for Gandhi, though it may be noted that in 1968 President Kaunda of Zambia accepted an invitation to address the fourth Assembly of the World Council of Churches in Uppsala, the only head of state, apart from the King of Sweden, so to do. And there remains the striking fact of the exceptional importance of religious figures, and religious issues, amongst the early and protonationalists in Africa. There is the dramatic, and, thanks to Shepperson, Price and Rotberg, now very well known story of the Reverend John Chilembwe in Nyasaland, who led the short, desperate, despairing revolt there in 1915 (surely the archetypal African proto-nationalist if ever there was one).[19] But there were numerous others as well,[20] like the Reverend Spartas Mukasa in Buganda,[21] or Kimbangu in the Congo,[22] not to mention the innumerable separatist church leaders in South Africa about whom Professor Sundkler wrote so splendidly in *Bantu Prophets in South Africa.*[23] Not the least interesting examples are to be found, moreover, amongst the Kikuyu of Kenya. Here protonationalism was intimately bound up with religious issues, and led to the founding of independent churches as much as of local political associations.[24] There seems no doubt indeed that it was men with substantial religious interests, rather than men with purely political interests (who are in any case difficul to locate), who first bore in their own lives the trauma of the break with European dominance which became in the end the central theme of African nationalism when it came to full flower. Historically, in other words, the genesis of African nationalism often lay in the issues which were central to a large number of isolated conflicts across the African continent which were first and foremost religious issues. And in some areas the intimate relationship between religious issues and political issues persisted[25] and has only just begun to be investigated. It was the same elsewhere. The genesis of

Indonesian nationalism lay in Islamic cultural movements,[26] as did the genesis of Malayan nationalism.[27]

How stands Christianity—the religion of imperial Britain—in all this? It is clearly part, even a large part, of the story. Consider first two, largely symbolic, examples. When, in the best 'British' tradition, they 'Beat Retreat' on Independence Day each year in front of the great Secretariat buildings in New Dehli, as the sun goes down, and the parade concludes, the massed bands play, of all things, *Abide with me*—because it was Gandhi's favourite hymn. (He interrupted his seminal discussions with Lord Irwin before the Gandhi-Irwin Pact in 1931 to discuss the hymn with the Viceroy, since he knew him to be a devout Christian: with such men, as with his old friend the Reverend Charlie Andrews, he always felt an especially close affinity.) Who, moreover, does not know of Nkrumah's use of Christian language as epitomised by his favourite slogan: 'Seek ye first the political kingdom, and all these things shall be added unto you'? (And if this should still strike a discordant note, let it be said that a visit to Accra, to the Ghanaian coast road, or to a town like Larteh—or more simply a perusal of Professor Baeta's *Prophetism in Ghana*—will soon dispel the notion that it was somehow inapposite to the intensely religious context which was there prevailing.)[28]

It is easy to argue that Christianity and the British Empire spread with arms linked. (Sir Thomas Fowell Buxton, for example, was at once a Director of the Imperial British East Africa Company and Treasurer of the Church Missionary Society.) It is easy, moreover, to quote—from the Baptist missionaries in Serampore, Bengal, in the first third of the nineteenth century, for example, or the Congregational missionaries in central Africa in the last third—statements by missionaries in support of British imperial rule.[29] Yet some of the connections which are offered between the Bible and the Flag are without warrant. It is plain, for example, that British missionaries secured very large numbers of converts in Madagascar in the nineteenth century quite outside the realm of any British colonial administration,[30] while the first key conversions in Buganda occurred a decade before British rule was established there;[31] and there was an even longer gap in Lesotho, in Yorubaland, and upon the Gold Coast.[32] The protracted opposition of the East India Company towards the advent of Christian missionaries to India provides a famous example, moreover, of the Flag's resistance to the Bible;[33] whilst, whatever may be said about some of the missionaries in Northern Rhodesia, nationalist criticisms against missionaries in Nyasaland plainly need to be tempered very carefully.[34] It is much more interesting to take a more precise look at why pro-imperialist missionaries spoke as they did. Alexander Mackay, the great Church Missionary Society missionary in Buganda, is an honoured figure there to this day. In his first few years in the country he remonstrated warmly with his original colleagues' insistence upon securing special privileges for themselves at the court of the ruler, Kabaka Mutesa I; they must, he insisted, accept the local situation as they found it. But by the mid 1880s his whole approach had changed and he was now looking for any European power he could find to come and establish its dominion over Buganda. By 1890, indeed, he was ready to enlist in the service of the Imperial British East Africa Company. What had happened in the meanwhile was that, following the accession of a new ruler, Kabaka Mwanga, some of his converts had been mutilated and martyred. 'Were your assistants . . . or your children, day by day taken and murdered before your eyes, no man could reproach you with appealing to an arm of flesh . . . or help you to protect yourselves from a repetition of such atrocities', he pointed out to those in London who protested against his new 'worldly' involvement.[35] His agony of mind as he wrestled with these issues comes through in his published letters: but we have yet to fathom all that was at stake here.[36]

The official doctrine upon the association between Christianity and British rule was put by Macaulay when he wrote in 1835: 'We abstain, and I trust shall always abstain, from giving any public encouragement to those who are in any way engaged in the work of converting natives to Christianity.' It was authoritatively reiterated in the Queen's Proclamation of 1858: 'Firmly relying on the truth of Christianity . . ., we disclaim alike the right and the desire to impose our convictions on any of our subjects . . . and we do strictly charge and enjoin all those who may be in authority under us that they abstain from all interference with the religious belief or worship of any of our subjects on pain of our highest displeasure.'[37] Departures from this doctrine had no official warrant. But there were such, and not only by men like Colonel Wheler of the 34th Native Infantry in India who, in the years before 1857, went preaching to his sepoys.[38] When Sir Harry Johnston was Special Commissioner in Uganda in 1900 he was appealed to by Bishop Tucker of the local Anglican Mission against the appointment of Muslim chiefs in Busoga: 'I must confess,' Tucker wrote, 'to feeling a considerable amount of dread as to the effects of even an appearance of Government patronage of Mohammedanism.' Johnston quickly assured him, however, that he had nothing to fear: 'if there is one thing to which I am doggedly opposed . . . it is the Muhammadanising of the Basoga'.[39]

For parts of the British Empire, and elsewhere, the so-called 'Missionary Factor' has been helpfully explored.[40] May it be possible, however, to open up some other issues in some rather different directions?

So far as India is concerned, there are three preliminary points to be made. First, all rulers prior to the British had by the British period come to be characterised by their religious affiliations. Thus there had been Hindu rulers, Buddhist rulers, Muslim rulers. There was a natural tendency, therefore, to think of the British as Christian rulers, and assume that they would have substantial Christianising concerns.[41] Secondly, it seems fairly clear that both amongst the elite and amongst the rural leadership there were profound fears, whenever Christian missionaries were encountered, of a real danger that they would secure a substantial number of conversions and that these would undermine the existing structure of society. This seems to have been the assumption in Bengal in the 1820s, as it was later on of the Arya Samaj leaders in the Punjab, and of Tilak in Maharashtra.[42] Thirdly, it must be remembered that from 1813 onwards there was an Anglican Establishment within the Government of India that was directly responsible for the Anglican Bishops in India and for many Anglican Chaplains. There was no counterpart to this in Africa, but it remained the case in India until as late as 1930.[43]

There are three very much more general considerations as well, applicable both to Africa and, indeed, to other areas as much as to India. First, notwithstanding Macaulay's dictum and Queen Victoria's proclamation, there can be no doubt that Christian missionaries generally enjoyed an unusual degree of protection and moral support within the British Empire from the imperial authorities.[44] They clearly enjoyed privileged access to them, and in many respects a considerable moral advantage over them. It is the existence of this special relationship that makes the investigation of the connections between Empire and Christianity especially important. It was a relationship which did not often survive the imperialist period, as missionaries in independent India, in independent Sudan, and those in the many other independent countries who now have to secure 'work permits' and 'entry visas' before they can set to work there can, in various degrees, testify. It has indeed now become unusual for Christian institutional leaders to have quite the freedom—or their converts quite the special protection—which the imperialist order gave them. It is difficult, for example, to think of anything comparable to the almost monopolistic hold which the missions were permitted to have over the educational system in large parts of 'British' Africa at all events, through most of the colonial period, or the influence which they once had over the Government of India—in securing, for example, the Caste Disabilities Removal Act of 1850.[45] Christianity in India and in Africa frequently had, it seems, under Empire a 'fair field' of relatively unusual order. Secondly, Christianity often enjoyed a quite particular moral authority as well. It was the religion of the supreme political power; the religion, in fact, of the conquerors. For this reason alone it possessed a quite unusual prestige. To put it pithily—though in many particular circumstances it is a description which those concerned would literally have allowed—the Christian God had not failed His followers, whereas other Gods had.[46] And there could be elaborations here. On handing the Kabaka of Buganda a Bible a Uganda missionary told him it was 'the key to the secrets of England's Greatness and Glory'[47] 'England' was certainly powerful: who was in a position to deny that this was in fact the reason why? 'The missionaries,' Professor

Ajayi writes in his account of southern Nigeria, 'were able to exploit the prestige and power of the white man already won by the colonial soldiers and administrators. It was then that, in the non-Muslim areas at least, the fabric of the old society gave way and people began to flock to the missions.'[48] Nothing illustrates better, moreover, the degree of moral advantage which Christianity possessed than the vehemence of the assaults upon it, as, for example, in India by the quasi-nationalist Arya Samaj.[49]

It owned, however, a third advantage as well. Clearly, for many people—though in greatly varying terms—the advent of Empire threw their whole world 'out of joint'. In one way or another this involved so many of them in having to think about some kind of restructuring of their *weltanshauung.* Christianity was not, they might tend to think, 'the obvious answer'. It was very well placed, however, to be considered as 'an answer', and from that a great deal more could follow. Once again this was to place it, for the nonce at least, in a formidable position.

Obstacles in India

Given all these circumstances, how did Christianity fare during the British period in India?

Nothing is more notable in the general histories of the spread of Christianity in India during the British period than the accounts they give of what they call 'mass movements' towards Christianity.[50] Indeed, it has been estimated that 80 per cent of Indian Protestants and 50 per cent of Indian Roman Catholics are descendants of 'mass movement' converts.[51] These 'mass movements' have still to be studied in the detail which should be possible,[52] but some of their characteristics are readily recognisable even so. There are many references in the accounts of them to large-scale group conversions to Christianity in the aftermath of a famine.[53] More generally, although there were certainly some 'mass movements' amongst caste Hindus (as, for example, amongst a number of sudra castes in Telegu country),[54] most 'mass movements' were either by tribal peoples who had never been within the Hindu fold, or on the part of low-caste or outcaste communities—those really downtrodden castes who, though often very numerous, were treated as marginal and worse to the main body of Hindu society. On other occasions and at other times such people have sought to escape from their Hindu thraldom by becoming Muslims or, as so often today, Buddhists. During the British period many of them chose to become Christians.

Consider here an account of just one of these movements, written in 1926. 'The Indian members,' it states, 'of the Anglican Church . . . in the Diocese of Travancore and Cochin, numbered at the end of the census [in 1921] 65,114 . . . Of the Indian Anglicans 39,000 are the fruit of the present Mass Movement. These are converts, or descendants of converts, from two outcaste communities, Pulayas and Parayas, who were admitted into the Church in families, or groups of families.' Here was a 'Mass Movement', that is (and it would seem a fairly typical example), which in a quite typical way won a following in a (sociologically speaking) 'marginal' community, by working along a caste seam. The account goes on to say as well: 'Today all the Mass Movement work is in Indian hands.' The processes of conversion were, that is, indigenous processes. On closer investigation these movements look indeed to be extraordinarily like Christian equivalents of those Hindu Bhakti and Muslim Sufi movements with which so much of the religious history of India in the last millennium is bespattered. The report on the Travancore-Cochin story alludes to some of the secessions from the movement (of a kind with which we are perhaps more familiar in the African context—to which we shall come in a moment): 'The chief is the Pratyaska Raksha Sabha (the Church of Revealed Salvation) . . . it still has between 5,000 and 6,000 adherents and once had 10,000.' 'It began as a doctrinally innocuous separatist movement led by a Paraya convert of unusual gifts connected with the Brethren, but developed into a blend of Christianity and animism with antinomian practices. But it is very largely social or, to use the now familiar word, communal—a symptom of the unrest among the outcastes.'[55] Here again, it is strikingly like the devotional movements within Hinduism, Islam, or for that matter Sikhism.[56] It looks, moreover, as if there was probably not very much to choose between the capacity of the leadership of these Christian movements and the capacity of the leadership of these other Indian movements; or between the access they all had to ritual, intellectual and organisational models—a point of some importance, to which we must return.

Yet the fact remains that, despite the dramatic advances of some of these 'mass movements', and despite all the more individualistic conversions to Christianity which did occur (despite, too, the dramatic character of the impact of such great Indian Christians as Sadhu Sundar Singh from the Punjab, or Bishop Azariah of Dornakal), the proportion of converts to Christianity within the total Indian population remained very small.[57]

There was no breakthrough into the elite. This is not to say that there were not magnificent efforts—not least by the quite outstanding group of early Baptist missionaries in Bengal, of which the great orientalist William Carey was the chief.[58] Nor that there were not converts. To many of the Hindu elite there were all too many. But there was, nevertheless, no real breakthrough. There would seem to be two considerations here. In the first place high caste converts had to face the dread certainty of outcasting; and all but a few found this difficult to contemplate. 'Of all the obstacles to the evangelisation of India,' Vaughan of the Church Missionary Society declared (writing in 1876 of a phenomenon that had long been recognised), 'this is by far the most formidable.... The judgement may be convinced, the heart impressed, but the fearful consequences of decision stare the individual in the face, and no wonder that he falters. The higher the caste, the heavier the cross which threatens him. To be loathed by all who once loved him, to be mourned for as *dead* by her who bore him, to have the finger of scorn pointed at him by all his associates, to be doomed for life to social ostracism as a polluted thing is the penalty of conversion which caste inflicts'.[59] It was not readily incurred. Secondly, standing in the way was the formidable figure of Ram Mohan Roy. Deeply interested in Christianity, and profoundly influenced by it as he was, he concluded in the end that it was not for him, and found solace and justification in a continued investigation of his own Hindu heritage, not least in the light of what Christianity, Islam and the European enlightenment could bring to it. 'With a Rammohun Roy,' one of the most recent commentators has remarked, 'Christianity very probably would have made much more rapid formal progress than it did. Reformed Hinduism, whether Roy's or a more orthodox variety, could and did withstand the attacks of Christian missionaries, and acted as a buffer between Christianity and Orthodox Hinduism . . . He did far more than any other single person to retard the growth of an indigenous Christian Church.' His was a formidable intellectual achievement—to venture as he did into the fiery furnace of Christian apologetics, but emerge warm, singed even, yet not at all burnt up: and there is a profound justness to the accolade accorded to him—the father of modern India.[60] Most of those who came after him, for all their differences from him, followed in his path: Dayananda, Aurobindo, Gandhi, to name but three.[61] They were all influenced by Christianity (in more ways than some of them cared to acknowledge). 'The power of organisation, active hatred of sin, and indignation against wrong-doing in place of indifference, a correct sense of the dignity of man and woman, active philanthropy and a feeling of fraternity, freedom of thought and action, these are Christian virtues which have to be incorporated into the national character, and this work is actively going on in all parts of the country."[62] So wrote not the least of them, Ranade. But Christians he and they did not become. Nor the enlarging elite either. Here it may be of some consequence to note that the prestigious educational colleges which sprang up in the early part of British rule were not, as in Africa,[63] Christian in orientation. They were named Hindu College, and to begin with were explicitly devoted to a measure of Hindu learning.[64] When in due course they came to be reconstructed, it was in a secular rather than any Christian direction. There were, of course, some very notable 'Christian' colleges (particularly in Calcutta, Lahore, Delhi, Allahabad and Madras); but they were to be found within universities that were primarily secular. And for all their importance, and their educational success, they never secured any substantial numbers of Christian conversions from amongst the educated elite.

Amongst the caste Hindus in the rural areas the general

lack of missionary success, even allowing for all the exceptions which must be remembered, was patent as well. For some explanation of this phenomenon two quotations can be offered from one of the many accounts which Christian missionaries have left behind them of their work in India.

> 'It is necessary to remember . . . ,' the Reverend Andrew Gordon, D.D., wrote in the memoir he published in 1886, 'that whenever a native identified himself with us—especially when he received Christian baptism—that from that very hour his neighbours, of whatever creed, began to hate him with a malignant hatred, and his own near relatives became his bitterest enemies. This hatred was shown by refusing to give him food or water, forbidding persons to sell anything to him, turning him out of house and home, depriving him of his just share of his father's property, setting his wife and children against him, cutting him off from all communications with them, raising a mob against him, beating him, threatening his life, shutting him up without food in a dark room, conveying him away in the night to parts unknown, administering poison, and other similar treatment. If any one felt inclined to speak a word in favour of the persecuted convert, he well knew that by so doing he would expose himself to similar contumely.'[65]

Or again:

> 'The Meg authorities of the village [the panchayat of the weaver caste that is] met in Council, and formally and officially issued their orders as follows: First, Pipo and his party must prepare a feast at their own expense, and give a general invitation to the Megs in Jhandran and all the neighbouring villages to come and partake of it; second, they must return all Christian books which they had received from the missionaries; and, finally, they must cease to have any communication whatever with the missionaries. Failing or refusing to obey these orders, they were strictly prohibited from eating, drinking or smoking with their former associates, and from drawing water from the wells; and all Megs were forbidden to give them water, sell them food, or have any dealings with them.'

When, as sometimes happened, such measures were backed by violence, their deterrent effect was considerable.[66] The self-sealing devices of Hindu society were, in short, highly effective.

Breakthrough in Africa

What of Africa, or at all events tropical Africa? Here, too, there took place what the Christian missionaries in India would have called 'mass movements'. Between the late 1870s and about 1940 Uganda, for example, became primarily a Christian country. At an earlier stage so did Madagascar, and Botswana, and many other areas besides.[67] Christian expansion in western, and especially south-western, Tanzania in the most recent quarter of a century, has been very considerable too. A recent study indicates that, whilst during the two decades before independence the population was increasing at the rate of 2·5 per cent per annum, the annual increase in the membership of the Lutheran church in Tanzania was approximately 8 per cent per annum.[68] Recent histories of Tanzania tend to concentrate upon the political developments which preceded independence.[69] But from the African point of view of this is to get the perspectives altogether right?

Detailed work on these conversion stories is still only at the beginning. After reading the most substantial recent study—of the first two decades of Christian expansion in Uganda[70]—one is left with the impression of an extraordinary similarity between the way Christianity spread (with African 'evangelists' very prominently to the fore) with the manner in which African indigenous cults have spread. (Mr. Welbourn speaks, indeed, in one and the same breath of 'Spirit initiation in Ankole and a Christian Spirit movement in Western Kenya'.)[71] The Uganda study makes it very plain that Christian expansion there was primarily an African achievement. The Tanzanian account says that the expansion it describes 'does not appear to be due to the work of the missionaries': of prime importance, it reports, have been 'unordained church workers': Africans, of course. 'They have been the driving wedge of the church into new communities.'[72] If there is a difference between the African indigenous cults and the Christian story it looks as if it lies in the greater equipment of the Christian leadership, and more especially in the advantages they possessed over the new cult leaders in having existing rituals, theologies, and organisational models on which to draw. The cults' leaders rarely possessed the 'education' of the Christian evangelists; and very often they were having to develop their rituals, their ideologies and their organisations as they went along. The Christian Church in tropical Africa may seem, by comparison with its varied resources in the West, to have been existing on a very few shoe-strings. But compared with the indigenous cults in Africa, of which we have some knowledge, it seems to have been richly endowed indeed. (And we may recall that Christianity does not seem to have possessed such a relative advantage in India.)

Even so, and even allowing both for the personal conversions which have occurred and for the importance, more particularly at the outset, of the conversions of groups of freed slaves and of refugees from tribal wars (those 'marginal' men in the African scene), it does begin to look clear that the processes by which Christianity spread in Africa south of the Sahara have been essentially indigenous—processes very similar to those by which anti-witchcraft and anti-sorcery cults, for example (for the most part, at all events) of conversions tions have been different from those in India. We cannot speak for example (for the most part, at all events) of conversions travelling along a caste seam.[74] But—and it really should not surprise anyone, even though the emphasis in most histories of missions is not always placed here—in both continents, where Christianity has gained a widespread hold, it has done it in ways that are native to the country, not exogenous to it.

But if there is this likeness betwen the way Christianity infiltrated India and Africa south of the Sahara, it is the differences in its reception in the two sub-continents which are most striking. To begin with, Christianity in Africa had its breakthrough into the elite. I feel bound to say that I have personally a strong impression that the prime reason for this was that there was all too little available from African indigenous religions to provide a resource from which viable religio-intellectual bulwarks against Christianity might have been constructed. Certainly there was no African Ram Mohan Roy. But then it seems unlikely that there could have been. Undoubtedly his task, for all its complexity and brilliance, was eased, probably alone made possible indeed, because he had the great scholastic traditions of Hinduism, and Islam and Buddhism, to draw upon. There are signs, most notably in

Jomo Kenyatta's early and memorable book, ***Facing Mount Kenya,*** but also in Dr. J. B. Danquah's *The Akan Doctrine of God,*[75] that there were men prepared to essay this task in Africa, if they could have mobilised the necessary resources. But these do not seem to have been available. And in many instances the tendency therefore was—as in the adoption later on of the nationalist creed itself—to take over Christianity and then adapt it to the African context rather than, as in the religious story in India, to build up or stabilise the bulwarks against it.

There were, as a consequence, a number of Christian revolutions across tropical Africa which made Christianity the vehicle for accommodating the religious dimensions of the trauma that overtook Africa with the advent of the Western impact and more especially of the Western empires.[76] Sometimes these Christian revolutions were at the behest of the ruler. There is the intriguing example of Khama of the Bamangwato, a remarkable Christian ruler if ever there was one.[77] In Ankole in south-western Uganda, the Christian revolution was heralded when the Omugabe, the ruler, formally broke custom by beating the sacred royal drum, Bagyendanwa.[78] Plainly a substantial boost was given to Christianity in Africa (as it was in Anglo-Saxon England) when it was espoused by the ruler: or by the senior chief in the area. Walter Sangree has given details of the impetus Christianity secured amongst the Tiriki of the Nyanza province of Kenya when it was championed in the 1920s and 1930s by their formidable Chief Amiani.[79] In other places it was the support given to Christianity by members of an elite which won control over the political institutions of their society to a quite new degree which was of first importance to its widespread adoption. This was the case in Madagascar in the 1860s,[80] as in Buganda by the 1890s,[81] while in other areas the espousal of Christianity by a more wide-ranging elite, more particularly in West Africa, when it found itself in a very largely new situation, was critical for its expansion.[82] By the mid-twentieth century, the picture one receives again and again in accounts of the 'districts' which the colonial administrations formed is of a local 'district' elite that consisted almost entirely of the leading local Christians.[83] None of this is to say that the actual quality of such people's adherence to Christianity was of an order that critics would find to be unimpeachable. But it is to say that Christianity so often constituted the 'mood' of the elite, to use Geertz's term. When present its hold could be 'totalistic': though, 'like fogs', it was liable to 'settle and lift'; 'like scents to suffuse and evaporate'.[84] All in all, however, it was something to be reckoned with (which, with tiny exceptions, it was not amongst the elite in India).

Christianity spread in Africa beyond the elite as well. Not that there was no opposition. Early on, so Walter Sangree reports, the elders of the Tiriki people harboured feelings of disgust 'towards the mission because of the aliens, outcasts, witches and irresponsible youth (by Tiriki standards) that the missionaries recruited for their first African helpers and converts'. During several periods when initiation ceremonies were held, moreover, Tiriki 'had severely beaten a number of Christian Tiriki girls who worked or attended school at the mission, and had kidnapped for circumcision and initiation the sons of several Christians who professedly did not want their sons to go through the traditional initiation ceremonies'. Moreover, 'when, in 1927, the circumcision and initiation period actually began, the beatings and kidnappings characteristic of the two previous initiation periods again took place. In the weeks that followed, however, the beatings of Christians and aliens reached a new frequency; the violence culminated in the burning of a mission school in East Tiriki, and in the burning of the homes of two of the Tiriki Christians who [had committed the ultimate horror and] publicly confessed the initiation secrets.'[85] It is reported, moreover, of more than one Kenyan people that they had a clear conception of what they call *chomba*—of that which is alien, which is foreign, which is Christian. The Kuria, a people who bestride the Kenyan-Tanzanian border, have called the Arabs with whom they have had contact, the Europeans, the local coffee plantations, the European-founded towns of Kenya, administrative chiefs, Christian converts and all other such manifestations of an alien presence, *chomba*. For them, this is a thoroughly impersonal, almost inhuman, category of those things that distort the emphasis which is placed in their ritual upon ordered growth and upon 'straightness' in society, and accordingly endanger what is good in society.[86]

In so many ways it all sounds so like India. But there is a critical difference. Plainly these were the sentiments of a great many African peoples. By and large, however, they did not have the societal mechanisms to give them effect. They possessed all too few of the self-sealing devices which we have seen being so formidable in India. Accordingly opposition to Christianity in Africa outside the Islamised areas was very often ineffectual, and in a large number of places substantial Christian conversions freely took place amongst its rural populations.

So two differences emerge. In the first place, whereas the elite in India was able to call upon a great recorded heritage and by reference to it to withstand the assaults of Christianity and much of its works, this was not the case in Africa south of the Sahara. In many ways the heritage was there in Africa —one has only to consider John Taylor's book, *The Primal Vision*[87] or glance at Marcel Griaule's *Conversions with Ogotemmeli*[88] to be clear about that; but it was not so readily available.

One can underline the point here by a secular comparison. When anxious to establish his 'Indian' identity the former Harrovian and Cambridge man, Jawaharlal Nehru, embarked on his momentous search for the *Discovery of India.*[89] He found what he wanted, even if he did not quite settle his own personal problem, by calling in aid the immense sequence of effort and achievement about which those who were learned in India's cultural history down the millennia could inform him. When Kwame Nkrumah faced the same issue he plucked 'Ghana' out of the savannah to the north, but for the rest had to go formulating the conception of 'the African Personality', as Senghor and others were formulating the conception of 'Negritude', out of little more than fragments.[90] It was not as if there had been no African cultural history. The basic trouble was that records of its distilled wisdom did not lie readily to hand.

Then, secondly, there were differences in the social mechanisms of exclusion as well. Not that Hindu society was totally exclusive. On the contrary, it was extensively absorptive.

Peoples with separate beliefs and practices were freely permitted to accommodate themselves within its fold. There were, moreover, mechanisms, which seem to have been accepted as legitimate, by which depressed groups could, if they were skilful, rise to a higher status. Both movements, however, were always ultimately on Hindu society's own terms. It was towards existing Hindu practices that other people's were required to shift. It was towards the practices of 'higher' castes that aspiring lower castes found themselves having to gravitate. Both, morever, were far from being speedy procedures. The second might well take two or three generations.[91] And anything more speedy than this—let alone anything which directly challenged the prevailing religious order—was not just seen as a threat to both society and culture. All the manifold weapons for maintaining the *status quo,* which were constantly kept in trim by the almost hourly emphasis upon inherited distinctions betwen persons of different socio-religious categories, were wielded in their defence. Social pressure, indeed physical pressure, which was driven by deep seated social and cultural imperatives,[92] composed, in all but a minority of places, an all but impenetrable barrier.

Sometimes it could be the same in Africa. Young Masai or Samburu *moran* in Kenya, for instance, having once been incorporated into their warrior age-group, and having thereafter become convinced of their society's superiority over all other peoples who were not similarly tempered, were scarcely any less impervious to Christian advocacy than most caste Hindus.[93] Within their inherited culture their strong sense of security remained supreme. But amongst many other tropical African societies this was not so. They might fear that which was alien to them, disdain it, rebuff it. They might even rise against it. But at the same time they were so often notably open-ended societies to an extent that Hindu societies were not.[94] African societies had traditions of aggregating others to themselves. And, very specifically, many of them had long since taken on the religious or quasi-religious cults of their neighbours. One thinks, under the first head, of the diffusion of age-set organisations in the Kenyan highlands in the nineteenth century,[95] or of the accommodation by all the Uganda kingdoms in the twentieth of many of the institutions of the

Kingdom of Buganda;[96] and one thinks under the second of the spread of Masai-type laibons through the Kalenjin peoples of Kenya in the decades preceding the European conquest,[97] and of the spread of Chwezi cults through the interacustrine region several centuries earlier.[98] Quite extraneous elements percolated through and even came to predominate within a great many African societies to a degree that they do not seem to have done in India. At the same time, precisely because of the quite different order of openness in the predominant cultural patterns of the two regions, there was relatively so much less in Africa south of the Sahara than in India that was tempered to withstand for long and effectively the kind of assault which Christianity mounted. We have already seen, indeed, enough of the record of hasty and ineffective contriving of new religious movements by which the early decades of contact were often marked in Africa, to illustrate the fragility of the barricades which were available for erection.

But we cannot leave the discussion there. A great deal is frequently made of the astonishing spread of Christianity in the last two thousand years into every continent and country; but nowhere has Christianity as yet made a decisive invasion of the strongholds of the other 'world religions'. It has nowhere been as successful, indeed, against any of them as some of them have been against each other, and as one of them has been against Christianity. There is no Christian parallel to the Buddhist victory over Hinduism; Hinduism's victory over Buddhism; Islam's successes in India against Hinduism, or Islam's major success against Christianity in North Africa. Christianity had a great triumph in the Roman world, and from there spread to the rest of the Western world. But outside the West, and outside the conglomerate area that is Latin America, it is only in Africa south of the Sahara that there have been major conversions to it in another major cultural area. The spread of Christianity in Africa is thus a topic of far greater importance to Christian history than is generally recognised.[99]

In this connection two things should be said. First, and perhaps most intriguing of all, there is a great deal of evidence to show that in contact with a great tradition (to use Robert

Redfield's term)[100] which they are free to interpret in their own way, many Africans have displayed a great deal of creativity and perspicacity. The striking example here is the use which the Christian independent churches have made of the Judaeo–Christian Bible. Dr. David Barrett (to whose analysis of over six thousand such movements in Africa anyone considering these issues must be deeply indebted) has forcefully argued that there is a casual relationship between the translation of the scriptures into African vernaculars and the emergence of African independent churches. 'Once the *zeitgeist* of disaffection engendered by the vernacular translations has become high enough,' he affirms, 'the secessions take place out of whatever type of mission happens to be at work in that area.' But is this not too simple, even perhaps *post hoc, ergo propter hoc*? For what was it that moved the 'numerous separatists' to pick upon those passages in the Bible which, as was so often the case, provided them with the legitimacy whch they sought for their actions? The likelier generalisation would seem to be Dr. Barrett's other, and contradictory, statement that 'the printed scriptures ... provided the necessary mechanisms whereby African Christians could articulate their grievances at the discrepancy they were beginning to perceive between the missions and biblical Christianity'.[101] Feeling alienated from what was alien to them, that is to say, great numbers of them distilled the essence of their own distinctive position from the great written tradition they now had to hand. This is extraordinarily like Ram Mohun Roy in India. But, unlike Ram Mohun Roy, it was not an indigenous great tradition that they had to hand but a borrowed one. The deeds, however, which they have accomplished with it go a long way to suggest what they might have done with an indigenous great tradition if they had had one to hand.[102]

And this is not all either. For independency is only the most striking example of the much more general African insistence that Christianity must be an African possession, or it has no place in Africa: that it should be, as one of the first Africans to become an Anglican Bishop, James Johnston, put it in 1877, 'not an exotic but a plant become indigenous to the soil'.[103] Often such insistence took the form of requiring that indigenous pre-Christian practices should coexist with those that belonged to Christianity. Hezron Mushenye, Chief of Tiriki, symbolised this attitude both by deciding to resume in later life his drinking of beer and by taking a second and then a third wife, as the custom of his people required: his church membership was thereupon withdrawn, but there was much local support for his subsequent statement that he was 'a man of God and a believer in Jesus Christ, but a man without a Church'.[104] Members of the staunchly evangelical, not to say puritanical, Revival movement in East Africa have clearly proceeded on the assumption that theirs is an African movement.[105] When, moreover, the gentle Professor Baeta writes about *Prophetism in Ghana*, or, more generally, about *Christianity in Africa*[106] it is plain that he is writing about what, for all its proximate source, he sees as Africa's own; while his younger colleague, John Mbiti, Professor of Theology and Comparative Religion at Makerere, after reviewing the evidence about Africa's indigenous religions, and frankly discussing the shortcomings of Christianity there, is firm in his conclusion that Christianity is 'also "indigenous", "traditional" and "African" '.[107] It should even be said that when African clergymen seem to be at their most conservative—when clinging, for instance, to their Victorian vestments—one senses that they are affirming that whatever the origins of these (ultimately, of course, Roman) these are now 'theirs', and they are not to be deprived of them lightly.

We are thus, it seems, left with the evidence that during the imperialist period Christianity was seen, both in India and in Tropical Africa, as a formidable force. The reaction, however, of each of the two sub-continents was in certain respects the mirror image of the other. There were few converts to Christianity in India. But Christianity had a substantial impact upon the thinking of many of India's most creative figures—upon, for example, the seminal prophet of non-Brahminism, Jyotirao Phule and the dynamic Bengali figure Keshab Chandra Sen,[108] to name but two of those not mentioned so far. By contrast in Africa there were many converts. But the striking fact is not so much, however, the influence which Christianity had upon Africa, but the adaptations by Africans of Christian practices so that they should match more readily with the propensities of their cultural and societal concerns.

Christianity and Social Orders

There are four final considerations. First, it seems plain that Christianity has spread in both places in the manner in which other religions have spread there.[109] In India, there have been some elitist shifts from Hinduism to Christianity which have close affinities with elitist shifts from Hinduism to Islam. At other levels, depressed caste movements towards Christianity are patently comparable to similar movements from Hinduism to Islam, or more recently from Hinduism to Buddhism.[110] It seems clear, moreover, that at the time when, during the nineteenth century, there were conversions to Christianity in the Punjab, there were parallel conversions to Sikhism.[111] It also looks as if when earlier on there were conversions to Christianity in the Nadia and Barisal Districts of Bengal, the ground had already been turned by a new Hindu sect called the Karta Bhajas (Worshippers of the Lord);[112] while a recent account of the conversion of a tribal people to Christianity looks to be on all fours with all that well described accounts of the incorporation of tribal peoples into Hinduism have indicated of such processes.[113] Similarly in Africa: despite certain very particular distinctions, the conversions in Buganda first to Islam and then to Christianity in the second half of the nineteenth century patently had close affinities with each other; whilst the welcome accorded to these religions from outside—because they seemed to meet a particular set of contemporary needs—has close parallels, as I have suggested elsewhere, with the earlier adoption by the Baganda leaders of the Lubale deities from the Sesse islands in Lake Victoria.[114]

And one could go on. Trances, *Mayembo*, Dr. Efraim Andersson reports, are 'an extraordinary faculty' possessed by many Congo tribes 'since time immemorial'. 'It is the fetish who arouses the *Mayembo* in his priest.' 'Even a superficial survey,' he then states, 'shows that the trance still plays an important role in popular religion.' When, for example, a great Revival came to the church he describes in January 1947, the seminal moment was a moving declamation by a young student which 'ended by [his] crying out in a trance, and expressing the distress he felt in his heart'.[115] We have to await a full study of the major East African Protestant Revival[116] but one cannot help noticing that it began precisely where the indigenous *Nyabingi* movement had been operating in the very recent past and that it displayed a similar intensity.[117]

From this and other evidence besides it even seems that Christianity only spread in accordance with the existing societal procedures for adaptation to new sets of religious beliefs. Thus decisions amongst untouchable communities to convert to Christianity in India were not individual decisions.

> 'When the Madigas of Jangarai [village] became Christians,' it is reported, 'the Madigas of Achampet heard much about the new religion from their relatives and other members of the same caste, and they cordially received the evangelist from Jangarai whenever he came to visit them. The five older Christians who remember when the congregation began said that the visiting evangelist gave money for a feast to some of the leaders of the Madiga community. Soon thereafter these leaders decided that the entire caste in the village should become Christians. The first baptism took place on June 26, 1932. All the Madigas are Christians (about twenty families), but none of the similar number of Malas [a comparable low caste] ever became such, even though they live very close to the Madigas in Achampet, and even though most of the evangelists working in the Madiga congregation have been Mala. Indeed, a rather bitter rivalry between Malas and Madigas has continued in this village.[118]

Indigenous conditions and indigenous procedures have firmly patterned the events which have occurred—as indeed historians of Empire should scarcely now need reminding! (It seems plain, for example, that Christian missionaries have had to be careful on many occasions not to offend the caste susceptibilities of their Indian Christian converts.)[119]

But, secondly, it seems also patent that Christianity, or at all events association with Christianity, has provided marked opportunities for social advancement, more especially within the order Empire maintained. Two examples must suffice here. The first is very striking. In his book on *The Nadars of Tamilnad*, Robert Hardgrave details the 'rise' of this originally half-polluting caste of toddy-tappers to the forefront of political power in Madras. 'An instrumental role in the Nadars' initial struggle to rise,' he writes, 'was played by the European missionary.' The first converts actually date from the seventeenth century. There were more in the eighteenth, and by 1830 there were five thousand Nadar converts in the area of southeastern Tinnevelly. 'Mass movements' followed in the 1840s, not least after the famine of 1847. Although the Nadars remained poor (as Caldwell, who was to be the first Anglican Bishop of Tinnevelly, wrote in 1869) Christianity had 'promoted their education and enlightenment . . . their position has been greatly improved, and many spheres of useful, remunerative, and honourable labour which were formerly closed against them are now almost as open to them as to any other class in the community'. In particular, missionary support proved to be vital to the success of the Nadars in neighbouring Travancore in their highly symbolic campaign to secure the right for their women to wear a breast cloth. And when the time came for the caste's aspiration to express itself in a claim to a higher status within the Hindu order, 'the Christians', Hardgrave reports, 'as the more literate of the Nadar community, initiated and sustained the caste literature of the new mythology, claimed traditional Kshatriya status, and took the title Nadan'. 'It has been the Christian Nadar, rather than the Hindus,' he reports as well, 'who have responded most to the opportunities for advancement through education in government services and in the professions. The background of the mission schools and the emphasis on education in the Christian home gave them an important headstart.'[120]

This last is so extensively the case in Africa south of the Sahara that it is superfluous to give detailed examples. We may just consider, therefore, one other instance from Africa of social advancement which attachment to Christianity provided. According to Walter Sangree, Tiriki women played a major role in their local church life, and he explains why:

> 'If one keeps in mind the lack of formal status and lack of direct participation in most of the principal tribal rites, and finally, the absence of any formal status-confessing or expressive organization for women *qua* women comparable to the men's

age groups and beer drinks, it becomes easy to appreciate not only the rapidity with which women responded to . . . Christianity and became Christians in order to escape the drudgery of beer-making but also it appears quite reasonable that women should have become such active participants in church organized social activities.'[121]

At the same time, of course, Christianity often provided the framework for the structuring of a new order which, with imperial rule, was in any event overtaking both India and Africa. Two very different kinds of example must suffice here. The first is once more from Sangree reporting upon the Tiriki: 'Amongst these people those unencumbered by strict missionary supervision, provide a ready-made framework within which a leader can fulfil some of the particularistic relationships traditionally expected of men in authority, while at the same time, with the aid of Christian ritual and symbols, increasingly eliciting more universalistic and functionally specific relationships in those areas where social, economic and political patterns have been most modified and broadened by European contact.'[122] More poignantly, there was the case of the young followers at Hindu College, Calcutta, of the magnetic Derozio, who, in the aftermath of his dismissal from his teaching post for being too anglicist, and of his early death in December 1831, had become 'beset', as David Kopf puts it, 'by the self-torment of cultural ambiguity'. 'Can I be saved? Can I be saved?' one of them, Gopinath Nundi, pleaded of the missionary Alexander Duff. What was included in this search was directly indicated by his contemporary Krishna Mohan Bannerji, who, following upon his baptism in October 1932, proclaimed aloud: 'Does not history testify that Luther, alone and unsupported blew a blast that shook the mansions of error and prejudice? Did not Knox, opposed as he was to bigots and fanatics, carry the cause of reformation into Scotland? Blessed are we that are to reform the Hindu nation.'[123]

Yet the last word must be upon a very different note. Whilst it must be said that missionary leaders often led the way in challenging illiberal conditions—one thinks of their role in championing the ryots of Bengal against the zamindars and indigo planters,[124] or of Dr. John Philip in South Africa,[125] or Archdeacon Owen in Kenya[126]—there can be little doubt that for a great many people in both sub-continents the critical relationships between Christianity and Empire lay in the support which the proponents of the one gave to the authorities of the other. Here a single testimony, by the Kenyan nationalist leader Oginga Odinga, must serve to represent a countless host of others. Africans, he wrote,

> 'were impressed by the superior material possessions of the Whites when they came, and attracted by their more elaborate Church organization and ritual, especially in the Catholic Church. But the Church not only demanded that the African reject his traditional marriage custom and much else, but, for all the preaching about brotherhood, the African priest was invariably graded inferior in the Church. It dawned that administration and Church were different representations of the same White authority. The policy of the Church was ever in accord with that of the administration'.

The result of this was, he added, somewhat sadly, that 'when there was general dissatisfaction among the people it created inevitably, disaffection with the Church'.[127]

If Christianity thus originally benefited from its associations with Empire—as in many places it plainly did—it found itself by the end suffering from its associations with Empire: as with any established order. When, moreover, a new order came to be established with independence, and Christians no longer held a privileged position, quite new doubts set in. As an ex-untouchable Andhra village Christian put it in 1959, when commenting on the fact that he and his like were not deemed eligible by the State government for the special concessions which were being accorded to members of the Hindu scheduled castes: 'We are still wondering if we have made a mistake in accepting Christianity.'[128]

NOTES

1. I am indebted to Dr. W. M. Hale for information upon this. See his 'Afghanistan Britain and Russia 1905–21', unpublished Ph.D. thesis, Australian National University, 1965. For another striking example see I. M. Lewis, *The Modern History of Somaliland*, London, 1965, Ch. IV, on Sayyid Muhammad Abdille

Hassan (whom the British called the Mad Mullah).

2. T. O. Ranger, *Revolt in Southern Rhodesia*, London, 1967.
3. E. E. Evans-Pritchard, *The Nuer*, Oxford, 1940, sub 'Prophets'; also his *Nuer Religion*, Oxford, 1956, pp. 303–10. For West African parallels, see J. F. A. Ajayi, *Christian Missions in Nigeria 1841–1891*, London, 1965, p. 19.
4. See especially Anne King, 'The Yakan Cult and Lugbara Response to Colonial Rule', *Azania*, V. 1970, pp. 1–25. For other examples see Robert I. Rotberg and Ali A. Mazrui [eds.], *Protest and Power in Black Africa*, New York, 1970, especially the articles by Elizabeth Hopkins and Audrey Whipper.
5. John Iliffe, 'The organization of the Maji Maji rebellion', *Journal of African History*, VIII, 1967, pp. 495–512.
6. Dr. M. M. Ali is writing a book which discusses this.
7. S. N. Sen, *Eighteen Fifty-Seven*, Delhi, 1957; W. K. Hancock, *Smuts. The Fields of Force, 1919–1950,* Cambridge, 1968, Ch. 5; *Report of the Commission of Inquiry into the Affray at Kalloa, Baringo*, Nairobi, Government Printer, 1950.
8. See *The Times* for February and July 1955.
9. Aziz Ahmad, *Islamic Modernism in India and Pakistan 1857–1964*, London, 1967.
10. Anil Seal, *The Emergence of Indian Nationalism,* Cambridge, 1968.
11. See especially Iqbal Singh, *Rammohun Roy. A biographical enquiry into the making of modern India,* Vol. I, *The First Phase*, London, 1958. There are interesting essays by Stephen H. Hay, e.g. his 'Western and indigenous elements in Modern Indian thought: the case of Rammohun Roy', in Marius B. Jansen, *Changing Japanese Attitudes towards Modernization*, Princeton, 1965, Ch. IX.
12. See Charles H. Heimsath, *Indian Nationalism and Hindu Social Reform*, Princeton, 1964, passim; and Ravinder Kumar, 'The New Brahmans of Maharashtra', in D. A. Low (ed.), *Soundings in Modern South Asian History*, London, 1968, p. 121.
13. Kenneth W. Jones, 'The Arya Samaj in the Punjab 1877–1902', unpublished Ph.D. dissertation, University of California, Berkeley, 1965.
14. A. H. Nethercot, *The Last Four Lives of Annie Besant*, London, 1963.
15. Stanley A. Wolpert, *Tilak and Gokhale, Revolution and Reform in the Making of Modern India,* Berkeley, 1962, p. 179.
16. Karan Singh, *Prophet of Indian Nationalism,* London, 1963.
17. Wolpert, *Tilak and Gokhale,* p. 158 sqq.
18. Perhaps the simplest way to look at all this a little more fully is by referring to Wm. Theodore de Bary, *Sources of Indian Tradition*, New York, 1958, esp. Chs. XXI–XXIV, XXVI, and XXVIII.
19. George Shepperson and Thomas Price, *Independent African:*

John Chilembe and the Origins, Setting and Significance of the the Nyasaland Native Rising of 1915, Edinburgh, 1958; George Simeon Mwase, *Strike a Blow and Die*, ed. R. I. Rotberg, Harvard, 1967.

20. Thomas Hodgkin, *Nationalism in Colonial Africa,* London, 1956, Ch. 3.
21. F. B. Welbourn, *East African Rebels*, London, 1961, Ch. 5.
22. E.g. Rene Lemarchand, *Political Awakening in the Belgian Congo*, Berkeley, 1964, p. 169. sqq.
23. London, 1948.
24. Welbourn, *Rebels*, Part III, passim; Carl G. Rosberg and John Nottingham, *The Myth of 'Mau Mau': Nationalism in Kenya*, 1966, passim, but especially Ch. 4.
25. There is the striking case of the Lumpa Church's conflict with UNIP in Zambia, see the chapter by Andrew Roberts in Rotberg and Mazrui, *Protest and Power*, pp. 513–68.
26. G. T. Kahin, *Nationalism and Revolution in Indonesia,* Ithaca, 1952, esp. Ch. III; Harry J. Benda, *The Crescent and the Rising Sun*, The Hague, 1958.
27. See the admirable study by William R. Roff, *The Origins of Malay Nationalism*, New Haven, 1967, esp. Chs. III and IV.
28. G. C. Baeta, *Prophetism in Ghana*, London, 1962; D. E. Apter, *The Gold Coast in Transition*, Princeton, 1955, passim.
29. Iqbal Singh, *Rammohun Roy*, has some typical quotations; also Rotberg, *Christian Missions and Northern Rhodesia,* see footnote 34 below.
30. The most substantial account is Phares Mutibwa, 'The Malagasy and Europeans . . . 1861–1895', unpublished D.Phil, dissertation, University of Sussex, 1969.
31. D. A. Low, *Buganda in Modern History*, London and California, 1971, Ch. 1.
32. Professor Leonard Thompson will be giving details about Lesotho in a forthcoming book; J. F. A. Ajayi, *Christian Missions in Nigeria 1841–1849. The Making of a New Elite*, London, 1965.
33. K. Ingham, *Reformers in India*, Cambridge, 1956, Ch. 1. The ordered combination of negative, limiting and positive attitudes towards Christian missionaries by the British administration in the Sudan is illuminated in Robert O. Collins, *Land Beyond the Rivers, The Southern Sudan, 1898–1918*, Yale, 1971, Ch. VII.
34. R. I. Rotberg, *Christian Missionaries and the Creation of Northern Rhodesia 1880–1924*, Princeton, 1965, passim, but especially the epilogue; Andrew C. Ross. 'The African—"A Child or a Man"—the quarrel between the Blantyre Mission of the Church of Scotland and the British Central Africa Administration, 1890–1905', Eric Stokes and Richard Brown, *The Zambesian Past*, Manchester, 1966, Ch. 14.

35. Mackay to Lang, 14 March 1887, C.M.S. archives G3/A6/04.
36. I have very briefly alluded to all this in a preface to the reprint of *Mackay of Uganda* by his sister, originally published London, 1890; reprinted Frank Cass, London, 1970.
37. Minute on Education 1835, G. M. Young (ed.), *Macaulay Prose and Poetry*, London, 1952, p. 728; C. H. Philips, *The Evolution Of India and Pakistan,* London, 1962, p. 11.
38. T. R. Metcalf, *The Aftermath of Revolt, India 1857–1870,* Princeton, 1964, Ch. III (and p. 48); also Potts, *Baptist Missionaries*, pp. 40–1 (see footnote 58 below).
39. Tucker to Johnston, 29 Nov. 1900, Entebbe Secretariat Archives, Uganda, A22/1; Johnston to Tucker, I Dec. 1900, ibid., A23/1. See also Collins, *Land Beyond the Rivers*, pp. 173–9.
40. R. A. Oliver, *The Missionary Factor in East Africa,* London, 1952; Firdtjov Birkeli, *Politikk og Misjon*, Oslo, 1952; A. A. Koskinen, *Missionary Influence as a political factor in the Pacific Islands*, Helsinki, 1953; I. Tufuoh, 'Relations between Christian Missions, European Administrations, and Traders in the Gold Coast, 1828–74' in C. G. Baeta (ed.), *Christianity in Tropical Africa*, London, 1968, pp. 34–60. Despite its somewhat similar title Bishop Stephen Neill's *Colonialism and Christian Missions*, London, 1966, focuses very particularly upon that relationship rather than upon the issues raised in this chapter.
41. E.g. Aziz Ahmad, *Islamic Modernisation,* pp. 19 sqq.
42. On all this see Ingham, M. M. Ali (footnote 45 below), Iqbal Singh, Jones, Wolpert, passim.
43. K. S. Latourette, *A History of the Expansion of Christianity*, London, 1947, Vol. VI, p. 108, sqq.; Vol. VII, p. 307. The records of the Ecclesiastical Branch of the Government of India are waiting to be worked upon; see D. A. Low, J. C. Iltis and M. D. Wainwright, *Government Archives in South Asia,* Cambridge, 1969, pp. 48, 94, 105, 178.
44. E.g. Metcalf, *Aftermath of Revolt*, Ch. III.
45. Muhammad Mohar Ali, *The Bengali Reaction to Christian Missionary Activities, 1833–1857,* Chittagong, 1965, pp. 117–36.
46. E.g. Ajayi, *Christian Missions in Nigeria*, pp. 19–20; Efraim Andersson, *Churches at the Grass-Roots*, London, 1968; and see the case in south-western Uganda of the 'Nyabingi', footnote 117 below.
47. O'Flaherty to Hutchinson, 30 March 1881, C.M.S. Archives G3/A6/0.
48. Ajayi, op. cit., p. xiii.
49. Jones. 'Arya Samaj'; and Heimsath, op. cit., sub 'Arya Samaj'.
50. Latourette, *Expansion of Christianity*; Vols. VI and VII contain extensive information in their 'India' chapters.
51. J. Waskom Pickett, *Christian Mass Movements in India,* Lucknow, 1934, pp. 5, 313.

52. Rosemary Keen, *A Survey of the Archives of Selected Missionary Societies*, Historical Manuscripts Commission, London, 1968, would provide some starting points, in the aftermath of reading Pickett.
53. Latourette, *Expansion of Christianity*, Vols. VI, VII, 'India' Chapters passim.
54. Pickett, *Christian Mass Movements*, Ch. XIII.
55. *Travancore Mass Movement Survey,* 1926, pp. 1–2, 11, 16. I am indebted to Dr. R. L. Rooksby for drawing my attention to this. See also the bibliographies in Hardgrave, footnote 120 below; and Luke and Carmen, footnote 118 below.
56. Aziz Ahmad, *Studies in Islamic Culture in the Indian Environment*, Oxford, 1964, pp. 119 sqq.; Lyall, see footnote 113 below; Stephen Fuchs, *Rebellious Prophets, A Study of Messianic Movements in Indian Religions*, London, 1965.
57. C. F. Andrews, *Sadhu Sundar Singh,* London, 1934; J. Z. Hodge, *Bishop Azariah of Dornakal*, Madras, 1946; J. H. Beaglehole, 'The Indian Christians—a study of a minority', *Modern Asian Studies*, I, 1967, pp. 59–80; Paul Wiebe, 'Protestant Missions in India, a sociological review', *Journal of Asian and African Studies*, V, 1970, pp. 293–301, and references there cited.
58. E. Daniel Potts, *British Baptist Missionaries in India 1793–1837*, Cambridge, 1967.
59. J. Vaughan, *The Trident, the Crescent, and the Cross,* London, 1876, p. 37, quoted G. A. Oddie, 'Protestant Missions, Caste and Social Change in India, 1850–1914'; *The Indian Economic and Social History Review*, VI, 3, September 1969, pp. 259–91.
60. Potts, *Baptist Missionaries*, pp. 227 and 242. See also Hay (footnote 11 above); Iqbal Singh, *Rammohun Roy*, passim; and M. M. Ali, *Bengali Reactions*, esp. pt. 1.
61. See de Bary, loc cit. The classic account is still J. N. Farquhar, *Modern Religious Movements in India*, New York, 1918; but see also Heimsath, *Nationalism and Hindu Social Reform*, passim.
62. M. G. Ranade, *Religious and Social Reform*, Bombay, 1902, p. 23, quoted Heimsath, p. 183. See also M. M. Thomas. *The Acknowledged Christ of the Indian Renaissance*, Madras, 1970.
63. For an account of one such school in Africa see G. MacGregor, *Budo*, Nairobi, 1967.
64. David Kopf, *British Orientalism and the Bengal Renaissance,* Berkeley, 1969, esp. Ch. XV (but elsewhere too); Kumar in Low, *Soundings*, p. 98 sqq.
65. Andrew Gordon, *Our India Mission*, Philadelphia, 1886, p. 179. I am indebted to my colleague Dr. Peter Reeves for drawing my attention to this item.
66. Ibid., pp. 204–5. Violence against converts is discussed in M. M. Ali, *Bengali Reaction*, Ch. VII.
67. J. V. Taylor, *The Growth of the Church in Buganda*, London,

1958; Mutibwa, 'Malagasy', etc.

68. Lloyd W. Swantz, *Church, Mission and State Relations in Pre and Post Independent Tanzania 1955–1964,* Program of Eastern African Studies, Syracuse University, Occasional Paper No. 19, 1965.
69. E.g. Andrew Maguire, *Towards Uhuru in Tanzania: the politics of participation*, Cambridge, 1969.
70. M. Louise Pirouet, 'The Expansion of the Church of Uganda (N.A.C.) from Buganda into Northern and Western Uganda between 1891 and 1914 with special reference to the work of African teachers and evangelists'. Unpublished Ph.D., University of East Africa, 1968.
71. In John Middleton and J. H. M. Beattie, *Spirit Mediumship and Society in Africa*, London, 1969.
72. Swantz, pp. 13, 16.
73. David J. Parkin, 'Medicines and the Minds of Men', *Man*, III, 3, Sept. 1968, pp. 424–39 and the other items there listed.
74. Conversions of courtiers in Buganda, and of Bahima and Bairu in Ankole in Uganda in the late nineteenth century nevertheless came close to this.
75. New ed. London 1953, esp. Chs. 10-12; and London, 1944.
76. The classic accounts are still in Chinua Achebe's novels, *Things Fall Apart,* 1962, and *Arrow of God,* 1966.
77. A. Sillery, *The Bechuanaland Protectorate,* Cape Town, 1952.
78. Pirouet, 'Expansion of the Church in Uganda', p. 230.
79. Walter H. Sangree, *Age, Prayer and Politics in Tiriki, Kenya,* London, 1966, Ch. V.
80. Mutibwa, 'Malagasy and Europeans', Ch. V.
81. D. A. Low, *Buganda in Modern History,* Ch. I.
82. Ajayi, *Christian Missions in Nigeria,* passim.
83. E.g. Edward H. Winter and T. O. Beidelmann, 'Tanganyika: a Study of an African Society at National and Local Levels', pp. 154 sqq. in Julian H. Steward, *Contemporary Change in Traditional Societies,* London, 1967, Vol. I.
84. Clifford Geertz, 'Religion as a Cultural System', in M. Banton (ed.), *Anthropological Approaches to the Study of Religion,* London, 1966, p. 11.
85. Sangree, *Tiriki,* pp. 128-9.
86. I owe this information to Dr. Malcolm Ruel; see his 'Religion and Society among the Kuria of East Africa', *Africa,* XXV, 3, July 1965, pp. 295-306; see also B. Bernardi, *The Mugwe, A Failing Prophet,* London, 1959 p. 159, pp. 170-5.
87. London, 1963.
88. London, 1965.
89. New ed., London, 1956.
90. Kwame Nkrumah, *I Speak of Freedom,* London, 1961, Ch. 15, for an early statement.
91. M. N. Srinivas, *Social Change in Modern India,* Berkeley, 1966,

contains the most accessible summary of the information on all this.

92. For a study of this phenomenon see Morris Carstairs, *The Twice Born,* Indiana, 1967.
93. Paul Spencer, *The Samburu,* Berkeley, 1965; P. H. Gulliver, *Tradition and Transition in East Africa,* London, 1969, pp. 223-42.
94. E.g. R. G. Abrahams, *The Political Organization of Umyamwezi,* Cambridge, 1967, pp. 151-5.
95. E.g. Robert Levine and Walter H. Sangree, 'The Diffusion of Age-Group Organization in East Africa: a controlled comparison', *Africa,* XXII, 2 April, 1962, pp. 97-110.
96. Low, *Buganda in Modern History,* Ch. 7.
97. D. A. Low, 'The Northern Interior 1840-1885', in R. Oliver and G. Mathew, *History of East Africa,* I, Oxford, 1963, p. 309.
98. Luc de Heusch, *Le Rwanda et la civilisation interlacustre,* Brussels, 1966.
99. Baeta, *Christianity in Tropical Africa,* p. 123, for the first statement of this passage.
100. Robert Redfield, *Peasant Society and Culture,* Chicago, 1956.
101. David B. Barrett, *Schism and Renewal in Africa. An Analysis of Six Thousand Contemporary Religious Movements,* Nairobi, 1968, pp. 141, 134, et passim.
102. Cf. in particular the 'Orthodoxy' of Reuben Spartas, Welbourn, *Rebels,* Ch. 5.
103. Quoted Ajayi, *Christian Missions in Nigeria,* p. 235.
104. Sangree, *Tiriki,* p. 145.
105. Personal recollection.
106. See footnotes 28 and 40.
107. John S. Mbiti, *African Religions and Philosophy,* London, 1969, p. 277. See also Andersson, *Churches at the Grass-Roots,* p. 200 sqq.
108. D. Keer, *Mahatma Jotirao Phooley,* Bombay 1964, pp. 13-15, 72, 92, 125-7; Keshab Chandra Sen, 'Jesus Christ: Europe and Asia', *Lectures in India,* Calcutta 1854, quoted Oddie, 'Protestant Missions', p. 283. See also Robin Boyd. *An Introduction to Indian Christian Theology,* Madras, 1969.
109. Prickett, *Christian Mass Movements,* p. 26 touches on this. Studies of 'conversion' seem very few and far between, and there seems nothing yet to supersede A. D. Nock, *Conversion,* Oxford, 1933.
110. Cf. Aziz Ahmad, *Studies in Islamic Culture in the Indian Environment,* Oxford, 1964, pp. 82, 136, *et al.*
111. E.g. Teja Singh, *Essays in Sikhism,* Lahore, 1944, pp. 168-9. I am much indebted to Dr. Hew Macleod for information upon this.
112. M. M. Ali, *Bengali Reaction to Christian Missionary Activities,* p. 44, footnote 5.

113. Barbara M. Boal, 'The Church in the Kond Hills', in Victor Hayward (ed.), *The Church as Christian Community. Three Studies of North Indian Churches,* London, 1966; Sir Alfred Lyall, 'Missionary and Non-Missionary Religions', in *Asiatic Studies, Religious and Social,* 2nd ed., London, 1907.
114. Low, *Buganda in Modern History,* Ch. 1.
115. Anderson, *Churches at the Grass Roots,* pp. 136, 139, 158 *et al.*
116. Max Warren, *Revival: an Inquiry,* London, 1954, has not yet been systematically followed up.
117. Elizabeth Hopkins, 'The Nyabingi Cult in Southwestern Uganda', in Rotberg and Mazrui, *Power and Protest,* p. 258 sqq. and authorities there cited.
118. P. Y. Luke and John B. Carmen, *Village Christians and Hindu Culture, Study of a rural church in Andhra Pradesh, South India,* London, 1968.
119. G. A. Oddie, 'Protestant Missions', in *Indian Economic and Social History Review,* VI, Sept. 1969, esp. pp. 260-71.
120. Robert L. Hardgrave, *The Nadars of Tamilnad,* Berkeley, 1969, pp. 42, 52, 94, 152 (et al.)
121. Sangree, *Tiriki,* p. 158. For interesting discussions of variations on this theme see Andersson, *Churches at the Grass-Roots,* Chs. 8, 13 *et al;* and Norman Long, *Social Change and the Individual,* Manchester, 1968, *circa* pp. 239-41.
122. Sangree, p. XXXI. For a sympathetic study of the general problems involved here see Michael Whisson, *Change and Challenge, a study of the social and economic changes among the Kenya Luo,* Nairobi, 1964.
123. Kopf, *British Orientalism and the Bengal Renaissance,* p. 262.
124. M. M. Ali, *Bengali Reaction,* Ch. VIII; Blair B. Kling, *The Blue Mutiny, the indigo disturbances in Bengal, 1859–1862,* Philadelphia, 1966, passim.
125. W. M. Macmillan, *Bantu, Boer and Briton,* London, 1929, passim.
126. J. M. Lonsdale, 'Political Associations in Western Kenya', in Rotberg and Mazrui, *Power and Protest,* p. 589 sqq.
127. Oginga Odinga, *Not yet Uhuru,* London, 1967, pp. 74-5. For a discussion of the wider issues here see Welbourn, *Rebels,* passim.
128. Luke and Carmen, *Village Christians,* p. 69.

5

Sequence in the Demission of Power

There was a time when it could be said that Lord Wavell, the penultimate British Viceroy of India, had had a uniformly bad press. He was notorious for his silences, and Attlee removed him from his position for being unimaginative about Britain's final withdrawal from India. But a different view has also been advanced. He has been presented as a man sympathetic to nationalist aspirations who strove to go the extra mile with them. A full portrait is still awaited.[1]

It will have to take cognisance of one intriguing consideration. Wavell's most relevant experience before becoming Viceroy in 1943 was not that he had been Britains' Commander-in-Chief in India or spent much of his life there. It was that he had been Allenby's biographer. Who was Allenby? He was Britains' victorious military commander in the Middle East who suddenly found himself pitchforked at the end of the First World War into control of the threatened British Protectorate over Egypt. Appointed because he was believed to be a 'strong' man, he soon infuriated the then British Foreign Secretary, Lord Curzon, because he made it his business to seek a settlement with the Egyptian nationalists; and thereafter presided over the ending of the British Protectorate in Egypt in 1922. Remaining, however, as the British High Commissioner he found himself faced in the years that followed by the inadequacies of his initiatives, and in the end allowed himself to be driven, in the immediate aftermath of the murder of Sir Lee Stack, the Sirdar of the Egyptian army, into a dramatic military demonstration, in which he forced Egypt's leading nationalist, Zaghlul Pasha, to resign from its Prime Ministership. All this Wavell had just set out in detail[2] when he found himself pitchforked into the Viceroyalty of India in 1943. He had only very recently 'been here before'.

So had Sir Charles Arden-Clarke, Governor of the Gold

Coast in the 1950s. He had just come from being Governor of Sarawak, neighbour to revolution-wracked Indonesia; while his Chief Secretary was an ex-Indian civil servant.

Earlier chapters have generally eschewed chronology. In this one the ultimate emphasis is upon chronology, since it looks as if one of the shortcomings of some of the accounts of the end of empire which focus upon individual countries is that they do not take sufficiently into account the larger decline and fall of empire of which their stories are only a part. There is no need here to advance a Whig interpretation of history. There was little 'inevitable' about the whole process. There were countless 'fits and starts'; and plenty of 'nothing long'. There were, nevertheless, occasions when questions of principle were being determined, and others when only the application of principles was at stake. There were occasions, too, when the precedents were very confusing; but others as well when these provided a very precise model for those who were involved in the confrontation between nationalism and imperialism. An outline of the whole story still seems worth pondering, particularly since the Indian part, to which considerable attention will be given here, has not always been sufficiently incorporated into it.

White Precedents

The classic, and very long-standing, precedent in the whole story was the British one. Under the British Tudor sovereigns the initiative in governmental matters, both executive and legislative, lay with the Crown and its servants. Under the first two Stuarts the elected House of Commons sought to win the initiative in legislative matters from the Crown, and used the so-called power of the purse to this end. Despite the 'Glorious Revolution' which followed, there remained a separation of powers between the executive and the legislature, as a glance at Montesquieu or the American Constitution—conceived, of course, essentially according to the then prevailing precedents—readily indicates. Not until the late eighteenth and the early nineteenth century did the power of the Crown wane. (And was not Labouchere kept out of the Cabinet in 1892 because his republican views were anathema to Queen

Victoria?)[3] The notion that flowed from all this—that constitutional change should advance by stages and at distinct intervals—was reinforced by the great succession of legislative Reform Acts from 1832 to 1928.

These somewhat untidy precedents became elaborated, as every schoolboy knows, in the later British Empire, into the progression from what was called Crown Colony Government, to Representative Government, to Responsible Government, and finally to Dominion Status. In Britain the moves forward had involved protracted struggles, and those who came afterwards were the beneficiaries of the English and British parliamentarians who established the principles to which they gave birth. At one stage there was even a major violent conflict: the English Civil War of the 1640s. Subsequently Representative Government in the colonies had frequently to be 'won'. But the Crown's resistance was always thereafter critically weakened, because the essential principle, neatly symbolised by the slogan 'no taxation without representation', had been conceded.

The next step, however, was a very different matter, since to give to the people of a colony local control over its executive as well as its legislature involved a good deal more than popular control over its government (such as had been the case in England). Logically it involved separation of the colony from the imperial centre. Failure to settle this issue to the satisfaction of the first colonial nationalists involved another war—the war of the American Revolution. In its aftermath various ways around the problem were attempted. Efforts were made, for example, to maintain some totally autocratic colonial governorships (in the 1820s it was said that in the Cape they knew no law but the will of Lord Charles Somerset). Alternatively, the Irish Act of Union provided for one hundred Irish MPs to take their seats at Westminster. But the first expedient did not last. It proved impossible to resist the principle of Representative Government. The second was the one the French employed—still employ—even for some of their most far-flung imperial possessions. But where oceans, and some very long sea journeys, intervened, British colonial territories, heirs to a long tradition of colonial representative government (did not the Virginia Assembly date from 1619?), regularly preferred some locally operative representation to submergence within the metropolitan legislature.[4]

The 'crisis of Representative Government' thus persisted. For it still had to be asked what was to happen when the locally elected legislature pressed its claims to control the colonial executive? Here the next great moment came, of course, in Canada in the 1830s, 1840s, and 1850s. Some last minute expedients were thought about—that, for example, the Governor should be his own Prime Minister. But they could not detract attention from the critical point. And as it chanced the issue came to be satisfactorily resolved here, on the one hand because neither the French-Canadians, nor the descendants of the United Empire Loyalists, nor so many of the later migrants, wished for separation—with its very probable corollary, absorption into the United States; while on the other hand Britain did not want another revolutionary American war; an articulate group of 'Colonial Reformers' argued the case for the positive merits of self-government for the colonies; and Lord Durham, in his Report on Canada of 1839, eased the way forward with his notion that there could be a separation between matters of purely local concern—where there was no objection, as he saw it, to responsibility being transferred to a government 'responsible' to a local legislature—and matters of imperial concern, control of which, he believed, should be retained in imperial hands. There were evidently posibilities here. It opened up, indeed, the distinction between Responsible Government and Dominion Status and thus the way around the old dilemma.[5]

Once the Canadian precedents had been settled—above all when Elgin had shown that a colonial governor really could be a colonial constitutional monarch—there were many awkward moments before it was universally applied (a very typical crisis blew up at the Cape, for example, under Governor Sir Philip Wodehouse in the later 1860s): but once conceded, in the white Commonwealth at all events, there was no going back. With some qualification the principle was even allowed to apply, for the largely exclusive benefit of British settlers, where they were extensively outnumbered by people of other colours. It was applied in South Africa (in what at the time was seen as a most magnanimous gesture) to those recently defeated in the bitterly fought Boer War; and in the first quarter of the twentieth century (once the South African Protectorates had been excluded) no real objection was raised to the process by which even the Union of South Africa gained Dominion Status. It was only where the European settler community really was an infinitesimal proportion of the total population (as in Northern Rhodesia), or where contrary considerations were adduced with quite exceptional skill (as in the 1920s over Kenya) that a halt was called. Such, however, was now the strength of the precedents that, in spite of their very small numbers amid a very much larger African population, the British settlers in Southern Rhodesia were in 1924 granted an all but complete Responsible Government.[6]

Meanwhile legislatures, even with non-white members, had been introduced in India, in West Africa, and elsewhere too; and there were those who believed (some local people in fact continued to believe) that the Canadian precedents would in due course be made to apply to these areas as well. By the end of the nineteenth century, however, another major crisis was looming up upon the horizon. For all sorts of doubts came to be expressed as to whether the white precedents could be allowed to apply to the coloured empire as well as to the white. There was a critical debate before the Indian Councils Act of 1892. Salisbury, the British Prime Minister, argued strongly that the white precedents could not be allowed to apply to India, that the nature of Indian society made them wholly unsuitable, and that any move to apply them there would be fatal to the British position. His opponents agreed with his premisses. Such, however, was now the strength of the established tradition that they started to put it into practice even while they did so.[7]

Their double think persisted. Because of this it becomes really extremely difficult to be clear about the critical dimensions of the major encounter between the forces of Indian nationalism and the British Raj which then ensued. Its relationship to what went before remains very uncertain, whilst its influence upon all that followed is so very clear, that it seems worth a very preliminary effort to explore its contortions in some detail.

Brown Struggle

It has to be remembered that at the outset there were many Indian politicians who were very fully prepared to laud the empire 'on which the sun never sets'.[8] The worst that they would say in criticism of it was that some of its actions were unworthy of its British overlords.[9] But with the opening of the twentieth century there were marked changes. At the meeting of the Indian National Congress in Calcutta in 1906 the veteran Indian political figure, Dadabhai Naoroji, declared that the object of their endeavours should now be 'swaraj'; and for someone so conversant with English constitutional language the use of an Indian term was doubly symbolic—of a distinctively Indian view of India's future, and of a recognition that to use any of the more specific English terms was to invite a fruitless controversy.[10]

There was at this stage no sign whatsoever that the British were prepared to apply the white commonwealth precedents without ado to India. On the contrary, everything was now pointing to very considerable resistance to any such idea; and in the years that followed there was little to dispel this fear. It is very clear, for example, that there were British figures who took an all but absolute stand upon this issue: Salisbury in the 1890's, Winston Churchill in the 1930s, to name but two; and when one takes a close look at those who saw themselves to be of a more liberal cast of mind—Kimberley, Morley, Hardinge, Montagu, Irwin, Hoare, Amery, to name some clear examples—it soon becomes apparent that their attitudes were only marginally different. 'Whatever may be the future political development of India,' Lord Hardinge, the sometimes liberally inclined Viceroy minuted in 1912, 'Colonial self-government on the lines of the British Dominions is absolutely out of the question'.[11] Whenever, moreover, such men managed to push things forward along lines which patently implied that the white commonwealth model was being adduced, there were vehement efforts to deny that its complete application could be presumed, and almost invariably their statements simply referred to a still as yet very distant future. Montagu's seminal declaration in 1917 merely promised, for example, 'the gradual development' of self-governing institutions 'with a view to the progressive realization of responsible government in India as an integral part of the British Empire', while Irwin's declaration in 1929 only spoke of the attainment of Dominion Status as 'the natural issue of India's constitutional progress'. His own negotiations with Gandhi in that year and the next broke down precisely because it was clear that the British had no intention of introducing Dominion Status for India in the immediate future.[12]

Two comparisons with the white commonwealth will serve to highlight the deep disparities which prevailed. In 1912 a substantial number of Congressmen won seats to the Bengal Legislative Council. In Surendranath Banerjee they had a forceful political leader, and (as John Broomfield has shown) in Lord Carmichael a sympathetic Governor. All the ingredients were present for an orderly shift here from Representative Government to Responsible Government. But a complete move from the one to the other did not come until a quarter of a century later.[13] Secondly, in 1923, as we have seen, the British settlers of Southern Rhodesia secured Responsible Government: but in the very next year the Secretary of State for India told the House of Lords: 'I am not able in any foreseeable future to discern a moment when we may safely, either to ourselves or India, abandon our trust.'[14] As this suggested, two considerations reinforced the British resistance: deep suspicion of the elites of other cultures, and profound concern for the sanctity of that lodestar of Britain's version of itself as a great world power: the Indian Empire.

The result was that those Indians who sought 'swaraj' for their country found themselves up against most formidable obstacles. There was never a sign (as Nehru rightly insisted to Lord Lothian in their famous exchange of letters in the mid-1930s) that the British would move of their own accord.[15] A major conflict was not to be avoided.

It was made all the more vehement because by the end of the nineteenth and the beginning of the twentieth century there was besides the 'white' commonwealth precedent another precedent as well—British policy in Ireland. Here for nearly forty years successive British parliaments had made it their business to see that Irish demands for Home Rule for Ireland were at once resisted and repressed. There can be no doubt that British conservative policy towards India and British unionist policy towards Ireland had intimate connections with each other. They were both concerned with Britain's standing in the world. They both avowed the unsuitability of independencc for the country concerned, and stood out forcefully against it. There came to be parallels upon the other side as well. Dadabhai Naoroji sought to emulate the Irish counterattack by securing election to the British Parliament in 1892. Like some of the Irish, the Bengal terrorists took to arming themselves, drilling themselves, and assassinating a symbolic selection of their oppressors; while the Ghadr party, like Sinn Fein, actually mounted an armed uprising.[16] None of this availed (the British-officered Indian police with a long tradition of apprehending 'criminal' tribes behind them, seem to have found professional revolutionaries relatively inexpert opponents). But thereupon Indian 'Home Rule' agitations followed, for the first time on an all but countrywide scale. At their climax, however, the nerve of their leadership failed,[17] and by the end of the First World War the Indian national movement was in deep disarray. Instead of widening to a straight, broad highway, the constitutionalist path seemed to have narrowed to the meanest of thicket-covered tracks. Armed uprising had proved abortive, and Home Rule agitation upon Irish lines had lost its thrust.

It was at this moment that, finding little which was encouraging for its encounter with the British Raj in either the white commonwealth or the Irish precedents, the Indian national movement took unto itself a style it was soon to make its own. It turned to Gandhi.[18] For here was a man who offered a very different political technique from those they had employed hitherto, one which on a number of occasions already, albeit on a small scale, had brought discernible results. To a quite new degree Gandhi seemed able to enlist the support of large numbers from both the urban and the massive rural communities. He displayed a dedication to the cause, and a commitment of a moral, indeed of a religious, order which not only put other people to shame but placed him in a unique position *vis à vis* both the rank and file of the movement and the British. Above all, he brought together so many who had hitherto been divided. To the 'moderate' or moderate-minded nationalist he promised a non-violent political campaign; to the 'extremist' or extremist-minded nationalist he proffered vehement activity and an absolute personal commitment. As a result, in 1919–20 the movement closed in behind him.[19]

Thereafter it did not always obey his orders blindly. It is a mistake, moreover, to imply that the ensuing quarter of a century was marked throughout by persistent Gandhi-led non-cooperation and civil disobedience campaigns. It is indeed, fairly easy to distinguish three great phases in the agitation of the Indian national movement which took place from about the time he came into its leadership. The first ran from about 1915–16 to 1922–3, the second from 1927 to 1934–6, and the third from 1939 to 1946. One of the striking facts about these phases is the family likeness between them.

Each began with a fairly long agitational run-up, gravely aggravated in each instance by some great affront to Indian feelings: in the first case a combination of Annie Besant's arrest in 1917[20] and the Rowlatt Bills of early 1919; in the second, the appointment of the all-white Simon Commission in 1927; and in the third, Linlithgow's declaration in 1939 that India was at war before ever any Indian public body had been consulted. In each case there was then a first Gandhi-led agitational campaign: on the first occasion the Rowlatt *satyagraha* of 1919; on the second, the first civil disobedience campaign, the so-called Salt *satyagraha* of 1930; and on the third, the individual *satyagraha* campaign of 1940–41. Thereafter there followed on each occasion a very striking mid-course break, when important figures in the leadership of the movement attempted to reach a settlement with the British. On the first occasion Gandhi proposed at the Amritsar Congress in 1919 that Congress should accept, and not boycott, the Councils which were then being established under the Montagu-Chelmsford reforms; in March 1931 he himself made the Gandhi-Irwin pact; and in March 1942 two of his closest followers, Maulana Azad and Jawaharlal Nehru, came within an ace of reaching a settlement with Sir Stafford Cripps.

Every time, however, these attempts at some mid-course settlement were swept aside by a profound undertow of unfulfilled agitational feeling which then erupted in a second agitational campaign: on the first occasion the non-cooperation movement of 1920–2; on the second, the renewed civil disobedience campaign of 1931–2; and on the third, the 'Quit India' campaign of 1942. It is no less striking, however, that when these second campaigns had broken, or—as on the second and third occasions—been broken by the British, there was no third campaign. Before very long, indeed, agitational energies dramatically receded and there was then talk of what was called 'council-entry': that is, participation in the legislatures and executives which the British were hesitantly instituting. This usually eventuated in two stages. In 1923 and 1934 some Congressmen participated in the legislative elections; in 1926 and 1937 most of the others; while in 1946 Congress very soon entered the legislatures, but delayed its entry into the central Cabinet.[21]

I shall have occasion to return to this analysis on more than one occasion later on. Immediately, however, four points should be made about it. First, it ignores a good deal—and it may well be that there are here considerations which will be fatal to its usefulness. It ignores, for instance, the differences in the concurrence of each phase with a world war, with the absence of war, and with the immediate aftermath of war (to read the sequence backwards). It says nothing, moreover, about the increased adhesion to the movement which each phase brought to it. Even so, it serves to emphasise the switchback features of the story which were so characteristic of it. Secondly, it serves as well to underline the great achievement of the Indian national movement in rarely being at a loss from the first world war onwards about what it should do next. It played upon the two themes of agitation and council entry alternatively, and as a result remained in the public eye throughout. It thus maintained an unrelenting pressure upon the British. Thirdly, it is reasonable, I think, to suggest that by the third time around there was an elaborated rhythm to the movement of which its participants were now instinctively aware. Certainly there was a plainly ritualistic quality to Gandhi's individual *satyagraha* campaign of 1940–41; and, personally, I am much struck both with his firm reluctance to compromise with Cripps in 1942 (as he himself had done with Irwin on the previous occasion in 1931) and with his readiness to go along with the build-up to the fierce confrontation of August 1942. He seems by this time to have had an extraordinarily keen appreciation of the dynamics of Indian agitational processes; and in the last stages of the encounter with the Raj (when he was no longer in as much control over the movement as he had been previously) to have been very careful indeed to go along with these so as not to do anything to break the movement asunder. Fourthly, and precisely in this connection, few things are more striking than the manner in which, during each of the agitational phases, the leadership's mid-course attempts at a settlement with the British were subsequently swept aside by the unfulfilled propensity of the movement which, on each occasion, erupted in a second and even more substantial outbreak. We still need to know a great deal more about this undertow: but its presence seems indisputable.

Nothing in the end, however, is more striking about these agitational campaigns than the plain fact that none of them succeeded in actually breaking the immediate hold of the British Government of India over its Indian Empire. 'Swaraj in one year' did not come in 1921. The British did not 'Quit India' in 1942.

Although there are issues here which are still very inadequately researched, a first, quick glance suggests that there were three phases to the Government of India's response to the nationalist agitations which it faced in India. Each, moreover, was climaxed with a grim *dénouement*. They did not, however, coincide with the nationalist agitational phases as they have been adumbrated here—which is another reason for treating that analysis cautiously.

When the first substantial agitation of the twentieth century erupted in Bengal over Lord Curzon's partition of that province in 1905, the 'Home Department' of the Government of India blandly assumed that once the Secretary of State for India had spoken firmly against it, it would blow itself out.[22] They were wrong; and by 1910 the Home Department was issuing instructions to all officials of importance in India about how to deal with 'sedition' (for so, like other colonial administrations, they instinctively called strong nationalist agitation when it first raised its head).[23] And in the years that followed nothing less than a directly 'hawkish' policy predominated in the Home Department of the Government, under the direction between 1912 and 1917 of the redoubtable Sir Reginald Craddock, much the ablest exponent of his views, on paper at least, of any senior British official in India during the twentieth century. He it was who fulminated against the 'soft' policy of the Government of Bengal under Lord Carmichael; who helped to deny an Executive Council to the United Provinces in 1915; and who disagreed with his colleagues over the 'reforms' to be introduced into India after the first world war. He it was, moreover, who used the Defence of India Act against political offenders during the war, and instituted the discussions for the continuance of its provisions for dealing with 'revolutionary crime' in peacetime, which eventuated in the notorious Rowlatt Acts.[24] It was his spirit which precipitated the Home Department into their immediate acceptance of Sir Michael O'Dwyer's call for martial law in various parts of the Punjab in 1919. 'It remains for the Governor-General in Council,' a Government of India Resolution declared in April, 'to assert in the clearest manner the intention of Government to prevent by all means, however drastic, any recurrence of these excesses. He will not hesitate to employ the ample military resources at his disposal to suppress organized outrages, rioting or concerted opposition to the maintenance of law and order.' It was this same spirit which reached its terrible climax in General Dyer's massacre in the Jallianwallah Bagh in Amritsar in that same month.[25]

By that time, however, a change of policy had been set on foot in the Government of India by Craddock's successor as Home Member, Sir William Vincent. Vincent had already resisted O'Dwyer's demand that martial law in the Punjab should be extended to Delhi.[26] And by 1920 he was responsible for the formulation of a quite new approach by the Government of India towards nationalist agitation in India. The Government of India, it came to be decided, would not attempt 'forcibly to suppress the non-cooperation movement' which followed, since 'we should in all probability', it subsequently affirmed, 'not only have provoked widespread disturbances—we have never doubted our capacity to deal with such—but should . . . have diverted to the enemies of Government, that support which . . . has been ranged more and more, by the excesses and blunders of the non-cooperationists, on the side of Government'.[27] There were opponents to this policy. 'Forces in support of Government can only be reckoned upon . . .', Sir Reginald Craddock, now Governor of Burma, wrote to his successor in 1920, 'if action is taken to suppress this non-cooperation conspiracy, before it has gained further ground . . . It is quite possible . . . that active suppression of this movement . . . will produce outbreaks of violence . . . But it is much better that these should occur and be dealt with when they can be dealt with, than that events should be watched until the situation has passed out of control . . . The outcry and excitement, and possibly violence . . . will rapidly die down as soon as people at large realise that the British Government is not the setting sun which they are rapidly learning to believe it to be.' Vincent, however, was firm in his mind against such views. 'We are fully alive,' he replied to Craddock in October 1920, 'to the dangerous situation created by the acute racial feeling that prevails but we doubt whether it would be improved by repressive action on the lines you suggest.' And in a memorable sentence he added: 'I hope you will also realize our difficulties recognizing that the gradual change from Autocratic to responsible Government cannot be effected without taking risk (indeed we have few historical examples of such changes ever taking place peacefully) that our difficulties in this matter are increased by many factors which are of world-wide character and that they are not to be remedied by drastic repressive action alone.'[28]

Elsewhere I have detailed the astonishing success of the Government of India's handling of its confrontation with the first non-cooperation movement of 1920–22.[29] Because the movement collapsed without the Government having to revert to the Craddock stance, and without the Government collapse which had occurred in both Egypt and Ireland, the Vincent policy still held the ring when the next agitational phase opened in 1927. This is nowhere better illustrated than in the way the Home Department handled in 1929 the more alarmist demands of the Government of Bombay (which had had the Bardoli agitation on its hands, and was now faced by a large communist-led mill-workers' strike as well). The Home Member, Sir Harry Haig, made it very plain that he was not prepared to have a repetition of the events of 1919.[30] He resisted demands for a Rowlatt-like Public Safety Bill and O'Dwyer-like demands for stern repression. Even when he was propelled in 1929 into instituting the Meerut Conspiracy case against the Indian communist leaders he insisted that 'we should be very cautious in taking action against communism which may rouse for the communists any general sympathy among the nationalists or provide the nationalists with what they are searching for at the moment, namely a good rallying cry for an intensive anti-Government agitation'.[31] When, in the next year, this did erupt there was a marked attempt, as in 1920–22, to avoid arresting Gandhi as long as it was thought possible to do so.[32] Although in response to the Civil Disobedience movement of 1930 there were several new 'Ordinances', a great many arrests, and, at the *dénouement*, some brutal confrontations—as, for example, at the Dharasna salt works in May—there was no Jallianwallah Bagh; not many lengthy sentences were imposed by the courts, and certainly there was no comprehensive Emergency Powers Ordinance. There was a readiness, moreover, on the part of the Government to have negotiations with the nationalist leaders, the third of which eventually culminated in the Gandhi-Irwin pact of March 1931.[33]

But there was now a further shift in the Government of India's position. 'I confess I have been getting the impression during the last week or two from various parts of India.' Haig himself wrote to the Governor of Bombay on 25 May 1930, 'that in spite of all that has been done Government may not be retaining that essential moral superiority, which is perhaps the most important factor in this struggle.'[34] The details of this shift must be left to another occasion. Suffice it to say that it stemmed from the bureaucracy's increasing concern that unless the nationalist movement was now sternly resisted the Indian members of the army, the police and the subordinate bureaucracy, would not face the strain of the civil disobedience movement very much longer. By early 1931, indeed, they became adamant that they would not accept the 'don't-treat-the-movement-too-harshly' doctrine ever again.

The ensuing change of policy is usually blamed on Willingdon (Viceroy 1931–36), but in critical respects it had already occurred by the time he assumed office. My own impression is, indeed, that the bureaucracy only accepted the Gandhi-Irwin pact on one condition: that, if there was any renewal of civil disobedience ever again in India, they must be free to move immediately and uncompromisingly against its leaders in whatever numbers and wherever they were to be found. The discussion centred upon the drafting of a full-scale Emergency Powers Ordinance.[35] This was shelved in the immediate aftermath of the Gandhi-Irwin pact, but in the light of what were felt to be the subsequent breaches of it by so many Congressmen it was soon taken down again. If Gandhi had not gone to London in August 1931 it would have been put into effect immediately. Following the events later in the year, in the North Western Frontier Province, in Bengal, and in the no-rent campaign in the United Provinces, the bureaucracy firmly insisted that it should have its *quid pro quo*. Gandhi's efforts on his return from London in December notwithstanding, the full panoply of the new policy was put into force on 2 January 1932.[36] It did not involve martial law or massacre of the Jallianwallah Bagh type. But it did involve what was called 'civil martial law': some very serious momentary violence, widespread proscriptions, innumerable arrests, substantial prison sentences, and an adamant refusal to enter into any negotiations with the nationalist leaders, Gandhi in particular. For all Gandhi's efforts in the next three years to secure what in effect would have been a 'Gandhi-Willingdon' pact, the Home Department resolutely refused to allow him even to see the Viceroy,[37] and made it their business as well to see that emergency powers were fully maintained until civil disobedience had been completely abandoned.[38]

By 1934 there can be no doubt that the new policy had succeeded. In May 1934 Gandhi himself advised 'all Congressmen to suspend civil resistance for Swaraj as distinguished from specific grievances; they should leave it to me alone',[39] and by 1937 Congressmen who in 1930 had demanded immediate independence were arguing about who should be members of the provincial cabinets established under Britain's new and much hated Government of India Act of 1935.[40]

As the 'successful' policy of 1921 held the field in the

thinking of the Government of India during the 1920s, so the no less 'successful' policy of 1932 held the field for a decade thereafter too. This time, moreover, not only was there no reversal: in the final confrontation with Indian nationalism the repressive policy of the Government of India was elaborated to its fullest extent. As early as April 1940 the later Home Member, Sir Reginald Maxwell, decided that if civil disobedience were to be renewed, as was beginning to seem likely, he would insist that immediate action should be taken with all the vehemence of 1932.[41] Detailed instructions were sent to all local governments on 2 August 1940,[42] and a few days later the Viceroy, Lord Linlithgow, followed these up with a personal letter to all his provincial governors in which he declared that he felt 'very strongly that the only possible answer to a "declaration of war" by any section of Congress in present circumstances [and it ought to be remembered that this *was* the summer of 1940] must be a declared determination to crush that organization as a whole'.[43] When the Cabinet in London heard of such instructions they were much put out, and formally told him to change his approach.[44] But in a further letter to provincial governors in December 1940 Linlithgow stated that, although 'His Majesty's Government and I are of opinion that, given the turn things have taken, and given also the importance of considering reactions outside India, the wiser tactics in the present circumstances would be . . . to deal with the Congress on the line adopted in 1932, this modification of method in the light of the development of the *satyagraha* movement *does not represent any modification of policy or any alteration in our attitude towards Congress* and those of its activities which infringe the law' (my emphasis).[45] In the event, the action taken against the 'Quit India' movement of August 1942 was explicitly in terms of the Government of India's instructions of August 1940.

Because Gandhi did not launch a mass *satyagraha* in 1940 but only his 'individual' *satyagraha,* these instructions were shelved in the meanwhile. The mind of the Government of India at this time is, however, readily revealed in an exchange of letters in October 1940 between Sir Maurice Hallett, the Governor of the United Provinces (and himself a former Home Member of the Government of India) and Sir Reginald

Maxwell, his successor in Delhi. 'Having said,' (as was the case) Hallet declared, 'that the future constitution of India will, subject to certain safeguards, be decided by Indians themselves it seems anomalous for us to go out and smash the Congress on any other ground than that they are interfering with the war.' But to this Maxwell replied:

> 'This view seems to me to assume that Congress does in fact represent the Indian people as a whole. We deny this: we see no reason why the Congress Working Committee should be allowed to set themselves up as the political dictators of India; and we think that on the wider view the time may be approaching when it may be possible to expose the insincerity and opportunism of its political leaders and give the people of India a chance of deciding their future constitution in some other way than under the domination of a political party which has led them badly since the beginning of the war and no longer represents their views correctly.'

And he went on to make a classic statement of terminal imperialist *hauteur*:

> 'But even if the Congress were the only people we had to deal with in shaping the political future of India I should not for a moment admit the proposition that when certain things had been promised to be done at a certain time and in a certain way the Congress were entitled to hold a pistol to our heads in order to compel us to implement these promises at a different time and in a different way, nor would I be deterred from resisting such a movement by the amount of support which Congress might be able to enlist by methods known to you as well as to me. I hope I have said enough to convince you that the conclusions at which we have arrived on this whole question have not been adopted without full consideration.'[46]

The Viceroy, he added, had approved his reply; and one has only to read Secretary of State Amery's justifications for the suppression of the 'Quit India' movement[47] to see that, the earlier Cabinet disapproval notwithstanding, it was this totally hostile policy which operated in 1942. It required, in August and September 1942, 57½ battalions of troops to give it effect, and there were killings in Bihar and eastern U.P. on a scale which had not been seen even in the conflicts in the Punjab in 1919.[48]

But the British position held. The number of Indian resignations from Government service was minute. Congress leaders thereafter served long periods of imprisonment; and the adamantine face towards the Congress of the Government of India was resolutely maintained until the second world war was near its close.[49]

There had been three really anxious moments for the Government of India during the three preceding decades. First, in the third week of December 1921 when it looked as if the policy adopted towards the first non-cooperation movement was collapsing, and the Viceroy, Lord Reading, came within an ace of having to concede Responsible Government for the Provinces fifteen years before it actually happened: he was saved by Gandhi's failure (probably because of his commitments to the imprisoned Ali brothers) to grasp the opportunity, and the moment of crisis passed.[50] (It should perhaps be emphasised that since Britain had at this very moment taken the hard decisions to give up its dominion in both Egypt and Ireland it was never more likely to have conceded something of substance in India precipitately as well.) Secondly, in 1931 when the bureaucracy could not be quite sure, especially whilst there was still a Labour Government in London, that if civil disobedience should now be renewed they could have their Emergency Powers Ordinance as they demanded; there was a change, however, to the National Government in London and the new Conservative Secretary of State, Samuel Hoare, soon promised them that they would.[51] And thirdly, in the aftermath of the 'Quit India' movement when the Government of India became extremely worried lest on a future occasion the troops available would prove sufficient both to withstand the Japanese and a further nationalist upheaval as well;[52] but, again, the movement of gravest anxiety very soon passed. We may note in passing, however, that each of these anxious moments occurred at a critical point in the confrontation with the second campaign in each of the three agitational phases to which we have referred.

Throughout, however, the major fact was that the Government of India was never actually forced to the wall as its equivalents had been in both Egypt and Ireland. In its protracted encounter with the Indian national movement it has to be said that it won all the battles.

But it lost the war.

This was not because it had no support in London. On the contrary, a series of stances were adopted there which buttressed the resistance it offered in India. There were changes here (and, again, it is of consequence that they did not occur *pari passu* with the changes in the other sequences which we have outlined). To begin with, there was the whole resistance in principle to the application of the white commonwealth precedents to which allusion has been made. This was undermined by the Montagu declaration of 1917, and in the immediate aftermath a conservative 'line' was not easy to discern (except as a severe distaste for Montagu: his political career was successfully destroyed by Lord Curzon in 1922).[53] During this hiatus some substantial constitutional advance (at all events in the provinces) might have been effected. Hailey, who was Finance Member of the Government of India, said in March 1921 that the present scheme of Reforms cannot . . . last ten years or anything like it'.[54] (It lasted fifteen.) In December 1921 Reading, as we have already seen, nearly had to concede full Responsible Government in the provinces; and, as is well known, Willingdon, as Governor of Madras, was quite prepared to go ahead with it there in 1922.[55] When, moreover, the Government of India saw nationalist pressure rising up against it once again, it told the Secretary of State in 1924 that it believed 'we should not . . . be justified in refusing to contemplate any advance at all within the scope of the present constitution'.[56]

Even the new Labour Secretary of State, however, made it very plain that he was not in any way prepared to contemplate any such changes 'arising merely from impatience with transitional position'[57], and his successor, Birkenhead, thereupon formed the first of what were to be three further conservative stances for withstanding India's advance towards independence. Essentially he formulated the doctrine which became embodied in the attitude on constitutional progress of the Simon Commission that followed: that, although some advance would probably have to be allowed, no commitment of any substance should be conceded about advance at the centre.[58]

To the fury of those who took this line the Conservative Viceroy, Irwin, issued his 'Dominion Status' declaration in 1929, which made promises about the future which went far beyond this. Prompting Irwin to it was his now strong feeling that if Britain were to stand pat, a major conflict with Indian nationalism would very soon erupt, and could be fatal to her future relations with India.[59] There were many who found his arguments persuasive, yet who, like him, were still not prepared to accept a programme of early independence for India. In 1931–2 they managed to formulate the essence of the next conservative position: an all-India federation with responsibility at the centre but with controlling safeguards, and in particular a blocking third of princely votes.[60] 'As you know,' Hoare, who became the chief exponent of this line, telegraphed to the Viceroy, Willingdon, in March 1932, 'it has always been my view that if we do not succeed in getting majority of [princely] states into a Federation prospects of early and steady Constitutional progress for India will be very seriously impaired.'[61]

The great debate which had by then broken out in Britain over Indian constitutional development, with Churchill in the lead on the die-hard side, and Hoare on the other, was not merely a debate mainly within the Conservative party itself, but essentially an encounter between two conservative positions. Churchill stood on the Simon Report and the Birkenhead line; Hoare on the blocking third of princely votes. It was only after a five-year debate; after a display of consummate ability on the part of Hoare against the uniquely eloquent Churchill; and, in the last analysis, because of the support for the Irwin-Hoare position of the leader of the Conservative Party, Stanley Baldwin (who was determined that the British parties should not be divided from each other over India as they had been over Ireland), that the federation policy was accepted in Britain, and found fruition in the Government of India Act of 1935.[62]

The trouble then was that this further conservative device was rendered fruitless because the protagonists of the earlier position secured an undertaking that in the formation of the federation the Princes would not be coerced into joining it.

The Princes used this lever to fatal effect, and the Federation idea foundered at birth. The result was that by 1940 the two conservative camps had succeeded in destroying each other's position, and the British were without policy in India.[63] The emphasis was then clumsily shifted to the third position: that there should be no independence until after the war (an idea which found expression in both the August 1940 and the Cripps offer), and to the Maxwell-Linlithgow-Amery glosses upon this, as already recounted.

The internecine defeats of the earlier conservative lines over India did not, of course, take place on their own. It would be very wide of the mark, however, to suggest that they stood over against any effective radical counterview upon India's independence. It was not just that the Conservative Party happened to dominate the government of Britain throughout most of the relevant period. Despite the Brockways, the Sorensons, the Edward Thompsons and the Agatha Harrisons, the official 'left' persistently showed a marked tendency to accept the conservative arguments. Attlee was a member of the Simon Commission; Macdonald was prime minister when the federation formula came to be constructed; Cripps was still a member of Churchill's Government at the end of 1942.

As the structure of the political coalition which eventually put through the 1935 Act indicates, it was the centre right and the centre left in British politics which in the end was the decisive *mélange* in the critical decisions on the British side.[64] It never moved fast. The most it would do was to propound statements of the 'jam-tomorrow' kind. Moreover, it never moved unless the existing conservative posture looked to have lost its vitality, and unless it was persuaded that a move ahead had just an outside chance of de-escalating the open conflict which threatened in India.

This last consideration emerges to a really very surprising extent if one plots the moments when British Governments made their seminal statements about policy on India's future political development upon the switchback graph of each great phase of nationalist agitation as outlined previously. Each was issued either before the first agitational campaign had begun, or at those very significant mid-course breaks to which reference has been made more than once already. This is true, under the first head, for the Montagu declaration of 1917, the Irwin declaration of 1929, and the August offer of 1940; and, under the second, for the decision to implement the Montagu-Chelmsford reforms in 1919, the Macdonald responsibility-at-the-centre statement of 1931, and the Cripps offer of 1942. In each instance the first was an attempt to head off a first agitational campaign before it had yet burst forth: the second to find grounds for calling it off before it should renew itself again.

It was upon these lines that the agitation of the Indian nationalist movement won independence for India and Pakistan. Not by overthrowing the Government of India—which it never did. Not by renewing the agitation in the major second campaigns: these presented the Government of India with its moments of greatest strain, but they never succeeded in moving it, or the British Government in London; indeed, they usually served to reinforce the attitude epitomised by Sir Reginald Maxwell in his letter of October 1940 to Sir Maurice Hallett (as quoted above). It was the threat of agitation, and the threat of renewed agitation, with which the Indian national movement moved the British—which is not, of course, to say that agitation itself was of no consequence: the threat would plainly have been vacuous if the reality was not known to be substantial. The linkages here are complex, and contorted—not as straight as has sometimes been suggested.

As Dr. Danzig has shown for the Montagu declaration of 1917,[65] and as seems to be the case for the later ones too, once such declarations had been made they became the ruling foundation for eventual British policy thereafter; and in a conflict in which the hold of the Government of India was never broken, and in the course of which there was a succession of conservative blocking procedures, which each in turn had widespread support in British politics, their extraction from the British Government was of very considerable consequence. And, of course, the striking fact is, if I can come back to where I began, that whenever the *mélange* that was the British 'centre' was looking around for new formulas to offer to India, they reached for the only models which they had to hand: those of the white commonwealth. This, however, was the way the model was applied to India; and not (if I may look at it from another angle) as a consequence of a long-approved policy. 'The reforms of 1919,' as the Simon Report correctly put it, 'did not make provision for a steady evolution towards an ultimate object.'[66]

There are two points to be added here. First, although the great debate between the die-hards and the proponents of the 1935 Act was plainly a debate *within* conservatism, and thus upon a singularly narrow front, its outcome was, no less plainly, quite momentous. It took a few years more for it to be fully realised that British public opinion would not be prepared to have such a debate over India again. Such, however, was the case. I have elsewhere quoted evidence to show that there can be very little doubt that by the time of the second world war the great debate on India, in Britain at least, was over.[67] Let me, however, add some evidence from a man who at the time of writing would have been the last to have believed in the good faith of Conservatives. In November 1939 Sir Stafford Cripps wrote from London to tell Jawarharlal Nehru. 'There is one good sign and that is the quite remarkable change of opinion even amongst Conservatives which is most remarkable and may have its influence on Governmental action. The Winston-Woolmer view is definitely in a very small minority and apart from the former's influence in the Cabinet is not influential otherwise.'[68]

Secondly, in essaying what turns out to be the exceedingly difficult task of determining what it was that secured India independence—how it was, in my earlier terminology, that the Government of India won the battles but lost the war—there is a sentence in one of Jawaharlal Nehru's long reports on his visit to London in 1938 which catches one's eye. He had an informal meeting with the Labour executive (Attlee, Dalton, Cripps, and Morrison amongst them) who included, as he put it, 'all the moderate and most cautious of the Labour group', and found their attitude 'very different this time from what it was two and a half years ago'. However, he wrote, 'the gap between the position of the Congress and that of the British Government is so great and the whole background is such that a conflict some time or other seems likely . . . At the same time there are other factors which affect the situation profoundly—*the knowledge of the great strength of the national movement and the obvious difficulty of suppressing it by force'.*[69] (My emphasis.)

In 1942 it was, of course, so suppressed. Why, then, was there a conflict in that year? Especially if, as would seem very clear, Cripps's assurance to Nehru in 1939 was right? There was clearly British ham-handedness in 1939-40 (for which Dr. Moore has recently made it plain Linlithgow was only partly responsible).[70] Moreover, Churchill's 'influence in the Cabinet', to use Cripps's phrase, was in 1940 in all senses peculiar.[71] Furthermore, once the old wounds had been reopened, Congress reached for its old civil disobedience formula, and the well oiled dynamics of an agitational phase began to move once again. The Government of India reached, quite literally, for its secret history of *The Civil Disobedience Movement 1930–34*[72] (with its appendices of draft Emergency Powers Ordinances), and blew the dust from all its previous procedures, especially in respect of the need to keep the 'Indian' services loyal by being prepared to take draconian action. In addition, British conservative opinion seized on its last, yet absolutely typical, formula: "after-the-war-not-now". There were abortive attempts to head off both the first agitational campaign (the August 1940 offer) and the second (the Cripps offer); these (despite the fact, incidentally, that the second was not 'accepted') became the ruling formulas from there on: but as before, there was no further offer in response to 'Quit India' and the second campaign it represented. There were three features to this last conflict which deserve a further comment. As we have seen, there were those in the Government of India ready to use the occasion for a final, desperate effort to 'crush' the Congress. In August 1942, when great force was used, British—and American—opinion turned a blind eye, because this was an exceptionally critical moment in the second world war. The white commonwealth model displayed, moreover, one of its worst weaknesses. It was based on the principle of the great leap forward from one whole system (e.g. Representative Government) to another (e.g. Responsible Government). Because both the British leadership and the Indian leadership had it in mind, they saw—quite fatally—at the height of the Cripps negotiations the question of who was to hold the Defence portfolio in the Government of India as a great issue of principle—when, if they had been thinking in the much more incremental terms (which came to prevail later on, as we shall see), it is difficult to see that they would have done so.[73]

However, when the Second World War came to its close, the pre-existing elements conspired very quickly to bring about the final British decision to withdraw. The point in the rhythm of the nationalist movement's agitational phases for 'council entry', and of real compromise with the British, had come around once again. 1942 had shown the Government of India that the stiff-terms-of-imprisonment-but-no-massive-shooting policy of 1932 would not work again. 'Tomorrow' had come for the last 'jam-tomorrow' statement (the Cripps offer); and Wavell could set out to do his Allenby. 'So far as India is concerned.' *The Times* leader writer on Indian affairs wrote on 7 August 1940 to an old Indian friend, 'the situation can be described in a single sentence. The die-hards are extinct, public opinion is united in desiring India to obtain her independence just as soon as it can be arranged.'[74]

Importantly, the bureaucracy had lost one battle: they had not, as some of them had certainly wished, 'crushed' Congress. And, of course, there remained the momentous issues of partition, the actual transfer of power, and the Punjab massacres to follow.[75] But these are not issues to be pursued here.

The critical point is that by 1945 Britain had eventually decided that it really would do in its brown commonwealth what it had previously done in its white. One can see the significance of this very clearly by taking a look at Indonesia, where in 1945 the Dutch were still very far from making any such decision, and where there was both a revolution and two periods of sharp Dutch-Indonesian warfare—not to mention considerable American and United Nations intervention—before the Dutch conceded Indonesian independence at the Hague conference in 1949.[76]

Black Sequel

It may be felt that some apology is necessary for allocating so much space in such a chapter as this to the Indian story alone. No apology is offered, for of all the latter-day stories the Indian one is much the most momentous. What if it had been a story of war, like the American or the Algerian? What if it had not eventuated in independence, as in southern Africa? Aside from these, it always needs to be remembered that its great encounters were spread not over one or two years, or even ten, but over thirty. Such precedents as existed, moreover, were long denied to it, and were certainly only very tardily applied. As an anti-imperialist conflict it has scarcely an equal. At the same time, for the subsequent story, it established a major principle, not just for the brown commonwealth (Burma and Ceylon were soon independent too), but for the black commonwealth as well.

Far be it from me to belittle the force of African nationalism (I have first-hand experience of it *en train,* as I do not of Indian). It must be said, however, that some of the critical battles of African nationalism were fought, not so much on the banks of the Volta or the Niger, or even the Zambezi, but on the Ganges—and, if the argument above has any validity, on the Thames as well. This is not to say that the battles of African nationalism were not substantial battles. Some of them were very substantial inded. It is simply to insist that Africa owes a great deal to the Indian precedents.

It seems plain that their influence was not very obvious. Sir Charles Arden-Clarke came to the Gold Coast, as I have said, from Southeast Asia; and many an African leader, from Nkrumah to Kaunda, claimed that he was a follower of Gandhi. But these are insubstantial considerations. The crucial one is that there was never any kind of great debate in Britain about independence for her West African colonies, as there had been over India in the 1930s, or even as there was to be in the late 1950s over East and Central Africa.[77] There was much anxiety in Britain about West Africa's advance towards independence, and, from the African point of view, much dragging of feet. But the same men who had met Nehru in 1938 (as I quoted him earlier)—Attlee, Dalton, Cripps and Morrison—were the key figures in the British Government ten years later when the critical point in the West African story was reached. They had been through the fundamental argument over India already, and do not seem to have shown any interest (or their Conservative opponents either) in going through it once again over West Africa.

This, let it be emphasised, is very far from saying that Nkrumah (very patently the key figure here) had nothing to do. On the contrary, he had still to get the British actually to do in the Gold Coast what they had already done in India; and he made, as well, his immensely bold effort to get them to do it very much faster than they had done it in India. On both scores he was triumphantly successful. He and his associates were assisted no doubt by their relatively favourable circumstances. The somewhat different Sudan story was unfolding in front of them. By contrast with the Gambia, the Gold Coast was substantially bigger. It had neither the north/south cleavage of Nigeria nor the colony/protectorate divide of Sierra Leone. With about the same population as Uganda, it had twice the national income. The alternative pressures of 'positive action' and 'tactical action' provided just that combination of threat and readiness to cooperate which was calculated to move the British as Nkrumah wished them to be moved. Nkrumah was bold enough, moreover, to accept office under a British Governor at a very much earlier stage in the nationalist encounter than the Indian leaders ever had; some Congress leaders had taken office in 1937, but Nehru and Patel did not do so until 1946. And, in the event, whereas it had taken thirty years since the Montagu declaration of 1917 before India gained its independence, it was a bare ten years between Nkrumah's return to the Gold Coast and the independence of Ghana in 1957. With that, moreover, independence for Nigeria and for Sierra Leone was only a matter of time, and of some resolution of their internal divisions.[78]

But before leaving the Ghanaian story two of its features deserve heavy emphasis. In the first place it did not have to be delayed because the rest of British Africa could not keep up with it. Because the British Empire in Africa was not a united whole, Ghana was in a position to go ahead on its own, as Bengal had not been in India. There were, of course, obvious advantages here for Nkrumah: but for the British as well, since elsewhere in Africa they were able to point to what was happening in Ghana as evidence of the bona fides of their promises about African self-government; and that made their life very much easier.[79]

Secondly, Ghana saw the abandonment of key features of the old constitutional progression which had operated in the white commonwealth, and to which appeal had been made for the brown. In 1920, as a result of the Montagu-Chelmsford reforms, there had been established in the provinces in India the system known as 'dyarchy', by which a local government's responsibilities were divided between those subjects that were 'transferred' to the hands of Ministers drawn from the local legislature, and those subjects which were 'reserved' in the hands of British officials.[80] Variations upon this theme were applied elsewhere as well (and there was the never repeated experiment of the Donoughmore Constitution in Ceylon). For the most part, however, the old white commonwealth thinking continued to hold the field, even though it was becoming extremely confused. When Martin Wight came to compile his *British Colonial Constitutions 1947*,[81] he found himself having to use terms like 'Semi-Representative Government' and 'Semi-Responsible Government', to describe some of the situations he found himself confronting.

In the African story—with one critically important exception—much of this was done away with. The white commonwealth progression was no longer applied, and a new one took its place. It had always borne within it the fatal defect of what I have termed 'the crisis of Representative Government': when the localised legislature clashed with the autocratic executive; and as the Indian story had shown it was, as well, a very ponderous procedure, sometimes indeed dangerously so.

Quite who worked out the new progression is not at all clear.[82] Its genesis still wants working upon. But its principles are clear. First, no 'great-leaps-forward', but a whole series of small steps that could be taken without having to wait for a full dress review. Thus, on the executive side, Nkrumah began by being a Leader of Government Business, then became Premier, and eventually Prime Minister, and along with this went the small-step by small-step withdrawal of British officials from the Executive Council (later the Cabinet), until the British Chief Secretary was transformed into the Deputy Governor responsible for those limited items (Defence and

External Affairs) that constituted the residue which the British held on to in the period immediately preceding independence. In principle, similar small gradations were instituted on the legislative side as well. Secondly, the old programme by which the legislature was largely localised first, and the executive only subsequently, was abandoned for a piecemeal advance on both fronts at the same time. As a consequence, British Governors in Africa and in the rest of the colonial empire were able to avoid the great confrontations which the crisis of Representative Government had meant for their predecessors; and they found themselves with a whole series of cards up their sleeves which they could play, not at intervals separated by decades, but every one or two years, one or two at a time.

Despite what I have just said when speaking of Africa, I have been careful so far to speak specifically of West Africa. It is of first importance to note that East and Central Africa were critically different. The Ghanaian precedents applied in many places: but not on the other side of the continent. Far from independence in East and Central Africa following as day follows night, it looked to most Africans—if things went on as they were doing in the early 1950s—that no dawn would ever break there. If there was relatively little conflict over West Africa, there was major conflict over East and Central Africa, as the uniquely violent Mau Mau revolt, and the Nyasaland disturbances of 1959[83] (not to mention Rhodesia's UDI), quickly serve to demonstrate.

The fundamental reason for this was that in these parts of Africa there was a head-on collision between what were by now two classic British imperial policies, both of them stemming ultimately from Durham. Under the first, power was transferred to British settler communities scattered across the globe as soon as they were in sufficient numbers to support the governmental structure which this required. Under the second, power was transferred to non-British peoples within the Empire when their demand for it seemed to have become irresistible. The first had by 1923, despite some minor qualifications, brought Responsible Government to the settlers of Southern Rhodesia. Some slight appreciation of the force of the second had checked at that time the spread of Responsible Government to the British settlers of Kenya, and throughout the 1920s, 1930s and 1940s, despite the widespread establishment of settler influence over all the British territories of East and Central Africa, there was, thanks to the coordinating efforts of a 'liberal' lobby in Britain, no transfer to the settlers of political control in Kenya.[84]

But by the opening of the 1950s the British Colonial Office was confronted by the likelihood of an early collision between the two policies. To meet this situation they (and, to begin with, both British political parties as well) formulated the doctrine of 'Partnership'—of 'Multi-racialism'—which during the 1950s found both actual and symbolic embodiment in those balancing formulae for the racial membership of the legislative and executive councils of the British east and central African territories which were such a feature of the time.[85] On first introducing, in 1952, non-official members into the Uganda Executive Council, even that reforming Governor, Sir Andrew Cohen, appointed two Asians, two Europeans and two Africans, while in central Africa the Colonial Office agreed to the creation of the Federation of Rhodesia and Nyasaland because, so it claimed, it embodied the principles of 'partnership' and contained in its constitution the variation of the 'balancing formula' principle which was appropriate to the political realities of that region. I myself heard James Griffiths, Labour Secretary of State for the Colonies, propound in 1951 the merits of the partnership doctrine for Uganda. It won the vehement support of the linch-pin of the old liberal lobby of the 1920s and 1930s, J. H. Oldham.[86] And it was preached as a doctrine far superior to the white and black racialisms which were denounced as its alternatives.

The trouble was that to Africans it was simply a smokescreen for an unjust misallocation of political privilege in direct contravention of the prevailing population ratios to be found in their countries.

The fight was soon on. Its focus was ultimately upon central Africa. But some of the major developments occurred elsewhere.

In the first place in Uganda. Despite Colonial Office efforts, James Griffiths' speech, and Cohen's first reform of his Executive Council, Uganda was never convincingly subsumed beneath the partnership doctrine. The Capricorn Africa Society, for example (the doctrine's most articulate pressure group), never succeeded in making any headway there. In 1953 there came the crisis in Uganda over the deportation of the Kabaka of Buganda. Only in part was this provoked by any concern for multi-racialism. It precipitated, however, the seminal statement by the new Conservative Colonial Secretary that Uganda was to be viewed 'as primarily an African country', though in deference to the still prevailing dogma he was careful to add 'with proper safeguards for minorities'. More important, in the course of the efforts to resolve the conflict in Buganda at the so-called Namirembe Conference of 1954, the British took the critically important steps of changing the balance in the racial composition of the Governor's Executive Council from 2:2:2 to 1:1:5—the five being Africans—and restructured the Uganda Legislative Council so that it should always in the future have a majority of African members (though, because of the 'new progression', and more specifically because of the nomination of African members to the Government side, this did not as yet mean 'an African controlling majority'). The *coup de grâce* came in Uganda in 1959 when the local Wild Committee pushed aside its original terms of reference and recommended the constitution of a non-racial legislature, i.e. one that *followed* the population ratios rather than flew in their face.[87]

The next step came in tiny Zanzibar, where by 1956 the younger Arabs in the Zanzibar Arab Association persuaded its older members to forego their previous attempts to stand on a claim to specially allocated seats and embark on the risky, and all but successful, attempt to make themselves the leaders of the African majority.[88] Thereafter, the next most critical moment came in Tanganyika when TANU, instead, as they were first inclined, of boycotting the elections in 1957–58 under Professor Mackenzie's carefully devised 'multi-racial' constitution, decided to contest them, ran a campaign to enrol as many Africans who were qualified to vote as they could, and succeeded in driving a coach and four through Governor Twining's efforts to secure a multi-racial balance of political power, which the Mackenzie constitution had been devised to ensure. The right numbers of new Legislative Councillors of each race were returned, but TANU not only won the African seats: it was obvious that most of the successful Asian and European candidates owed their victories to their readiness to espouse the African cause, and, very specifically, to African votes.[89]

That meant that Kenya was left entirely isolated. Both its so-called Lyttelton and Lennox-Boyd Constitutions, of 1954 and 1957, for all the greater *entrée* which they successively gave to Africans, were typical 'partnership' contrivances, which maintained the predominance of local European influence in Kenya. The great revolt against this, Mau Mau, had by 1957 been suppressed. There was considerable African political activity in Kenya; but the decisive events occurred elsewhere.

They came to fruition in 1960. Not only was the Kenya construct isolated by that time in British East Africa. It was isolated in a wider context as well.

Ghana had become independent in 1957, Guinea in 1958. Upon General de Gaulle's advent to power the French territories had been given the choice of independence or membership of the French community. Only Guinea had chosen the former. But by 1960 there was change afoot here. Togo and Cameroons, as U.N. Trust Territories, were both due to have independence in 1960. So was another Trust Territory, Somalia. And so was Nigeria. The French territories already enjoyed a substantial measure of local autonomy under the *loi cadre* of 1956. The temptation for them to take the final step into full independence was now becoming quite irresistible. Already, moreover, the transfer of power within them had had a deeply unsettling effect upon the hitherto strongly authoritarian Belgian administration in the Congo; and in 1959 and 1960 the Belgians embarked upon their fateful attempt to win a Congolese alliance by a precipitate grant of independence.[90]

When the British Conservative Prime Minister started on his tour of Africa at the beginning of 1960 these developments were already tumbling over each other. As he put it in his speech in Cape Town in February: 'The wind of change is blowing through this Continent.'[91] To a degree which is not always appreciated that speech was of seminal importance for Kenya. For in it Macmillan propounded a doctrine of equality which was at variance with the regime which had hitherto prevailed in Kenya. At a time, moreover, when more than half Africa was about to become self-governing, its immediate effect upon Kenya was dramatic. At the Lancaster House Conference which met within the fortnight, the previous predominant influence of the Europeans in Kenya was decisively broken.[92]

There remained the central African territories incorporated in the Federation of Rhodesia and Nyasaland. A statement in 1957 after talks with the Federal Prime Minister suggested that London was on the point of relinquishing its final control. But there was then a substantial debate in Britain, which was pushed forward by the Nyasaland riots of 1959 and the highly critical Devlin Report upon them, and then centred upon the work of the Monkton Commission on the future of the Federation.[93] Following developments in British Conservative policy over East Africa which finally broke the European hold in Kenya, the case for a similar development in Nyasaland was patent. There followed, however, an exceedingly tense political struggle in Northern Rhodesia which eventually culminated in a statement by Maudling, by this time Britain's Colonial Secretary, on 1 March 1962, in which, by making a minor change in the details of the voting procedures which were to be embodied in its new constitution, he finally opened the way in Zambia to an African majority and an African government.[94] Public support in Britain for these moves had been generated by an active political lobby; and the dismantling of the Central African Federation followed thereafter (as in due course did the independence of Swaziland, Lesotho and Botswana).

The black commonwealth eventually, therefore, trod the road of the brown, as at long last the brown had of the white. But in East and Central Africa it had been touch and go to a degree that it had not been in West Africa. And although there were substantial nationalist efforts on the ground, it was contemporary all-African developments, and the successful public campaign in Britain against the Central African Federation and all which it stood for, that were of major importance to the outcome.

What remained was Rhodesia. And if one wants to see

something of the remaining strength of the white commonwealth model one has only to consider how, following UDI, the British Government felt itself unable to break the hold of the 'Responsible Government' long since established in Salisbury, yet could still hold back what, to the illegal regime, would have been the inestimable gift of Dominion Status, and/or the recognition of its independence.

Perhaps there are two matters to which to refer in conclusion. First, next to nothing has been said of the strategic and global considerations which weighed in the minds of the British in London—for example in the Defence departments and in the British Foreign Office. There is no reason to think that these were not important. For the moment, however, there is little public knowledge upon them—and in any event they would entail a further chapter to themselves.[95] Secondly, it should be said that there were some obvious sequences on the nationalist side which have not been touched on here, but which would be worth tracing out. One could begin by comparing the highly elitist circles in which Indian nationalism began with the thoroughly non-elitist nationalist movements which were characteristic of East and Central Africa in the 1950s.[96] One could then trace the ebb and flow of nationalist attitudes towards the British, beginning with Dadabhai Naoroji's increasing disillusionment with 'Un-British' rule in India, to his demand for 'Swaraj' in 1906, through Gandhi's denunciation of Britain's 'satanic' Government in India, and into Nehru's riposte to Lord Lothian's plea in 1936 ('the road is wide open whereby India can attain to independence represented by the Statute of Westminster') that 'ruling powers and ruling classes have not been known in history to abdicate willingly'.[97] One could then note Nkrumah's verbal echo of this in 1953 that 'never in the history of the world has an alien ruler granted self-rule on a silver platter'; but note as well not only that his own actions implied that by this time a rather different situation was prevailing,[98] but that Nehru (who had always seen independent India as the champion of a great, world-wide anti-imperialist campaign) was very clearly acting in the 1950s as if everything was over bar the shouting.[99] In this context the violence of Mau Mau in Kenya clearly represented the vehemence of Kikuyu feeling at the thought that they were being arbitrarily excluded from this process;[100] while the *dénouement* (as I have myself suggested elsewhere) came in a country like Uganda where by the mid 1950s it really *did* seem that self-rule was in fact being granted 'on a silver platter', and some of its political leaders were much more worried about the prospect thereafter.[101] At this point a great deal could be said—from the Irish story, through the Indian, the Palestinian, the Malayan, the Ghanaian, the Nigerian, the Ugandan, and even the Kenyan and the Zambian—about this other issue, which if it did not surge to the fore immediately prior to independence, more than once erupted—in Nigeria for one—not long afterwards: not the issue of whether independence would ever be attained; but the question of the distribution of power upon its attainment. In all this there is much to be said too about the methods the nationalists adopted—from 'terrorism' to 'tactical action'; and in the end there is the striking fact that in the final stages there was often a coming together of the nationalists and the last representatives of their opponents—Nehru and Mountbatten, Nkrumah and Arden-Clarke, Nyerere and Turnbull, Kenyatta and Macdonald—because, it would seem, the British were by this time badly in need of a responsive elite to whom they could actually transfer power, whilst the nationalists were now primarily interested in ensuring that at the last moment power should not slip from their grasp.

NOTES

1. John Connell, *Wavell, Scholar and Soldier: to June 1941,* London, 1964. The second volume remained unfinished at Connell's death. For the more favourable view of Wavell see Maulana Abul Kalam Azad, *India Wins Freedom*, Bombay, 1959, R. P. Masani, *Britain in India*, London, 1960.
2. Field Marshal Viscount Wavell, *Allenby in Egypt*, London, 1943.
3. D. L. Keir, *The Constitutional History of Modern Britain,* London, 1938.
4. Malta toyed with the Franco-Irish alternative in the 1950s, but decided in the end against it. So, indeed, a long time since, had the (southern) Irish, whilst most of the 'French' territories were soon to give it up as well.
5. Earl of Durham, *Report on the Affairs of North America,* ed. C. P. Lucas, 3 vols., Oxford, 1912.

6. Martin Wight, *The Development of the Legislative Council 1606–1945,* London, 1946; W. K. Hancock, Survey of British Commonwealth Affairs, Vol. I, London, 1937; E. A. Walker (ed.), *The Cambridge History of the British Empire,* Vol. VIII, South Africa, 2nd ed., Cambridge, 1963.
7. There is a useful M.A. thesis on all this by Penelope Rogers, 'British attitudes to India and the Indian Councils Act of 1892', University of Queensland, 1969.
8. G. S. Khaparde at the 1st Central Provinces and Berar Provincial Conference, April 1905, National Archives of India, Home (hereinafter 'H') Public, 217–227A, Oct. 1906.
9. E.g. Dadabhai Naoroji, *Poverty and Un-British Rule in India*, London, 1901.
10. R. P. Masani, *Dadabhai Naoroji*, London, 1939.
11. Hardinge's note, 30 June 1912, H. Deposit, No. 7 Sept 1912.
12. On Montagu, see C. D. Waley, *Edwin Montagu,* London, 1964; on Irwin, S. Gopal, *The Viceroyalty of Lord Irwin,* Oxford, 1957.
13. J. H. Broomfield, *Elite Conflict in a Plural Society. Twentieth-Century Bengal*, Berkeley, 1968, Ch. I.
14. 61 House of Lords Debates, 5s., cols. 1091–2, quoted S. R. Mehrotra, *India and the Commonwealth 1885–1929*, London, 1965, p. 226.
15. J. Nehru, *A Bunch of Old Letters*, Bombay, 1958, p. 129, sqq.
16. Amles Tripathi, *The Extremist Challenge: India between 1810 and 1910*, Bombay, 1967.
17. H. F. Owen, 'Towards Nation-Wide Agitation and Organisation: the Home Rule Leagues, 1915–1918,' in D. A. Low, *Soundings in Modern South Asian History*, London, 1968, p. 159 sqq.
18. Sir Keith Hancock has an interesting essay on Gandhi's technique in *Four Studies in War and Peace*, Cambridge, 1961, but see also Joan V. Bondurant, *Conquest of Violence: The Gandhian Philosophy of Conflict,* Princeton, 1958 (paperback, Berkeley, 1965): and Lloyd I. Rudolph and Susanne Hoeber Rudolph, *The Modernity of Tradition*, Chicago, 1967, Part two.
19. Judith M. Brown, *Gandhi's Rise to Power, Indian Politics 1915–1922*, Cambridge, 1972.
20. There is interesting evidence of this in Meston to Chelmsford, 20 June 1917, and enclosures, H. Political (hereinafter Poll.) 86–106A, August 1917.
21. The material upon all this is so voluminous that it is almost superfluous to give references. See, for example, J. S. Sharma, *India National Congress. A Descriptive Bibliography*, Dehli, 1959, and D. G. Tendulkar, *Mahatma: Life of Mohandas Karamchand Gandhi*, 8 vols., Bombay, 1951–4. I am inclined to think the most useful summary is still in the first half of M. Brecher, *Nehru: a political biography*, London, 1959.
22. Risley to Godley, 12 July 1906, H. Public 124C, A, July 1906.

23. Secretary Home Dept. to all Governments, 4 March 1910, H. Poll., 42–46A, March 1910.
24. E.g. Craddock's notes, 14 Oct. 1913, H. Poll., 83–85A, March 1914; 13 Oct. 1914, H. Poll., 39–48A, Nov. 1914; 21 Feb. 1916, H. Poll. 225–232A, Aug. 1917.
25. H. Poll. 74–108A, May 1919, passim; H. Poll. 318–323A, May 1919.
26. Notes by Vincent, 22 March, 19 April 1919, H. Poll; 144–162A, June 1919.
27. Viceroy to Secretary of State, telegram, 7 June 1922, H. Poll. 410/II 1922.
28. Vincent to Craddock, 14–15 Nov. 1920, Craddock to Vincent, 27 Oct. 1920, H. Poll. 271–276A, Dec. 1920.
29. D. A. Low, 'The Government of India and the First Non-Cooperation Movement, 1920–1922', *Journal of Asian Studies*, XXV, 2, Feb. 1966, pp. 241–59 (reprinted in R. Kumar (ed.), *Essays in Gandhian Politics*, Oxford, 1971).
30. H. Poll. 18/XVI/28 passim.
31. Haig's note, 9 Jan. 1929, H. Poll. 18/XVI/28.
32. E.g. Home Dept. to all local Governments, telegram, 22 April 1930, H. Poll., 257/VIII/II of 1930 and K.W.
33. I have reviewed this in 'Sir Tej Bahadur Sapru and the First Round Table Conference', Ch. 10, in Low, *Soundings*.
34. Haig to Hotson, 25 May 1930, H. Poll 257/V and K. W. 1930.
35. E.g. H. Poll. 13–8/31 and K. W. and 5/45/31. I hope to give details elsewhere.
36. [Home Department] *The Civil Disobedience Movement 1930–34*, 1935.
37. E.g. Haig's note, 26 Oct. 1933, H. Poll. 169/1933.
38. E.g. Haig's note, 22 May 1934, H. Poll. 4/4/34.
39. Quoted ibid.
40. Jawaharlal Nehru Papers—for 1937—Nehru Memorial Museum, New Delhi, passim.
41. Maxwell's note, 24 April 1940, H. Poll. 3/13/40.
42. Home Dept. to all Provincial Governments, 2 August 1940, H. Poll (I), 13/40.
43. Linlithgow to Governors, 8 August 1940, H. Poll. (I), 6/13/40.
44. Exchange of telegrams, Viceroy and Secretary of State, 11–14 September 1940, H. Poll. (I) 3/16/40; and Secretary of State to Viceroy, 12 Dec. 1940, H. Poll. (I), 3/22/40.
45. Viceroy to all Governors, 30 December 1940, ibid.
46. Hallett to Maxwell, 10 Oct. 1940, Tottenham's note, 18 Oct. 1940, Maxwell to Hallett, 4 Nov. 1940, H. Poll. (I), 3/14/40.
47. E.g. Amery to Smuts, 10 Aug. 1942, Smuts Papers, Vol. 67, No. 12.
48. E.g. 'Summary of events . . . during which Communications in Bihar were dislocated', H. Poll. (I), 3/30/42, Pt. II; 'Statement

made by the Honourable the Home Member to the National Defence Council . . .', 8 Sept. 1942, H. Poll. (I), 3/26–42 (2).

49. E.g. Tottenham's note, 26 July 1944, H. Poll. (I), e/28/44. See more generally, Francis G. Hutchins, *Spontaneous Revolution, the Quit India Movement*, Delhi, 1971, and Spear, 'A Third Force in India' in Philips and Wainwright (see footnote 60 below).
50. Low, 'Government of India and First Non-Cooperation movement'.
51. H. Poll. 14/12/31.
52. E.g. Maxwell's note, 1 Sept. 1942, H. Poll. 3/34/42.
53. E.g. Waley, *Montagu*, Ch. XIX.
54. Hailey's note, 22 March 1921, H. Poll., 3C and K.W. Deposit (Print), July 1921.
55. Willingdon to Vincent, 1 July 1922, H. Poll. 418/1922 and K.W.
56. Viceroy to Secretary of State, 28 Jan. 1924, H. Public, 166/1924.
57. Secretary of State to Viceroy, 2 Feb. 1924, ibid.
58. *Report of the Indian Statutory Commission* (Vol. I Survey, Vol II Recommendations), Cmd. 3568–9, 1930.
59. Low, 'Sapru and the Round Table Conference'.
60. R. J. Moore, 'The Making of India's Paper Federation, 1927–35', Ch. 2 in C. H. Philips and M. D. Wainwright, *The Partition of India*, London, 1970.
61. Secretary of State to Viceroy, P. and P. telegram, 23 March 1932, National Archives of India, Foreign and Political, 7–R/32.
62. Low, 'Sapru and the Round Table Conference'.
63. Urmila Phadnis, *Towards the integration of the Indian States 1919–1947*, London, 1968, Ch. VI–VIII. The period is reviewed in John Glendevon, *The Viceroy at Bay*, London, 1971.
64. Low, 'Sapru', pp. 320–21.
65. R. Danzig, 'The Announcement of August 20th 1917', *Journal of Asian Studies*, XXVIII, I, November 1968, pp. 19–39.
66. Cmd. 3569, p. 7, quoted Mehrotra, op. cit., p. 224.
67. Low, 'Sapuru', pp. 295–6.
68. Cripps to Nehru, 16 Nov. 1939, Jawaharlal Nehru Papers, Nehru Memorial Museum, New Delhi, Cripps file.
69. Nehru's notes for Working Committee, 30 July, 6 Sept. 1938, J. Nehru Papers, Notes for 'W.C.'.
70. R. J. Moore, 'British Policy and the Indian Problem, 1936–40', in Philips and Wainwright, *Partition of India*, Ch. 3.
71. See footnote 68.
72. See footnote 36.
73. I read a paper that discussed this, called 'Congress and the Raj: Sir Tej Bahadur Sapru and the antecedents of the Cripps Mission 1942', to a conference at the Australian National University in September 1969. See especially Nicolas Mansergh, *The Transfer of Power, 1942–7,* Vol. I, The Cripps Mission January–April 1942, London, 1970.

74. Rushbrook Williams to Sapru, 7 Aug. 1945, National Library of India, Sapru Papers.
75. See the two major recent studies Philips and Wainwright, op. cit., and H. V. Hodson, *The Great Divide*, London, 1969, and the bibliographies there cited.
76. G. M. Kahin, *Nationalism and Revolution in Indonesia*, Ithaca, 1952.
77. Some of the issues are reviewed in David Goldsworthy, *Colonial issues in British Politics 1945–1961*, Oxford, 1971.
78. *The Autobiography of Kwame Nkrumah*, Edinburgh, 1957; Dennis Austin, *Politics in Ghana 1946–1960*, Oxford, 1964; James S. Coleman, *Nigeria: Background to Nationalism*, Berkeley, 1965; Kalu Ezera, *Constitutional Development in Nigeria*, Oxford, 1960; Martin Kilson, *Political Change in a West African State. A Study of the Modernization process in Sierra Leone*, Harvard, 1966, Part III.
79. E.g. D. A. Low, *Buganda in Modern History*, London and California, 1971, Ch. 6.
80. For its origins, see L. Curtis, *Dyarchy*, Oxford, 1920.
81. Oxford, 1952.
82. It is not adequately dealt with in Sir Kenneth Roberts-Wray, *Commonwealth and Colonial Law*, London, 1966, or in Sir Charles Jeffries, *Transfer of Power, Problems of the passage to self-government*, London, 1960. The starting points might be first the article on 'The Member System in British African territories', *Journal of African Administration*, 1949, pp. 54–5, and second the Report of the Coussey Commission in the Gold Coast, which remarked upon the crisis of representative government (as I have called it) which had developed there, *Gold Coast Report to His Excellency the Governor by the Committee on Constitutional Reform, 1949*, Col. 248.
83. Carl G. Rosberg and John Nottingham, *The Myth of Mau Mau, Nationalism in Kenya*, London, 1966; *Report of the Nyasaland Commission of Enquiry*, July 1959. C. 814.
84. Dame Margery Perham, who was heavily involved in this herself, is understood to have embarked upon a full study of the first half of this story.
85. 'Statement about Colonial Territories in East Africa', 13 December 1950, *Hansard*, 1950–1, Vol. 482, cols. 1167–9.
86. J. H. Oldham, *New Hope in Africa*, London, 1955.
87. Low, *Buganda in Modern History*, Chs. 4 and 6.
88. Michael Lofchie, *Zanzibar, Background to Revolution*, Princeton, 1965, Ch. V.
89. For some of the bare facts, see Henry Bienen, *Tanzania. Party Transformation and Economic Development*, Princeton, 1967, Ch. II.
90. Catherine Hoskyns, *The Congo since independence, January 1960–December 1961*, London, 1965. I attempted to outline the

all-African events in my 'The Colonial Demise in Africa', *Australian Outlook*, 14, 3, Dec. 1960, pp. 257–68.

91. There is a useful reprint of Macmillan's speech of 3 Feb. 1960 in Nicholas Mansergh, *Documents and Speeches on Commonwealth Affairs 1952–1962,* London, 1963, pp. 347–51. See also Dan Horowitz, 'Attitudes of British Conservatives towards Decolonization in Africa', *African Affairs,* XIX, 1970, No. 274.
92. G. Bennett and Carl G. Rosberg. *The Kenyatta Election: Kenya 1960–61*, London, 1961, p. 17 sqq.
93. E.g. Philip Mason, *Year of Decision Rhodesia and Nyasaland 1960*, London, 1960; Edward Clegg, *Race and Politics: Partnership in the Federation of Rhodesia and Nyasaland*, London, 1960; Colin Leys and Cranford Pratt, *A New Deal in Central Africa*, London, 1960.
94. D. C. Mulford, *Zambia, The Politics of Independence 1957–1964*, Oxford, 1967, esp. Ch. V.
95. Professor Max Beloff has set out to tell this story, see his *Imperial Sunset*, Vol. I, London, 1969; see also Oxford *History of East Africa*, Vol. III, Ch. I.
96. Cf. Anil Seal, *The Emergence of Indian Nationalism*, Cambridge, 1968, with Andrew Maguire, *Towards Uhuru in Tanzania*, Cambrige, 1970.
97. E.g. Masani, *Naoroji*, and Nehru, *Bunch of Old Letters*, passim.
98. Nkrumah, *Autobiography*, passim.
99. Brecher, *Nehru*, the second half.
100. Nottingham and Rosberg, *Mau Mau*.
101. Low, *Buganda,* Ch. 6.

6

Political Authority in the Aftermath of Empire

On 19 January 1964, just over two years after Tanganyika had become independent, a mutiny occurred at Colito barracks outside Dar-es-Salaam of the 1st Battalion, the Tanganyika Rifles. Led by an Education Sergeant, Hingo Ilogi, the mutineers locked their British and African officers in the guard room, seized the radio station, set up a number of road blocks, and went on a rampage through the town. Perhaps twenty people were killed. There were sympathetic outbursts at two other military stations up-country. President Nyerere went into hiding, and the Government came to a halt. One hears indeed that train and air services in the rest of the country stopped running as well. The Minister of Defence, Oscar Kambona, managed, however, to make contact with the mutineers, and two days later Nyerere emerged from hiding. But it was only with the landing of a British Royal Marine Commando on 25 January 1965, and its efficient rounding up of the mutineers immediately afterwards, that the Government's authority was restored.[1]

The tenuousness of its position had been brutally revealed. A few rampaging soldiers had forced it to its knees. There were some sympathetic moves in the armies of Uganda and Kenya, and all three independent Governments suddenly found themselves having to face the bitter fact of appealing to their ex-imperial masters for assistance in reconstituting their authority. In the aftermath they took great care with the handling of their armed forces. But in January 1971 a military takeover occurred in Uganda. So common by this time, however, had such occurrences become in Africa that the fact that this was the first successful military coup in East or Central Africa was scarcely remarked upon.[2]

From the outset the fragility of territorial authority in Tanganyika had been recognised both by the last British

Governor, Sir Richard Turnbull, and by the nationalist leader, Julius Nyerere. Within weeks indeed of independence in December 1961, Nyerere had gone so far as to resign the Prime Ministership of his country so as to consolidate his own control over its nationalist party, TANU. The first legislative act of the independent government provided moreover for TANU party officials to be appointed to the governmental posts of Regional and Area Commissioners, while shortly afterwards, when Chiefs as such were abolished, the most reliable of them were reincorporated into a new centrally-controlled administrative structure. Owing to the switches from a system of direct rule through appointed chiefs (based on an Arab model which the Germans had adopted) to Sir Donald Cameron's 'Indirect Rule' in the 1920s, and then in the 1950s to a variety of local 'Councils' (some of them, multi-racial), Tanganyika's Government inherited at independence no well entrenched local government authorities—neither a strong centrally-controlled local bureaucracy, nor a strong African local government system. Because, moreover, independence had come to Tanganyika relatively swiftly TANU was not a strongly disciplined party either. In a situation therefore in which all territory-wide structures of local authority were inherently frail, there was much to be said for tieing together all the delicate strands which did exist—even at the cost of having to take steps thereafter to prevent overmighty subjects emerging.[3]

These measures did not, however, prevent the humiliation of 1964. It was said at the time that the Tanganyikan mutineers represented nobody. In many respects this was perfectly correct. They allied with no politically ambitious group. There is no evidence that they secured any popular support. There was, even so, a real sense in which the mutineers represented everybody in Tanganyika—outside the governing elite. For their three demands were for better conditions, better pay and 'africanisation': the three things which the governing elite (which had little or no inherent claim to them) had secured at independence but which most of the rest of the population (in a very impoverished country) had not. The point, however, seems to have been taken. For thereafter President Nyerere took steps to curb the various pretensions of the elite. At the elections in 1965 he instituted the ingenious arrangement by which, although Tanganyika was by now a one-party state, the electors in each constituency were permitted to choose between two rival candidates from the governing party, while in the Arusha Declaration of 1967, and in various other statements which followed, he committed his Government to an avowedly egalitarian social and economic policy. In so doing he not only displayed his own considerable idealism. He displayed as well his acute awareness of the tenuousness of the political authority of his Government, and of the need to reconstitute a new socio-economic order upon which his regime would be based.[4]

Very similar issues were close to the heart of post-independence events in Uganda to the north-west. Here, by contrast with Tanganyika, remarkably strong local governments had been built up during the colonial period. They were indeed the major political resource which Uganda possessed at independence. Inherently, however, they constituted a limitation upon the authority of Uganda's national government. To begin with, Milton Obote, as Prime Minister of Uganda, felt himself obliged to acknowledge their strength. Faced, however, in 1966 by an open challenge from their prototype, the kingdom of Buganda, he swept its kingdom structure away, and shortly afterwards put an end to its replicas in the rest of the country as well. But in so doing he destroyed the major element in Uganda's political heritage and thereby laid bare his own personal political autocracy. No one, however, seems to have sensed the exiguousness of his political legitimacy thereafter more than he did, and in a sustained campaign to reconstitute his position he first insisted that a new Constitution should be extensively discussed, and then embarked upon a series of 'meet-the-people' tours in which he appealed for popular support for his regime by affirming that he and his Ministers had come to 'meet their masters'. When neither approach proved to be very effectual he altered course, revived his long-standing interest in 'the common man', compiled *The Common Man's Charter*, and, with evident trepidation, set on foot his own development of Nyerere-style parliamentary elections. Since his coup d'état against Uganda's local governments in 1966 had in the event turned upon a violent assault by the Ugandan army against the palace of the Kabaka of Buganda, his most conspicuous achievement in the five years which followed was to maintain a civilian regime in Uganda.[5] But such was the fragility of his position that when he was eventually ousted in the army coup of 1971 before the elections could be held, his going was the work of but a few hours. The old issues however remained, as his successor General Amin very soon discovered. Although he took steps to assuage the country's royalists, he soon announced as well that he would not restore their kingdoms. At the same time he forbade any 'political' activity; made his Ministers swear allegiance as if they were army officers, and then embarked on his own 'meet-the-people' tours, during which he not only issued sharp denunciations of any rumblings against his regime, but (in an effort to assuage popular demands) distributed lavish promises of new roads, new hospitals and new schools.[6] Although he no longer talked of 'the common man' he went out of his way, moreover, to put himself in touch with local 'elders', and even went so far as to raise the possibility of a land reform.[7] Acceptance of the national leadership's authority was still evidently very uncertain, and in this unhappy situation successive Presidents found themselves having to respond to a host of urgent popular claims, and needing a new base in some socially viable political order.

In Kenya the basic compounds were similar. Only the mix was different. Like Tanganyika, and unlike Uganda, it inherited no strong African local governments from its imperialist past. As in both other countries, moreover, its political party structure was frail. But unlike its two neighbours it possessed at independence an unusually strong centrally-controlled provincial and district administration (the outcome in the first place of successive failures by the colonial administration in Kenya to enlist any indigenous authorities in its structure of government,[8] and then of the marked expansion in its administrative bureaucracy during the conflict with Mau Mau in the 1950s), and in Jomo Kenyatta, a head of state who by East African standards had a uniquely sustained record as a nationalist leader. In the years that followed it was upon the conjunction of these two—Kenyatta's personal standing, and his deliberate maintenance of the imperial legacy of centrally controlled civil servants at the local level—that the authority of the Kenya Government rested. But the lengths to which its leadership then went to determine in its own interest both the 'little general election' of 1967 and the General Election of 1966, and the harassment it meted out throughout these years to its opponents in Oginga Odinga's Kenya Peoples Union, revealed not only its own low estimate of its own strength, but its recognition of the explosive potential that lay in the generalised demands which (as in Tanganyika and Uganda) were reaching it from various quarters in the country. At the same time, however, the early years of Kenya's independence were marked by the most vigorous debate in East Africa about the course that the country's development should take, which reached its climax when Kenyatta declared that: 'There are some individuals who claim that I should give everything free to the people. . . . We believe [on the contrary] we must safeguard the personal and property rights of all our people as a vital element of our hard-won freedom'[9]—a socio-political manifesto if ever there was one.

For all the variations in detail, therefore, the major political issues in East Africa in the years which followed independence were thus the same: limited political authority at the national level, coupled with numberless popular demands upon it for increased benefits, and a seminal concern about the course which the future socio-economic and political order should take.

As independence came to the countries previously under imperial rule, so the focus of their political attention shifted. No longer was it primarily directed against their imperial rulers. It was reoriented towards the multiple issues of economic development and internal articulation. Analysis of their political condition has tended to concentrate upon their (more recent) 'political development', and, more specifically upon their party, constitutional and educational attainments, their patterns of 'political communication', their experience of societal 'conflict and consensus', the role of their elites, and the character of their administrations. One sometimes wonders however just how much of this touches the core of their lot.

But what is this? On the basis of the accounts offered above it may be suggested that it is made up of three elements: the nature and condition of the political authority which obtains; the impetus in the demands that are made upon it; and the structure of the agrarian regime associated with it. Since in each instance there again appear to be significant differences between East Africa and India we shall consider these once more comparatively.

Structures of Authority

As we have seen, nothing has been more disconcerting about the experience of the countries of East Africa since independence than the accumulating evidence of the vulnerability of their political systems—and we may remember that Zanzibar, Rwanda, Burundi and Somalia have each had their political upheavals as well. Other countries like Burma, Pakistan and even Ceylon have of course been similarly afflicted. But India has not. It may be that there is one quite special reason for this. At all events it is important to remember that in the quarter-century which followed independence there was scarcely an Indian State in which, for one reason or another, 'state' government did not break down. If the immediate consequences were not so serious as in Africa, this was no doubt initially due to the provision in India's Constitution for 'President's rule'. Under this the Government of India was entitled to assume control over the operations of a State government when its normal constitutional functioning seemed for any reason to be politically impossible. If there had been a central government in Africa with similar powers, perhaps the history of its post-independence coups would have been different: one has a hint of the possibilities here in the flying-in of troops from elsewhere in Africa to the Congo in 1960 and to Tanganyika in 1964. Plainly, however, this was not the whole story. For, while India's ills have not been confined to periodic breakdowns in its State governments, it has not only had to face the strain of episodes like the Naga revolt, the linguistic states controversy, and the national language issue; it has also had to face the campaigns for the division of Bombay State, for Punjabi Suba, even for Dravidistan (not to mention the more general tendencies towards fissiparation which at one time were widely remarked upon, and which the National Integration Council was set up in 1962 to combat). India's poverty has, moreover, been much more extreme than Africa's, its vast population always far more unwieldy, and spasmodic violence much more frequent.[10]

And yet, for all the more gloomy prognostications which have been advanced,[11] there was never in fact, in the decades which followed independence, a traumatic breakdown in the authority of the Government of India. The legitimacy of its claims to authority was accepted when crises developed at the State level; while survey evidence suggests that, for all the discontents which have existed, the authority of government in India, and all which that has implied there, was widely acknowledged even in the more unexpected quarters.[12] As regards, therefore, the political authority it has enjoyed, the Government of India seems to have been much more happily placed than any of the East African Governments we have considered—and much better placed, too, than the Governments of Burma and Pakistan.

One preliminary way of glimpsing why this should have been so is to apply the yardstick of Max Weber's 'three pure types of legitimate authority'. These, we may remind ourselves, rest their claims upon

1. 'Rational grounds—resting on a belief in the "legality" of patterns of normative rules and the right of those elevated to authority under such rules to issue commands (legal authority)
2. Traditional grounds—resting on an established belief in the sanctity of immemorial traditions and the legitimacy of the status of those exercising authority under them (traditional authority);
3. Charismatic grounds—resting on devotion to the specific and exceptional sanctity, heroism or exemplary character of an individual person, and of the normative patterns or order revealed or ordained by him (charismatic authority).'[13]

So far as traditional authority is concerned (if we may vary the order here slightly) we may note, as is readily apparent in Delhi, that the independent Government of India is the heir to the British, who themselves were heirs to the Mughals, who (via a series of other Muslim dynasties) were ultimately heirs to the Guptas, who likewise were heirs to the Mauryas. The concept of the supreme ruler—of the *chakravartin*[14]—has, moreover, been prevalent in India for two or three millennia; and it is in no way fanciful to suggest that the present Government of India is its current embodiment.

On its own, of course—as India's history exemplifies as well as any other—a heritage of traditional rulership does not by itself ensure the existence of a persistently strong political authority. But the Government of India does not just possess a degree of traditional authority. It has a goodly heritage of legal-bureaucratic authority as well. It is now indeed 150 years, plus or minus, since this was first in instituted in India (and in many respects it even then drew upon the pre-existing patrimonial system of the Mughals).[15] During the British period, moreover, there was a heavy emphasis upon the rule of law, upon the system of legal codes, and upon the operation of legal-bureaucratic authority much more generally. During much of the British period the rulers were themselves primarily bureaucrats, and they bent their chief efforts to elaborating an immensely detailed legal system of land ownership and land revenue.[16] At the same time elitist Indians became extensively involved in the British legal system in India, and following a relatively lengthy association with it (and despite Gandhi's civil disobedience campaigns) developed a warm attachment to the rule of law and to the system of parliamentary government to which it was ultimately linked.[17] This inheritance passed over virtually intact to post-independence India. Since it happened, moreover, that neither the British Government of India nor the independent Government of India ever had to suspend the Constitution, and since the transfer of power from the one to the other was a 'non-revolutionary' transfer, there was never in two-hundred years a break in the system at its apex. What is more, just about half the elite Indian Civil Service (and, of course, a vastly greater proportion of its subordinate Services) was Indian at the transfer of power, so that the continuity of bureaucratic personnel (reinforced as all this was by the deliberate policy of the first Indian Home

Minister, Sardar Patel) was substantial as well.[18] The uninterrupted constitutional and administrative heritage of India is as old, indeed, as that of the United States.

To all this has to be added the charismatic authority which the new Cabinet Government of India enjoyed upon independence. We have earlier noticed the value to Kenya's independent Government of Kenyatta's longstanding reputation as a devoted nationalist. It is no reflection upon this to say that it was capped by Jawaharlal Nehru's reputation, to which was added the explicit investing by Gandhi of his own mantle as India's leader upon Nehru, which enhanced Nehru's standing still further.[19] In some ways, however, this was the least of it. For in this connection the really notable fact about India's independence Cabinet was that it was formed by the leaders of the Indian National Congress, the uniquely successful organ of a uniquely extensive nationalist movement with an unbroken record of endeavour stretching back to 1885.[20]

No independent East African Government had any of these advantages. None of them had any 'traditional' authority worth the name. In Tanganyika Julius Nyerere recognised this very fully when, as independence drew near, he declared: 'Tanganyika is not a traditional unit at all. . . . There is nothing traditional in the Central Government of Tanganyika today.'[21] Outside north Africa there was hardly any African national Government indeed with any real claim to traditional authority of the kind which Weber had in mind.[22]

In so far, moreover, as the East African Governments inherited a measure of legal-bureaucratic authority from the British, they rarely succeeded to a system which had anything more than fifty years behind it. And it was not such an elaborated system as India's either: it was not reinforced by, for example, anything comparable to the elaborate edifice of of the Indian land revenue system. Moreover, unlike some of the Indian elite, the East African elite had little acquaintance with either the British legal system or the British parliamentary system. And at the transfer of power nothing like 50 per cent of the top bureaucracy in the East African territories was African (while many in the middle levels were Asians).[23] There were thus marked disjunctions here; not as in India a marked continuity.

Beyond this, not only was Kenyatta's personal charisma less than Nehru's. Nyerere's was by any similar comparison less still, whilst Obote's in Uganda was difficult to discern at all. More to the point: at independence TANU in Tanganyika was not yet ten years old, whilst KANU in Kenya, and the UPC and Kabaka Yekka in Uganda, were less than five.[24] All of course had had their predecessors; but so had the Indian National Congress. None of them, however, possessed anything like its sixty-three years of uninterrupted service in the nationalist cause by the time that independence came.

One can trace the attempts of all three East African Governments to combat the serious deficiencies which they faced under each of these three heads. Thus, as the 1970s opened, the Presidents of Kenya, Uganda and Tanzania were officially and popularly called, respectively, 'Mzee', Respected Elder, 'Dada', Grandfather, and 'Mwalimu', Respected Teacher (and some historians, wishing to respond to the needs of the country in which they worked, went out of their way to publish an anachronistically entitled *History of Tanzania*.)[25] At the same time (and despite various public displays to the contrary), careful attention was given to the cohesion and integrity of the top African civil servants in these countries.[26] Considerable emphasis came to be placed moreover upon legal proprieties. Nowhere was this more paradoxically displayed than in Uganda, where, following the upheavals of 1966, great play was made of two successive new Constitutions, and where after the 1971 coup, in an effort to regularise its claims, the new military regime went out of its way to call itself 'The Second Republic of Uganda'.[27] All three Governments moreover took special care in the years after independence to extol the charismatic attributes of their Presidents. There is nothing however, surprising about that. For, as Weber's insights should lead one to expect, where both traditional and legal-bureaucratic authority were as thin as they were here, there was really no alternative but to bolster the leadership's charisma in every possible way.

In so far as Pakistan and Burma, each of which has had more than one political and military upheaval, stood in these terms closer to the East African countries than to India, this analysis goes part of the way to explain why. Neither a government based upon Karachi (nor later upon Islamabad), nor one based upon Rangoon, had the traditional authority of a government based upon the ancient capital Delhi. Interestingly, the time-depth to the legal-bureaucratic authority of the government, in Burma and West Pakistan at all events, was several decades less than for India's. More pertinently, unlike India, Burma did experience a sharp break with its legal-bureaucratic past just prior to independence; while in 1947 (again by contrast with India), the Government of Pakistan had in a great many respects to start from scratch. At the same time neither Government was anything like as well endowed at the moment of independence with experienced senior bureaucrats of its own as was India's. In Burma the governing party was as new at the moment of independence as those in East Africa; while in Pakistan the Muslim League—more particularly in the greater part of those areas which in 1947 became Pakistan—possessed none of the claims deriving from long, sustained and devoted service which were enjoyed by the Congress Government in India. What was more, both countries lost at critical moments their most spectacular figures: Aung San was murdered in 1947; Qaid-i-Azam Mohammed Ali Jinnah died in 1948, and Liaquat Ali Khan, Pakistan's much respected first Prime Minister, was assassinated three years later (Jawaharlal Nehru on the other hand lived on until 1964).[28]

But all this is only a beginning, and if we are to appreciate to the full the contrasts which there have been in the strengths of the Governments that have succeeded the British we must look at their inheritance in another perspective as well. In particular, consideration needs to be given to the distinctive characteristics of the structures of political authority which have persisted into independence from the imperial era; and once more there are striking contrasts between India and East Africa for us to consider.

It is a commonplace, but an important one, that, aside from the Partition of 1947, Indian political history over the last few centuries has known no sudden traumatic break. As any historian attempting to understand it can avow, one prime fact about modern Indian history is that it has not—as yet, at all events!—had a French 1789, a Japanese 1868, a Russian 1917, an Indonesian 1945 or a Chinese 1949. Neither the advent, nor the departure of the British constituted anything at all comparable; the former was spread over a century; the latter occurred—as between the British and India—without a tumultuous upheaval.[29]

Concomitantly, nothing has been more striking about the modern political history of India than the continuity in its levels of political decision-making. The starting point for an understanding of what is involved here lies in a first-rate piece of historical research by Bernard S. Cohn. In a pithy study of 'Political Systems in Eighteenth Century India' with special reference to 'the Banaras region'.[30] Professor Cohn describes the various levels of political authority which were to be found in the political structure of India at that time and the delicate nature of the relationship between those who occupied them. At the apex, he reminds us, stood the Mughal Emperor in Delhi. Below him—so far as Benares was concerned—there was the Nawab of Oudh, with his capital at Lucknow, whilst below him stood the Raja of Benares; and below him again there were sometimes (more especially in the central areas of the Rajadom) dominant Rajput clans with their direct associations with village leaders, but elsewhere (more particularly in the Rajadom's peripheral areas) lesser intermediate Rajas as well. At least one similar analysis (by A. M. Shah for Gujarat) has been published for one other region of India and as a general picture it is confirmed for other areas as well.[31]

In some vital respects it is a very familiar picture. If the late eighteenth century trappings are stripped away, it is closely commensurate with the late nineteenth-century position. A supreme Government once again stood at the apex—admittedly based in Calcutta, though after 1912 back in Delhi once again; a provincial government, covering broadly speaking the old Oudh territories, occupied the next level down; whilst below that, in descending order, there were three more levels of political authority at Division, District and Tehsil level before one came upon those who exercised authority in the villages. But what is more, in the second half of the twentieth century, the levels in the overall political structure (more particularly following the advent of Panchayati Raj) have been ordered in much this way again. During the 1960s there was still a supreme Government in Delhi; there was still a second-tier Government in Lucknow; and beneath them another triple-tiered political structure as well—for the most part Zila Parishads at District level, Panchayat Samitis at Block level, and Gram Panchayats at Village level.[32] There have of course been changes in the two intervening centuries (to some of which we shall return); but the levels of political authority and of political decision-making seem very largely to have persisted throughout.

It is no objection to this view to insist that the boundaries of particular units do not show the same consistency over time, or to complain that sometimes there seem to have been five levels of authority and sometimes six; for such variations are a separate issue (and are in no way a new development in India during the last two centuries). It avails little, moreover, to insist that one must take account of the variations in power between different levels of the structure at different times, for in part at least this is to miss the point. As the care with which a new Nizam of Hyderabad proceeded in 1830 to secure sanction for the legitimacy of his succession from the powerless King of Delhi illustrates (or the increasing embarrassment of the British during the first half of the nineteenth century at their maintenance of that same King of Delhi would further suggest),[33] a level of authority could persist even when its actual political power covered no more than a few acres. But more than this: as Professor Cohn's article makes plain, it is precisely when one recognises the coexistence of several successive levels of authority in the Indian political system that one can begin to ask some of the right questions about the distribution of power between them.[34] When, for example, after reading Philip Woodruff's persuasive volumes on *The Men Who Ruled India*, one is tempted to believe that in nineteenth-century India it was the British who did, one has only to read Robert Frykenberg's *Guntur District, 1788–1848: a History of Local Influence and Central Authority in South India*[35] to wonder whether on the contrary it was not some of the Indian service castes which did. Both temptations should be resisted, and in Cohn's footsteps we should proceed on the assumption that 'a balancing of relative weakness' between those who occupied the premier positions at the different levels which existed 'appears to have been central to the functioning of the system'.[36] And, throughout, the prime fact remains that in India the levels of political authority and political decision-making have remained remarkably consistent during all the vicissitudes of the past two centuries, particularly perhaps in their 'upper' reaches.

The contrast with East Africa could scarcely be greater. It is not just that there is not in Africa anything comparable in the size of its dominion to the Government of India (no 'Government of Africa', not even 'of East Africa'). It is rather that, far from the prime fact of modern East African political history being the persistency of levels of political authority and political decision-making, the prime fact has been the building up of the upper levels of political authority here for the first time.[37] One way of considering, indeed, the major occurrences in African political history over the last century or so is to note that around a century ago there were (to take a conservative estimate)[38] something like 600–800 actual or latent political systems in Africa, whereas in the opening decades of the second half of the twentieth century these have been aggregated into a mere forty. Perhaps one of the best ways, however, of seeing the processes at work here is to consider how some East African peoples have viewed them.

'*Suru*,' it is reported of the Lugbara of West Nile district in north western Uganda, 'has the meaning of a group of people who consider themselves and are considered by others to form a group because they share a territory and have ties between them based on common ancestry . . . Thus *suru* refers to major lineages and sections, clans, subclans and subtribes. The term is also used in a wider sense as the *suru* (peoples, tribes) of Madi or Europeans.'[39] It is reported indeed that in discussing the two world wars the terms by which Lugbara refer to two of the main protagonists are *Suru Germani* and *Suru Britishi*.[40]

The people of Nyansongo, a Gusii community in Kisii district in western Kenya, have been even more explicit. It has been reported that

'The social universe as Nyansongans see it is made up of units of increasing size and exclusiveness from the family to the nation, all of them referred to by the same term, *egesaku*, and all composed of a group of men who recognize a common patrilineal ancestor and occupy a common territory. *Egesaku* in its most general sense thus means "lineage", although it can refer to the group of father and sons in a single homestead, a lineage at one of four levels between family and clan, a clan, one of the seven Gusii "tribes", the Gusii people as a whole as contrasted with other ethnic groups (each one of which is also termed *egesaku*), or a nation such as Kenya, the United Kingdom, or the United States. Each unit within the Gusii ethnic group is spoken of as *egesaku* when considered as a separate entity, but when considered as one of several segments of a larger social unit, it is called *enyomba*, "house". Thus each social unit is thought of as subdivided into "houses", a pattern based explicitly on the polygamous extended family.'[41]

This sophisticated thinking represents a clear-cut theory of the way in which the larger political entities into which the peoples of East Africa have been aggregated have been formed. In particular, it takes account both of the internal autonomy of units at different levels and of their coexistence. Moreover, it views the situation in terms of a succession of levels (and is thus far more apposite than any adaptation of Western 'federalist' thinking which tends to confine its attention to two levels only). And it presents, of course, some notable parallels to Professor Cohn's account of eighteenth-century India. But there are contrasts as well. Some of these we must leave aside for the moment. We may note here, however, that whilst he proceeds from the top downwards, these East African models extended from the bottom upwards. But therein lies an important truth about the East African experience. For, in part at least, the multiple processes of aggregation which have been such a marked feature of recent East African (indeed of African) history have taken place from the bottom upwards. So many of its societies began three quarters of a century ago, like the *suru* of Lugbara or the *egesaku* of Gusii, as small-scale societies. As they entered the twentieth century, they became increasingly conscious that they were placed in some kind of association with other peoples, in a larger framework, and in a rapidly changing environment. Thereupon, for social, cultural, political and even economic purposes, they increasingly aggregated with their kith and kin, and with those who lived within their neighbourhoods who were ready to associate with them.[42] As a consequence there was very often a growth of what has been denounced as tribalism: a heightened sense of a common community amongst peoples who previously had not often emphasised the links they possessed with those who shared their own language, and their cultural and societal practices. It was in this way that in the twentieth century peoples like the Bakiga in southwestern Uganda,[43] the Sebei in northeastern Uganda,[44] the Tiriki in western Kenya,[45] and the Luguru in eastern Tanzania,[46] as scholarly studies in each instance have revealed, came not only to feel but to act as if they were part and parcel of one another (*egesaku* and *enyomba*, as the Gusii would translate these) to an altogether new extent. There were similar developments amongst the larger groups—amongst the Chagga, the Haya, the Sukuma of Tanzania; the Baluyia, the Luo, the Kamba, the Kikuyu of Kenya; the Langi, the Bagisu, the Basoga of Uganda—to mention only the most obvious instances. In the case of a Uganda kingdom like Buganda, the making of a larger entity had long preceded the present century; but even here, and in neighbouring Ankole and Toro as well, peripheral areas now came to be associated with their larger neighbours to a much greater extent than before.[47]

These processes were considerably advanced by the actions of the imperial power. The political boundaries it laid down served to delimit the lateral spread of the units which were being formed. The district administrative and later the representational institutions it formed frequently provided the key arenas within which the aggregative processes made their way, and as a consequence the district tribe and the tribal district became a common feature of East Africa's political map.

Developments in this direction varied of course in their detail and in their comprehensiveness. They also brought their strains. In Uganda, Teso District saw a cleavage in the 1950s between its two halves, the Iseera and the Ngoratok.[48] Bukedi District was never more than an administrative contrivance, an amalgam of peoples who did not even belong to the same linguistic groups.[49] A number of Banyoro districts never reconciled themselves to being incorporated in Buganda, and eventually broke away to rejoin Bunyoro;[50] while the Sebei, because they felt themselves to be distinct from the Bagisu with whom they had been administratively aggregated, successfully seceded in 1962 from Bugisu District.[51] When a similar dispensation was denied to the Bakonjo, who were anxious to free themselves from incorporation in Toro, some of them took to armed revolt.[52] (Elsewhere, in Kenya for example, larger, though more tenuous, aggregations, of the Kalenjin peoples of the south-west, and of the Mijikenda in the south-east, periodically attained some significance too.)[53]

For most of the imperial era the larger constructs, the territories, were embodied in no more than the institutions of their imperial governments. But because there was here the local centre of imperial power, and the commanding height of a network of overruling political structures, it was natural that as Africans aspired to supreme political power so as to determine their own future destinies themselves they should seek to secure control of them. Experience after independence quickly showed, however, that without the backing of imperial power the political authority these territorial centres possessed was very tenuous. Where, as in Tanganyika, the territorial government could occupy the interstitial position between a large number of tribes, none of which could dominate the others by itself,[54] or where, as in Kenya, the opposite applied and one tribe, the Kikuyu, could emulate the role of Prussia in late nineteenth-century Germany, there was something to proceed upon; but where, as in Uganda, neither the one nor the other operated, the territorial Government was in an exceptionally weak position. Everywhere, however, these upper levels of authority were so new, and so little linked to any active social networks outside those of a narrow elite, that their inherent fragility was stark.

Whichever way one looks at the position of the East African Governments after independence, it is evident that there was all too little on which they could rely in trying to maintain their political authority. Not only were their sources of political legitimacy weak; the upper levels of the political structures they topped were all too new and insubstantial. There was little here of the long-established structures of political authority and political decision making that one finds in India. Rather, at the parochial level, so often, new 'chiefdoms', new 'locations', and new 'counties', and at the next levels, new tribal districts, and new nations, where such units and such levels had never existed before.[55] If the units at the lowest levels did very often mesh with certain pre-existing social realities, this was decreasingly true the more one moved up the structure. At the territorial or national level the constructs were all quite arbitrarily composed, and because of their novelty and rootlessness the vulnerability of their governments was inevitably acute.

Circumstances of Authority

Their position was made all the more difficult because they were at the same time faced by a situation whose potentialities were dangerously tumultuous—as the East African Army mutinies of 1964 indicated. *Au fond* there were, apart from the travails of aggregation, four additional reasons for this. First, it has to be remembered that with few exceptions there was no fixed social stratification in East Africa (nor for that matter in much of the rest of tropical Africa either).[56] Even in many of the Uganda kingdoms, *la carrière* was *ouverte aux talents*, whilst elsewhere it was commonly accepted as fully legitimate that a daring and skilful individual should be able to thrust himself to the fore.[57] All this allowed for rapid mobility by the ambitious. Where, therefore, successful politicians came to exercise great power and place—especially after only a few years of effort and achievement—there was nothing to prevent others from aspiring to those positions, and in as short a time as well. Perhaps the classic example of this phenomenon in Africa was Patrice Lumumba of the Congo, who moved from postal clerk to Prime Minister in five years.[58] But to begin with, Nyerere or Obote's careers were scarcely more than twice that length, whilst meteoric careers were effected by other individuals in East Africa as well.[59] Such possibilities bred both personal and political uncertainty (and General Amin's coup in Uganda in 1971 did not suggest that the 1970s were necessarily going to bring about a change).

Secondly, there can be no doubt that in many areas the social order was changing substantially. There is, for example, the striking case of the Nyakyusa of south-western Tanzania. 'In 1935,' Monica Wilson has stated, 'the traditional rituals celebrated by lineages and chiefdoms formed a coherent system. They were directed towards the shades and the heroes, as was manifest in the sacrifices and in the dramas of death and rebirth. . . . By 1955 the ritual cycle was nowhere celebrated in full: what remained were bits and pieces of ritual, none of them fully intelligible without reference to the complete cycle.'[60]

Thirdly, despite the sprinkling of exceptions that can be adduced, the relative advantages in the man/land ratios in tropical Africa has meant that in the twentieth century people have become more prosperous than before; and in the light of their recent experience, they do not see their desires for still more prosperity as in any way unreasonable.[61] If there are not the connections between rising expectations and discontent which some people have suggested, there are clearly—to judge at least from the politicians speeches—close connections between rising expectations and rising demands upon the political system to deliver increased benefits.[62] Great improvements have therefore been sought in, for example, the ecenomic and educational spheres, because these appear to be the logical next step to the new benefits which have already been experienced. There is a tide here which the politicians fail to ride at their peril.

Fourthly, this proclivity is reinforced by the millenarianism which is abroad. The reasons for this are not hard to find. Immense changes have already occurred in East Africa in the past half century. An unbelievable new world has already opened up: all kinds of fundamentally new conceptions have recently come to this area. No one in 1950, moreover, could reasonably have expected that within fifteen years, the European rulers would have departed. But they did. So that, on the evidence, the unthinkable appears to be thinkable after all; and with their slogans of *Ujamaa* and *Harambee*, with their Arusha Declarations and their invocations of "the common man",[63] the political leaders have been trying to contain and direct the desires which have thus been set loose.

Once again there are marked contrasts here with India. There one finds next to none of these circumstances. In the first place—and for all the blurring of this picture both among the westernised elite and in the towns (even now, despite their growth, containing only a small proportion of the population) —there is still in India the most closed system of social stratification to be found anywhere in the world.[64] Its mechanisms for accommodating demands for social change are at once sophisticated and seemingly in good working order, and meteoric individual careers are all but unknown.[65] For all that the 'green revolution' may promise, moreover, the economic issue for most people is still to procure subsistence and rising expectations are thus for the most part still muted.[66] What is more, there have not been the radical changes in the ways of most people's worlds that one encounters in East Africa:[67] and although the European rulers have now departed, it was not the speed but the dilatoriness of their going that was so notable.[68] The popular thrust which the Government of India encounters, therefore, is not nearly as dynamic as that which assails the East African Governments,[69] and along with the differences in the hold which their political structures have over their countries, this makes for profound disparities in their political lot.

One might think, even so, that the misery and poverty which is so marked in India would by this time have bred a revolutionary upsurge there. But the experience of the proponents of violent revolution, the Naxalites of the Communist Party of India (Marxist-Leninist), suggests that this will be rather unlikely. The Naxalite leadership came in the main from disillusioned members of elite groups, especially, and understandably, from Bengal. But such limited successes as they have hitherto secured have depended, not upon the mass support of the most disadvantaged members of India's village societies (the Harijans or the grossly impoverished outcaste untouchables), who have a fixed social niche within them, but upon the more limited support of disadvantaged tribal peoples who feel themselves excluded from the usual Indian village society altogether.[70] This development is on all fours with other movements by tribal peoples in India who finding themselves unable to secure entry into the hindu village order have turned to other ideologies and other putative social systems in the hope that these will accommodate them instead—in the past to Islam, to Christianity, to Arya Samaj; then to revolutionary Maoism.[71] There is scarcely the basis here, as the Naxalites have discovered, for a mass revolutionary upheaval in India.

For most of India it would seem wise indeed to focus upon one other set of circumstances. We have earlier noted the persistence in India of a series of levels of political authority and political decision making. But once this is allowed for, it has to be emphasised that over the past two centuries the system has witnessed a succession of major changes even so. In outline these can be briefly described. As Cohn's article on eighteenth-century Banaras makes plain the middle and upper levels in the structure were occupied at that time by traditional rulers. The first of the major changes in the system since the late eighteenth-century is that almost without exception these have now gone. In what used to be called 'British India' they were mostly removed by the British during the last half of the eighteenth and the first half of the nineteenth-century.[72] Those who remained throughout the British period were subsequently set aside by the Government of independent India.[73]

In British India, the prime positions previously held by traditional rulers at different levels of the system came to be held during the British period, for the most part, by bureaucrats. The upper levels were of course largely occupied by British bureaucrats from the Indian Civil Service.[74] It is not always sufficiently emphasised, however, that, apart from the entry of Indians into the elite I.C.S., the middle and lower levels of the structure were usually occupied during the British period by *Indian* bureaucrats of the so-called Subordinate Services.[75] Very often these came from the hereditary service castes, as they were called; those elite communities within Indian society which had served traditional rulers in this role in the past. Their heyday came indeed in the nineteenth century when, under the British, they held the premier political positions at the subordinate levels.[76] There is a substantial story to be told about how during the later nineteenth-century such of these communities as were emigrés—and in particular who were either Bengali Bhadralok or Mahratta Brahmins—

were superseded by more obviously local elite castes;[77] and it has always to be remembered that it was from these same elitist, bureaucratically inclined communities that the earlier Indian nationalists were largely drawn.[78]

One major theme of Indian history in the first half of the twentieth century concerns, however, the ways in which these elite communities found themselves having to give way to others both within the persisting political structure and within the nationalist movement itself.[79] For along with the spread of nationalism and the attainment of independence there came another major change. In British India traditional rulers had so often given way before bureaucrats. Now bureaucrats gave way before those who commanded majorities within the new conciliar bodies of elected or delegated members—parliament and assemblies at the apex, panchayats by the 1960s at the three levels lower down. Unlike the traditional rulers, the Indian bureaucrats did not find themselves deposed altogether (the British had of course left) but they did find themselves relegated once more to the back room.

And along with this there came another development of quite outstanding importance. For, with all the variations and exceptions which a more detailed account could discuss, the striking facts are first, that despite the changes in the nineteenth and twentieth centuries in the institutions and personnel in the upper levels of the system, the ruling rural clans, as they were in some places, the 'village brotherhoods', as the early British administrators called them, the 'dominant castes', as the social anthropologists have called them, the richer peasants, as the economists think of them, usually remained in control of the villages they headed at the base of the political pyramid.[80] And then secondly, as ballot-box elections came to provide the royal road to the prime positions at the upper levels, it was men from these dominant rural communities—along with those who were dependent upon them for support—who came to hold so many of the key positions at all levels of the structure from the bottom to the top.

Such communities were the chief beneficiaries of so many of the measures taken by the British and by India's independent governments to assist 'the peasantry'. They began by having social, economic, political and often ritual primacy within their village settings.[81] They were greatly helped during the nineteenth and twentieth centuries by the Ryotwari settlements instituted by the British (which *inter alia* freed them from the obligation to make up for any shortfall in the revenue payments of their less fortunate fellow-villagers). They were also helped by the succession of Rent Acts and by all the measures which the British eventually introduced to curb the freedom of moneylenders.[82] They were helped, too, by the steady reductions in land revenue and by the resources put into the cooperative movement; and, after independence, they were helped as well by Zamindari abolition and by the maintenance of a high price for food.[83] The way in which factional politics operated within villages, particularly in a context where most rural social structures possessed relatively fluid centres,[84] meant, moreover, that their leaders could very often prevent horizontal cleavages occurring within village society by developing vertical ones.[85] And since, as the censuses made plain, these dominant rural communities were considerably more numerous than the elite bureaucratic communities,[86] they gradually began to oust the latter from the premier positions within nationalist politics.[87]

With the advent of independence the results were soon clear. 'Throughout rural India,' André Beteille wrote in 1966, 'one encounters dominant Peasant castes combining landownership with political power in the village. All through Western Uttar Pradesh and Hariyana one finds a succession of villages in which all, or almost all the land is owned by Jats, Ahirs or Gujjars, whichever caste happens to be dominant. Land seems to be similarly tied to the Marathas in Maharashtra, the Pattidars in Gujarat, the Kammas and Reddis in different areas of Andhra Pradesh and a variety of Peasant castes in the different districts of Tamilnad'.[88] A complementary calculation was advanced about the same time by Paul Brass, the political scientist writing about Uttar Pradesh: 'Elite proprietary castes dominate the district Congress and every other major political party in the state in every district without exception';[89] while, in terms directly applicable to the present analysis, M. N. Srinivas summed up his, and so many other people's impressions by that time, by declaring that: 'With independence and adult suffrage, the dominant peasant castes became so powerful that all political parties had to come to terms with them. They were well represented in State legislatures and cabinets, and the introduction of panchayati raj conferred power on them at village, *tehsil* and district levels'.[90]

The implications of all this were spelt out by the Swedish economist Gunnar Myrdal in the three volumes of his *Asian Drama*. 'Perhaps the most conspicuous result of post war politics in India and the other South Asian countries,' Myrdal wrote, 'has been the strengthening of the upper strata in the villages and a corresponding reduction in the position of sharecroppers and landless labourers. . . . The political consequences of the post-war trend of events are far-reaching. The evidence suggests that the opportune moment for a radical reshaping of the agrarian structure has passed.'[91]

It seems clear that this *dénouement* was deliberately sought by many of those responsible for zamindari (landlord) 'abolition' in India after independence. Charan Singh, the rich peasant ideologue from Uttar Pradesh, who for so long was Minister of Agriculture there, and at one time Chief Minister, made the point explicitly when he wrote in 1958 that: 'By strengthening the principles of private property where it was weakest i.e. at the base of the social pyramid, the reforms have created a huge class of strong opponents of the class war ideology. By multiplying the number of independent landowning peasants there came into being a middle-of-the-road, stable rural society and a barrier against political extremisms.'[92]

In so saying, remarkable as it may seem, he was, in effect, echoing Lenin. When, in Russia after 1906, the Czar's minister Stolypin set out to raise up just such a new class of peasants, Lenin had become greatly perturbed.

> 'It would be empty and stupid democratic phrasemongering', he wrote in 1908, 'to say that the success of the Stolypin agrarian policy in Russia is "impossible". It is possible! [If it succeeds] then Marxists who are honest with themselves will straightforwardly and openly throw all "agrarian programmes" on the scrap-heap altogether, and will say to the masses: "The workers have done all they could. . . . The workers call you now to join in the social revolution of the proletariat, for *after* the 'solution' of the agrarian question in the Stolypin spirit *there can be no*

other revolution capable of making a serious change in the economic conditions of life of the peasant masses".'[93]

In the event, Stolypin's reforms had only one decade to take root in Russia before the Revolution came. Their equivalents in India have had at the very least two to three decades, while in a number of places they have had as many as ten to fifteen. The Naxalites' experience (as outlined above) suggests, moreover, that Lenin's and for that matter Gunnar Myrdal's fears that rich peasant dominance is exceptionally difficult to undermine, and that in India 'the opportune moment for a radical restructuring of the agrarian structure has passed' could well prove justified. In an astonishing conclusion for a life-long social democrat, Gunnar Myrdal has at all events openly concluded of India 'that—as neither the political will, nor the administrative resources for a radical, or for that matter, any fairly effective land reform are present—it may be preferable to make a deliberate policy choice in favour of capitalist farming by allowing and encouraging the progressive cultivator to reap the full rewards of his enterprise and labour, while approaching the fundamental issues of equality and institutional reform from a different angle and by different policy means'.[94]

What then of East Africa? In two respects the position here has been obfuscated. In the first place too much animus has been directed against the narrow bureaucratic and political elite.[95] As the Indian story (and a great many others besides) would suggest, it is not their position which is crucial, except insofar as it overlaps with that of a rural elite. It is the structure of the agrarian regime itself which is crucial. If there prevails here a distinct category of wealthier peasants with persisting links with their rural settings and no landlords sitting above them, then it seems that short of uprooting them bodily[96] there will be little to stop them from determining what happens in the rural areas in which they live, and setting the bounds within which the political system operates. Whether this is or is not the situation in East Africa—as it is in India—is the critical question. Secondly, great play has been made with ideology. Thus Aaron Segal has written:

> 'Unlike the Kenya and Uganda vision of a yeoman peasant farmer moving gradually into the cash economy, financing his children's school fees, buying a bicycle, and paying taxes to the local council to improve secondary roads, the Tanzanian elite sees the country dotted with highly organized, communally owned cooperative villages directly linked to the party and government hierarchy; instead of yeoman peasant farmers, they see party and cooperative members driving tractors, operating sisal decorticators, practicing irrigation farming, living next to one another, speaking and eventually reading Swahili, and encouraging their children to intermarry on an intertribal basis.'[97]

In this particular situation ideologies have been one thing, actualities another. What are the actualities?

There are certainly some areas in East Africa where there have been severe land shortages and where as a consequence numbers of people have either become landless or have had to eke out their living upon economically unviable holdings.[98] There have also been some urban and rural working-class communities.[99] In certain areas, moreover, chiefs (though rarely hereditary chiefs) have held considerable powers as disposers of land.[100] Equally, in quite a number of areas chiefs, and occasionally other people as well, seem to have been able during the colonial period to gather into the hands of themselves and their families a degree of wealth and control over land which warranted their being called an African 'gentry'.[101] But outside one or two areas in East Africa—Zanzibar for instance[102]—there was not, and there is not today, a well entrenched, localised, hereditary landlord class. The classes therefore which Barrington Moore traced in various western and eastern countries in his *Social Origins of Dictatorship and Democracy—Landlord and Peasant in the making of the modern world*[103] are not often to be encountered, at all events in the relationships he discerned. At the same time communal landholdings do not seem to have been very extensive either. In the main, the rural areas of East Africa have been peopled by small individual farmers with the usufruct of the land on which they have dwelt, and with no landlords lording it over them. In one estimate, for Buganda in the 1950s, it was suggested indeed that 59 per cent of the population there could be described as 'Middling' or 'Poor Peasants', but only 20 per cent as 'Landless labourers'.[104] After land consolidation in Kikuyu country in the 1950s it was reckoned in Kenya that 'taking 7·5 acres as an average economic holding . . . only 8,700 out of 38,900 holdings in Kiambu, 4,400 out of 37,800 holdings at Nyeri and an estimated 2,700 out of 37,600 holdings at Fort Hall were 7·5 acres or more';[105] while at the end of the 1960s it was reckoned in Tanzania that amid a total population of twelve and a half million there were still over eight million 'small individual farmers' and their dependents.[106]

Fairly certainly there was a considerable development during the colonial period of a new individualism in the rural areas.[107] But this was not by any means always colonial policy. 'Naturally . . . ,' it was said of the Kenya administration in 1952, 'many officers are reluctant to initiate changes which may lead they know not where, and quite possibly cause political trouble at the same time. More specifically they shrink from the heavy responsibility of encouraging the growth of a landless class, which appears to be the necessary corollary of successful small-holdings; it is for this reason that the degree of official encouragement given to small holdings has varied greatly in Kenya from time to time.'[108] There were, even so, periodic attempts by East African colonial administrations, and not least in Kenya, to embark upon 'what amounts to an agrarian revolution . . . its nearest equivalent is the eighteenth and nineteenth-century enclosures in England', with a view to 'creating a solid middle-class . . . population anchored to the land who has too much to lose' by political radicalism;[109] and in the three surveys just quoted rich peasants do indeed figure. They were estimated to comprise 19 per cent of the population of Buganda in the 1950s. There were said to be '5,000 viable holdings in the whole of Kikuyu country' in 1960. While in Tanzania at the end of the 1960s it was reckoned that there were still 95,000 large farmers and their dependents who employed 'significant wage labour'.[110]

As empire departed, therefore, there appear to have been large numbers of small peasants in East Africa along with a generous sprinkling of rich peasants. But what was the relationship between them? And how did that relationship relate to the distribution of political power in the country? This has never been satisfactorily analysed;[111] but it is very clear that in the aftermath of empire each of the independent governments in East Africa has been preoccupied by the problems which these questions have presented to them. In Uganda the major political issue of the 1960s (concerning the relationship between the 'national' government and the 'local' governments) came to be framed in the language of 'the common man's' onslaught upon what was termed the 'feudalistic mentality'.[112] In Kenya the great political confrontation of the 1960s lay between those who affirmed that 'what we are interested in is the set up which will be for the interests of the majority of the people of this country' and those who argued that 'we are not going to rob people of property and then claim that we carrying out the tenets and the requirements of African socialism';[113] while in Tanzania President Nyerere roundly declared that: 'What is here being proposed is that we in Tanzania should move from being a nation of individual peasant producers [and] . . . gradually become a nation of Ujamaa (familyhood) villages where the people cooperate directly in small groups and where these small groups cooperate together for joint enterprises.'[114]

In practice—if we may take two quite contrasting examples—it may be that, as a northern Uganda case study has it, the elected committee of a local cooperative 'represented not the mass of peasant farmers but the choice of the big men of the community'. They very soon found themselves, however, being superseded by others.[115] While it may be, on the other hand, that whereas no one was living in a Ujamaa village in Tanzania at the beginning of the 1960s, over 10 per cent of the population was by the end.[116] A sympathetic observer felt bound to conclude, however, that 'the effect of developing commercialisation in Tanzanian agricultural systems appeared to undermine their communal features, and to encourage individualism'[117] (and early in 1972, with Tanzania's first political murder, there were intimations of sharp conflict between 'kulaks' and the proponents of TANU's Ujamaa policy).[118]

From these and many other instances it soon becomes clear indeed that major uncertainties attended the nature of the socio-economic orders which actually obtained in East Africa after independence and/or were coming into being there. Given the apparent fluidity in the situation it was natural perhaps that the politicians should have felt themselves to be presiding over the making of a quite new social, economic and political order.[119] But since the political authority they possessed was so tenuous, the political structures they headed so fragile, and the demands upon their largesse so multifarious, the uncertainties surrounding the directions in which their societies were actually moving made their whole situation uncommonly bewildering. In determining, therefore, the most effective nexus by which the frail political orders they headed—buffeted as they were by so many popular demands—should actually be linked with the societies under their aegis, they were faced by a signally taxing issue. One can sense the anguish which some of them felt in a *cri de coeur* from one of Obote's ministers in Uganda shortly before his regime was brushed aside. 'Our main concern, both as a Government and as a party,' E. Y. Lakidi, his Minister of Labour declared in July 1970, 'is with all the 9·5 million people of Uganda. What the Government is trying to do . . . is to establish a kind of conversation between officials or representatives of the party at all levels and all the people of Uganda. . . . There is no point in one side doing all the talking and the Government was not interested in proceeding in that manner.'[120] The expedient which emerged was the one-party national election, with one candidate for the Presidency, but multiple candidates from the one party in each constituency, which Nyerere first instituted in Tanzania in 1965, which Kenyatta adopted in Kenya in 1969–70 (with a distinctive emphasis upon primary elections), and which Obote was striving to introduce in Uganda during 1970–71.[121] Its combination of fixity with flexibility matched quite precisely with the institutional fragility of the East African state and the uncertainties attending its political linkages.[122]

Such were not the issues which India's politicians had to face in the aftermath of empire. There the political structure regularly revealed its remarkable resilience. It was extensively tied in with an agrarian order of immense tenacity. There was talk in the 1950s of establishing a 'socialistic pattern of society', and of a move towards communal farming; but, in no way surprisingly, nothing came of either.[123] At the beginning of the 1970s banks were nationalised, ceilings were imposed upon urban property possession, and the last vestiges of princely privilege were swept away; but on these matters socialist principles suited the rich peasantry very well. They would have no truck, however, with increases in land revenue,[124] or with too close a watch upon ceilings in land ownership. It was not, moreover, the brittleness of the political system they operated, nor even the impetus in the demands made upon it, let alone any deep uncertainty about the ordering of society, that preoccupied their minds; but hunger, poverty and size, and the vehemence of factional and communal strife.

In the end, of course, most of this discussion is unwarrantably tentative—even presumptuous. But to the extent that it does possess any force, it poses questions in plenty for historians of the imperial era to consider. Some of these have been suggested *en passant*, as have, indeed, the beginnings of one historian's explanations of them. Let it be said, moreover, that if one can have little respect for those who allow themselves to be blinded by hindsight, there is little to be said either for those who decline to ask the questions which hindsight suggests. Even now there is a real intellectual service to be performed by insisting that those two obfuscating tendencies—which see everything 'ending' with the attainment of independence, and everything 'beginning' with the attainment of independence—are to be firmly resisted. Now that some decades of independence are behind us, the time has surely come to consider some of the questions concerning the issues and circumstances they have displayed which have their roots in the past. Certainly there can be no doubt that the imperial era has left its legacies to the post-imperial period. It would seem now, therefore, part of the historian's responsibilities to discern what these are, how they came to be fashioned, and how they were carried over into the post-imperial era. That, at all events, is the primary consideration which it has been the ultimate purpose of this final chapter to advance.

NOTES

1. W. F. Gutteridge, *The Military in African Politics*, London, 1969, Ch. IV, and Henry Bienen, *Tanzania, Party Transformation and Economic Development*, Princeton, 1967, Chapter IX.
2. Unless the Somali Republic (which had a military coup in 1969) be thought of as in East Africa. See on this whole topic Ruth First, *The Barrel of a Gun: political power in Africa and the coup d'état*, London, 1970; and more generally S. E. Finer, *The Man on Horseback*, London, 1962.
3. Bienen, op cit.; William Tordoff, *Government and Politics in Tanzania,* Nairobi, 1967, p. 96 sqq.
4. Ibid.; and see also Julius K. Nyerere, *Freedom and Unity*, London, 1967, and *Freedom and Socialism,* Dar-es-salaam, 1968.
5. Low, *Buganda in Modern History,* Ch. 7.
6. *Uganda News* for 1971, passim.
7. See especially his speech to the 'Conference of Buganda Elders', 5 August 1971, ibid.
8. I have touched on this in Chapter 2 of V. T. Harlow and E. M. Chilver, *History of East Africa*, Vol. II, Oxford, 1965, pp. 38–50.
9. Cherry Gertzel, *The Politics of Independent Kenya*, London, 1970. For Kenyatta's Madaraka Day speech of 1 June 1966 see p. 88.
10. On India's fissiparous tendencies, see for example, Selig Harrison, *India the most dangerous decades*, Princeton, 1960; on its spasmodic violence see David H. Bayley, 'Public Protest and the Political Process in India', in John R. Gusfield, *Protest, Reform and Revolt*, New York, 1970, pp. 298–308.
11. Particularly those of *The Times* correspondent in Delhi at the time of the 1967 elections and the subsequent Congress split.
12. Dr. Rajni Kothari presented information on this, which was based upon the large-scale survey on which he is engaged, to a Conference in Canberra in September 1969. See also his *Politics in India*, Boston, 1970.
13. Max Weber, *The Theory of Social and Economic Organization*, paperback edition, London, 1964, p. 328.
14. A. L. Basham, *The Wonder that was India*, London, 1954, p. 83; Charles Drekmeier, *Kingship and Community in Early India*, Stanford, 1962, p. 157 *et al.*
15. B. B. Misra, *The Administrative History of India 1834–1947*, Bombay, 1971.
16. B. H. Baden-Powell, *Land Systems of British India*, 3 vols., Oxford, 1892.
17. B. B. Misra, *The Indian Middle Classes*, London, 1961.
18. David C. Potter, 'Bureaucratic Change in India', in Ralph Braibanti, *Asian Bureaucratic Systems Emergent from the British Imperial Tradition*, Durham, 1966.

19. Michael Brecher, *Nehru, A Political Biography*, London, 1959.
20. B. Pattabhi Sitaramayya, *History of the Indian National Congress*, New Delhi, Vol. I, 1935, Vol. II, 1947.
21. Bienan, *Tanzania*, p. 66.
22. The exceptions would be Ethiopia, and the small countries, Swaziland, Lesotho, Rwanda, and Burundi.
23. On this whole matter see Richard Symonds, *The British and their Successors*, London, 1966.
24. Bienen, Gertzel, and Low, loc. cit.
25. Edited by I. N. Kimambo and A. J. Temu, Nairobi, 1969. For the ensuing controversy see *African Affairs,* Vol. 69, no. 277, 1970 and Vol. 70, no. 278, 1971, pp. 50–61. For my own part I would draw the line at a statement like: 'At midnight on 9 December 1961, the people of Tanganyika regained their independence', J. Iliffe in B. A. Ogot and J. A. Kieran, *Zamani. A survey of East African History,* Nairobi, 1968, p. 308. Surely the most that one could properly say would be: '. . . the peoples of Tanganyika regained their independence as the people of Tanganyika'?
26. E.g. M. Crawford Young, 'The Obote Revolution', *Africa Report,* June 1966, pp. 8–14; Bienen, *Tanzania,* p. 317 sqq; Gertzel, *Kenya*, p. 169.
27. *Uganda News* for 1966, 1967, 1971.
28. A useful resumé which does justice to Burma and Pakistan as well as to India is Hugh Tinker, *South Asia, A Short History*, London, 1926, Ch. 9 and 10.
29. This is nowhere better adrumbrated than in Prakash Tandon, *Punjabi Century 1857–1947,* London, 1961.
30. Bernard S. Cohn, 'Political Systems in Eighteenth Century India: the Banaras Region', *Journal of the American Oriental Society*, 23, 3 July-Sept. 1962, pp. 312–20
31. A. M. Shah, 'Political System in Eighteenth Century Gujarat', *Enquiry,* I, i, Spring 1964, pp. 83–95; Eric Miller, 'Caste and Territory in Malabar', *American Anthropologist,* 56, 3, June 1954, pp. 410–20.
32. Henry Maddick, *Panchayati Raj: A Study of Rural Local Government in India,* London, 1970.
33. Percival Spear, *Twilight of the Mughals*, Cambridge, 1951, Ch. III.
34. These and other very pertinent matters are explored at some of the lower levels of the system in Richard G. Fox, *Kin, Clan, Raja and Rule. State—Hinterland Relations in Pre-Industrial India*, Berkeley, 1971.
35. 2 vols, London, 1953 and 1954; Oxford, 1965.
36. Loc. cit., p. 315. Seen in this context books by contemporary social scientists in which they discuss the articulation between levels in the present-day structure can be very illuminating: see especially, F. G. Bailey, *Politics and Social Change, Orissa in*

1959, California, 1963; Paul R. Brass, *Factional Politics in an Indian State. The Congress Party in Uttar Pradesh*, California, 1965; Balder Raj Nayar, *Minority Politics in the Punjab,* Princeton, 1966; and Marcus Franda, *West Bengal and the federalizing process in India*, Princeton, 1968.

37. Low, *Buganda in Modern History*, pp. 3–7, reviews this point.
38. I use G. H. T. Kimble, *Tropical Africa*, New York, 1960, Vol. I, p. 5.
39. John Middleton, *The Lugbara of Uganda*, New York, 1965, p. 39.
40. I am grateful to Anne King for this information from her field notes.
41. Robert A. Levine and Barbara B. Levine, *Nyansongo: a Gusii Community in Kenya,* New York, 1966, p. 18.
42. See on this topic generally P. H. Gulliver (ed.), *Tradition and Transition in East Africa,* London, 1969, and Ronald Cohen and John Middleton (ed.), *From Tribe to Nation in Africa. Studies in Incorporation Processes*, Scranton, 1970.
43. M. M. Edel, 'African Tribalism: Some Reflections on Uganda', *Political Science Quarterly,* 80, 1965, pp. 357–72.
44. Walter Goldschmidt, *Sebei Law*, Berkeley, 1967, p. 7.
45. Walter H. Sangree, *Age, Prayer and Politics in Tiriki, Kenya,* London, 1966.
46. Roland Young and Henry Fosbrooke, *Land and Politics among the Luguru of Tanganyika*, London, 1960.
47. D. A. Low, 'Uganda: the establishment of the Protectorate', in V. T. Harlow and E. M. Chilver, *History of East Africa*, II, Oxford, 1966.
48. Uganda Protectorate, *Report on the Commission of Inquiry into the management of the Teso District Council*, Entebbe, 1958.
49. Fred G. Burke, *Local Government and Politics in Uganda,* Syracuse, 1964, Ch. 6.
50. John Beattie, *The Nyoro State*, Oxford, 1971, p. 82 sqq.
51. Uganda Government, *Exchange of Despatches between His Excellency the Governor and the Secretary of State for the Colonies concerning the creation of Sebei District*, Entebbe, 1962.
52. Martin R. Doornbos, 'Kumanyana and Rwenzururu: two responses to ethnic inequality', in R. I. Rotberg and A. A. Mazrui (ed.), *Protest and Power in Black Africa*, New York, 1970 and the references quoted there.
53. Gulliver, *Tradition and Transition*, p. 28.
54. Nyerere once remarked: 'The more tribes we have the better: if there were only five tribes, there might be serious clashes', J. Clagett Taylor, *The Political Development of Tanganyika,* Stanford, 1963, p. 96.
55. John Lonsdale and I have discussed these matters in Chapter One, 'Towards a New Order 1945–62', *History of East Africa,* Vol. III, Oxford, forthcoming.

56. I say this despite the contrary impression that may be conveyed by Arthur Tuden and Leonard Plotnicov (ed.), *Social Stratification in Africa*, New York, 1970.
57. Amongst the Kikuyu such people were called 'athamaki', H. E. Lambert, *Kikuyu Social and Political Institutions*, Oxford, 1956, pp. 105–6; Peter Marris and Anthony Somerset, *African Businessmen*, London, 1971, Ch. 2. Amongst the Nyamwezi they were called 'ntwale', R. G. Abrahams in Cohen and Middleton, *From Tribe to Nation*, p. 104. Amongst the Lugbara 'opi' Middleton, *The Lugbara*, pp. 40–1.
58. Rene Lemarchand, *Political Awakening in the Congo*, pp. 199 sqq.
59. E.g. John Okello, *Revolution in Zanzibar*, Nairobi, 1967.
60. Monica Wilson, *Communal Rituals of the Nyakusa*, London, 1959, p. 211.
61. For example, Kenya small-holder coffee production increased in value from £172,000 in 1954 to £5m in 1964, H. Ruthenberg, *African Agricultural Production: Development Policy in Kenya 1952–1965*, Munich, 1967, p. 12.
62. See an interesting mimeographed paper by Anthony Oberschall, 'Rising Expectations, National Unity and Political Turmoil'.
63. See Nyerere, *Freedom and Unity*, and Jomo Kenyatta, *Harambee. The Prime Minister of Kenya's Speeches 1963–64*, Nairobi 1964.
64. F. G. Bailey, 'Closed Social Stratification in India', *Archives Europeenes de Sociologie*, IV, 1963, pp. 107–24.
65. E.g. F. G. Bailey, *Caste and the Economic Frontier*, Manchester, 1960; Robert L. Hardgrave, *The Nadars of Tamilnad*, California, 1969; Owen M. Lynch, *The Politics of Untouchability*, Columbia, 1969.
66. Michael Lipton makes this point regularly; see, for example, his 'Should reasonable farmers respond to price changes?' *Modern Asian Studies* I, i. 1966, pp. 95–9, and 'The Theory of the Optimizing Peasant', *Journal of Development Studies*, IV, 3, 1968, pp. 327–51.
67. E.g. Kusum Nair, *Blossoms in the Dust*, London, 1961; William and Charlotte Wiser, *Behind Mud Walls 1930–1960*, California, 1963.
68. It was thirty years from the Montagu Declaration of 1917 until Independence: the comparable period in East Africa was ten years or less.
69. It is difficult to think of an Indian Government feeling the need to require employers to take on 10 per cent more workers as a means of relieving unemployment pressure, as East African Governments have done on more than one occasion.
70. Gautam Appa, 'The Naxalites', *New Left Review*, 1970, no. 61, pp. 34–41 and various articles in *Liberation*, the English monthly published by the Communist Party of India (Marxist–Leninist) in

Calcutta since 1968. I am grateful to Abu Adnan who wrote a short dissertation for me based upon this material.

71. E.g. Martin Orans, *The Santals*, Detroit, 1965.
72. E.g. K. M. Panikkar, *The Evolution of British Policy towards Indian States*, Calcutta, 1929.
73. V. P. Menon, *The Story of the Integration of the Indian States*, Calcutta, 1956.
74. Woodruff, loc. cit.
75. See *Report of the Public Service Commission 1886–87* (Aitchison), Great Britain, Parliamentary Papers, Vol. XLVIII, C. 5327, 1888; and *Royal Commission on the Public Services in India* (Islington), Great Britain, *Parliamentary Papers*, Vol. VII, Cd: 8382, 1917.
76. E.g. Frykenberg, *Guntur District*.
77. E.g. ibid., p. 244; John G. Leonard, 'Politics and Social Change in South India: a study of the Andhra Movement', *Journal of Commonwealth Political Studies*, V, i. March 1967, pp. 60–77; V. C. P. Chaudhury, *The Creation of Modern Bihar*, Patna, 1964; Kenneth W. Jones, 'The Bengali Elite in Post-Annexation Punjab', *Indian Economic and Social History Review*, III, 1966, pp. 376–95.
78. Anil Seal, *The Emergence of Indian Nationalism*, Cambridge, 1968.
79. The classic short statement is Maureen Patterson, 'Caste and Politics in Maharashtra', *Economic Weekly*, VI, No. 39, 15 September 1954, pp. 1065 sqq.
80. This is endlessly apparent from the anthropological village studies which have been published. But see also Bernard S. Cohn, 'Structural Change in Indian Rural Society' in R. E. Frykenberg (ed.), *Land Control and Social Structure in Indian History*, Madison, 1969.
81. E.g. Adrian C. Mayer, *Caste and Kinship in Central India*, London, 1960.
82. E.g. Ravinder Kumar, *Western India in the Nineteenth Century*, London, 1968.
83. E.g. Daniel and Alice Thorner, *Land and Labour in India*, Bombay, 1962.
84. This is my reading of Mayer, loc. cit, especially as illustrated by the table on p. 36. See further, Henry Orenstein, 'Caste and the concept, "Mahratta", in Maharashtra', *Eastern Anthropologist*, XVI, 1963, pp. 1–9.
85. E.g. Ralph W. Nicolas, 'Structures of Politics in the Villages of Southern Asia', in Milton Singer and Bernard S. Cohn, *Structure and Change in Indian Society*, Chicago, 1968, Ch. II; Brass, *Factional Politics*, p. 243.
86. E.g. A. C. Mayer, 'The Dominant Caste in a Region of Central India', *Southwestern Journal of Anthropology*, XIV, 4, pp. 407–27. It should perhaps be emphasised that Bengal is signifi-

cantly different; but the 'Bhadralok' there are well over 10 per cent of the population.

87. E.g. Robert L. Hardgrave, *The Dravidian Movement*, Bombay, 1965; Myron Weiner, (ed.), *State Politics in India*, Princeton, 1968.
88. André Beteille, *Castes Old and New*, London, 1969, p. 62.
89. Brass, *Factional Politics*, p. 118; cf. Balder Raj Nayar, *Minority Politics in the Panjab*, p. 320.
90. M. N. Srinivas, *Social Change in Modern India*, California, 1966, p. III. By correlating information upon Panchayati Raj in Rajasthan, David Potter has written: 'it is possible to suggest that Panchayat members tend to be comparatively wealthy land-owning agriculturists or fairly prosperous village merchants', *Government in Rural India*, London, 1964, p. 34.
91. Gunnar Myrdal, *Asian Drama, An Inquiry into the Poverty of Nations*, II, London, 1968, p. 1367.
92. Charan Singh, *Agrarian Revolution in Uttar Pradesh*, U.P. 1958, p. 7; see also his *India's Poverty and its Solution*, New York, 1964. I like V. G. Kieman's remark that 'the single grand peasant revolt in pre-British India was that of the Sikhs'. *Socialist Register*, 1966, p. 312.
93. I owe this point to my colleague Beryl Williams. See V. I. Lenin, 'On the beaten track!', *Collected Works*, Vol. 15, March 1908–August 1909, London, 1963, pp. 44–5 For other such comments see, e.g., this volume and Vol. 13 of the *Collected Works* passim. See also D. Treadgold, 'Was Stolypin in favour of kulaks?', *American Slavic and East European Review*, XIV, Feb. 1965, pp. 1–14.
94. Myrdal, *Asian Drama*, p. 1380.
95. E.g. in René Dumont, *False Start in Africa*, London, 1966.
96. M. Lewin, *Russian Peasants and Soviet Power*, London, 1968. Lenin emphasised the economic hold that rich peasants have, see generally his 'Agrarian Question in Russia towards the close of the nineteenth century', *Collected Works*, 15, p. 69 sqq. In India nucleated settlement enables dominant castes to control what goes on in their villages especially effectively.
97. Aaron Segal, 'The Politics of Land in East Africa', *Economic Development and Tribal Change*, XVI, 2, 1968, pp. 280–1. See further G. Arrighi and John Saul, 'Socialism and Economic Development in Tropical Africa', *Journal of Modern African Studies*, VI, July 1968, pp. 141–69.
98. E.g. P. H. Gulliver, 'Land shortage, social change and social conflict in East Africa', *Journal of Conflict Resolution*, 5, i, 1961, pp. 16–26.
99. Mrs. Margaret Kiloh is developing work on this subject in Kenya at the University of Sussex.
100. E.g. D. A. Low and R. C. Pratt, *Buganda and British Overrule*, London, 1960, part I.

101. E.g. Beattie, *Nyoro State*, Ch. 8, and M. P. K. Sorrenson, *Land Reform in Kilkuyu country*, Nairobi, 1967, pp. 47–9 et al.
102. Michael F. Lofchie, *Zanzibar, Background to Revolution*, Princeton, 1965, Ch. III.
103. Boston, 1966; see also Samuel P. Huntington, *Political Order in Changing Societies*, Yale, 1969.
104. Quoted in Guy Hunter, *The New Societies of Tropical Africa*, London, 1952, p. 99.
105. Sorrenson, *Land Reform in Kikuyu Country*, pp. 224–5.
106. *Economic Survey 1970–71*, Government Printer, Dar-es-Salaam, 1971, esp. p. 48.
107. E.g. Lucy Mair, 'The Growth of Economic Individualism in Africa', *Studies in Applied Anthropology*, London, 1957, pp. 23 sqq.
108. R. O. Hennings, 'Some Trends and Problems of African Land Tenure', *Journal of African Administration*, IV, 4, Oct 1952. See also Sorrenson, op cit., Ch. IV.
109. C. M. Johnston, Special Commissioner for Central Province, Kenya, to members of the Kenya Regiment [June 1956], Provincial archives Nyeri, LND 33/3/11, quoted Sorrenson, op cit., pp. 117–8.
110. I am greatly indebted to Reginald M. Green for his kindness in preparing a note for me on this matter.
111. It has been more than once glanced at, but no more, by Lionel Cliffe, see his chapter in I. N. Kimambo and A. J. Temu (eds.). *A History of Tanzania*, Dar-es-Salaam, 1969, and in C. G. Widstrand, *Cooperatives and Rural Development in East Africa*, New York, 1970. Colin Leys begins his important article 'Politics in Kenya: The Development of Peasant Society', *British Journal of Political Science*, I, 3, July 1971, pp. 307–37, by saying: 'The central question ... is how we should understand the social structure that is emerging from the neo-colonial pattern of change in Africa, and what implications it has for politics ... As one proceeds it becomes steadily clearer that what we have here is a vast and astonishingly virgin territory for fundamental research.' David J. Parkin, *Palms, Wine and Witness, Public Spirit and Private Gain in an African Farming Community*, Aylesbury, 1972, provides a socio-economic starting point.
112. A. Milton Obote, *The Common Man's Charter*, Kampala, 1969.
113. Gertzel, *Politics of Independent Kenya*, pp. 68, 51.
114. Julius K. Nyerere, *Socialism and Rural Development*, Dar-es-Salaam, 1967, the conclusion.
115. Joan Vincent, 'Local Cooperatives and Parochial Politics in Uganda: Problems of Organisation, Representation and Communication', *Journal of Commonwealth Political Studies*, VIII, i, March 1970, pp. 3–17. See also her *African Elite, the Big Men of a Small Town*, New York, 1971.
116. Tanzania's *Economic Survey 1970–71*, Dar-es-Salaam, 1971.

117. David Feldman, 'The Economics of Ideology: some problems of achieving rural socialism in Tanzania', in Colin Leys (ed.), *Politics and Change in Developing Countries*, Cambridge 1969, p. 111. For uncertainties about the outcome of Tanzania's commitment to Nyerere's 'Education for Self-Reliance', compare chapters by Mwingira and Foster in R. Jolly (ed.), *Education in Africa,* Nairobi, 1969.
118. *The Guardian* 10 Jan. 1912; *The Times,* 14 Jan. 1972.
119. The key items are the Sessional Paper No. 10 on *African Socialism and its application to Planning in Kenya*, Nairobi, 1965; Julius K. Nyerere, *Ujamaa—Essays on Socialism*, Dar-es-Salaam, 1968; and Obote's *Common Man's Charter.*
120. *Uganda News*, 3 July 1970.
121. Bienan, *Tanzania,* Ch. XII; C. Legum and J. Drysdale, *Africa Contemporary Report. Annual Survey and Documents, 1969–70*, Exeter, 1970, pp. B126–7; A. Milton Obote, *Proposals for New Methods of Election of Representatives of the People to Parliament*, Kampala, 1970.
122. For an illuminating study of these elsewhere see Carl Landé, *Leaders, Factions and Parties: The Structure of Phillippine Politics*, New Haven, 1965: see also Alex Weingrod, 'Patrons, Patronage and Political Parties; *Comparative Studies in Society and History*, X, 1967–68, pp. 377–400.
123. E.g. B. D. Graham, 'The succession of factional systems in the Uttar Pradesh Congress Party, 1937–66', in Marc J. Swartz, *Local-level Politics, Social and Cultural Perspectives*, London 1969, p. 347.

Index